Studies in Economic Ethics and Philosophy

Springer
Berlin
Heidelberg
New York
Barcelona
Hong Kong
London
Milan
Paris
Singapore
Tokyo

Mark Casson · Andrew Godley
Editors

Cultural Factors in Economic Growth

With 2 Figures
and 11 Tables

Springer

Prof. Dr. Mark Casson
Dr. Andrew Godley
University of Reading
Department of Economics
Faculty of Letters & Social Science
P.O. Box 218, Whiteknights
Reading RG6 6AA
United Kingdom

ISBN 3-540-66293-6 Springer-Verlag Berlin Heidelberg New York

Cataloging-in-Publication Data applied for
Die Deutsche Bibliothek – CIP-Einheitsaufnahme
Cultural Factors in Economic Growth: with 11 tables/Mark Casson; Andrew Godley ed. – Berlin; Heidelberg; New York; Barcelona; Hong Kong; London; Milan; Paris; Singapore; Tokyo: Springer, 2000
(Studies in Economic Ethics and Philosophy)
ISBN 3-540-66293-6

Springer-Verlag Berlin Heidelberg New York
a member of BertelsmannSpringer Science+Business Media GmbH

Printed in Germany

Hardcover Design: Erich Kirchner, Heidelberg

SPIN 10734546 42/2202-5 4 3 2 1 0 – Printed on acid-free paper

Preface

This volume is the product of the "Sixth Annual SEEP-Conference on Economic Ethics and Philosophy" on the theme of 'Cultural Factors in Economic Growth' held at Marienrode Monastry, Hildesheim, in April 1998. Our thanks go to our colleagues (including Avner Offner, whose paper could not be included here), the staff at the monastry, and Professor Peter Koslowski of the Forschungsinstitut für Philosophie Hannover, and editor of this series, for contributing to a very enjoyable conference and, we hope, an interesting collection of essays.

Mark Casson and Andrew Godley
University of Reading,
March 2000

Contents

CONTENTS

Chapter 1

Cultural Factors in Economic Growth

MARK CASSON AND ANDREW GODLEY

I. The Concept of Culture

The importance of culture. Culture is a potentially nebulous concept. Many economists deny culture any place in their theories on the grounds that the concept is so imprecise. Yet economic models that exclude culture cannot fully account for the phenomena that they attempt to explain. This has forced many economists to reluctantly acknowledge culture as a 'residual element' in their explanations (a recent example is Landes 1998). The residual role of culture has been particularly important in the explanation of economic growth. There can be little doubt, therefore, that a book on cultural factors in economic growth addresses an important gap in recent economic literature. This book aims to begin the process of filling that gap. The contributors are from diverse social science backgrounds, although the largest number of contributions is from economic history. This is no accident. While sociologists and anthropologists are the two disciplines to have made the most intensive use of the concept of culture, economic historians have tried hardest to draw the links between culture and economic growth.

Definition. To employ culture as an explanatory tool it is necessary to be clear about what culture means. A simple definition of culture is 'shared values and beliefs'. This definition has two advantages. First, it is broadly consistent with the way that the concept is used in sociology and anthropology. Secondly, it fits well with the subjectivism that underlies the economic theory of rational choice.

Values. The behaviour of a rational economic agent is explained by the objective he pursues and the constraints he perceives on the means by which he can pursue it. The objective may relate to the agent's own standard of living, the well-being of his family, or his notion of the public good. Economic theorists describe the objective in terms of a utility function that the agent maximises. (The use of a utility function does not commit economists to 'utilitarianism' of the kind promoted by Bentham. The utility function is simply a mathematical device for specifying the agent's objective in a simple and rigorous way.) Many economists assume for simplicity that the agent's objectives are selfish and materialistic; this means that only quantifiable aspects of the agent's own consumption enter into his utility function. This restriction is not essential to the theory, however (Buckley and Casson, 1993). When analysing culture from an economic perspective it is convenient to take a wider view of human motivation. It is important to recognise that a rational agent who has a conscience (see below) will want their objective to be a legitimate one. Values confer legitimacy on objectives. Hence different value systems will lead agents to pursue different objectives, and therefore to behave in different ways.

Beliefs. If there were no constraints on the maximisation of utility then every rational individual would enjoy a state of absolute bliss. It is the existence of constraints that makes rational choice a substantive issue. Constraints reflect the scarcity of resources. However, it is not the constraints themselves, but the way that the agent perceives them, that affects the way that the agent behaves. The fact that an agent is rational does not mean that they have complete information about the situation they face. They may be uncertain about key facts. To fill the gaps in knowledge created by the missing facts, agents will appeal to theory. Theory suggests what the evidence would show if it were available. However, there may be several theories about how the environment operates, each of which suggests a different interpretation of the available evidence. Agents who subscribe to different theories will fill in the gaps caused by missing data in different ways. This will lead them to perceive different constraints, and therefore to behave in different ways. Thus people in the same situation, and with the same information, may act differently because their theoretical disposition leads them to interpret the available evidence in different ways. It follows that rational behaviour is conditional not only upon values, but upon beliefs as well.

II. Structure of the Chapter

Methodology. Having established the concept of culture that underpins the contributions to this volume, this introduction develops a conceptual framework that can be used to analyse the interaction between culture and economic growth. It uses the methods of economics to develop a general social scientific view of culture's impact on economic growth, and the impact of economic growth on culture. It integrates insights derived from a number of social science disciplines within the general framework of rational action. Readers simply interested in the individual case studies are advised to proceed to those chapters directly. This introductory chapter builds a broad conceptual framework (indeed builds on either a heroic or foolish scale depending on the reader's perspective!) developing the views of the editors published in their earlier work (Casson 1991, Godley 1999, chapters 1 and 7).

Instrumentalism. Part I examines the role of culture in the context of a simple social group. It develops the concept of culture as an intangible 'public good' which, like other public goods, such as defence and law and order, is shared by members of a social group. Culture is viewed in instrumental terms. It is argued that culture has functional value in promoting the economic performance of the group. Although cultural values may adapt to local circumstances, there are certain core values and beliefs which are useful under any conditions. These values promote trust within the group (see Chapter 2). It is argued that the dissemination of culture is a specialised activity, carried out by the leader of the group. The performance of the group depends crucially on how well the leader does his job.

Decentralisation and flexibility. As membership of a social group increases, and its economy grows, the question of decentralisation arises. How far should the leadership directly control the allocation of resources, and how far should they delegate decisions to individuals or smaller groups instead? This is a specific aspect of the more general issue concerning the types of organisation that may legitimately be used to control a social group. This is the subject of Part Two. Different cultures hold different views about the kinds of organisation that are natural to a social group. Some cultures favour a small number of large organisations that are collectively controlled, whilst other favour many small organisations that are privately controlled. It is argued that decentralisation of power to small organisations promotes flexibility within a social group. Decentralisation makes it easier to reconfigure organisations, and to internally restructure them, when circumstances change. The more volatile the group's environment, the more important is flexibility for its survival.

Scope and limitations of private enterprise. The most sophisticated form of decentralisation so far developed is the private enterprise economy. This is based on competitive markets, operating within a legal framework provided by a democratic government. Self-interest has an important role in promoting risk-taking by entrepreneurs. Competition is central to both the market process and the democratic process, because it neutralises attempts to exploit monopoly power. But self-interest and competition can bring out the worst in people. Their excesses cannot be constrained by law alone -

moral sanctions are important too. But it is difficult to know exactly where to draw the line, in moral terms, between acceptable and unacceptable behaviour. Those who endorse the value of competition tend to argue that competitive behaviour should never be restrained, whilst those who deny the value of competition justify cheating on contracts on the grounds that it helps to undermine the competitive system. The successful private enterprise economy is one which draws the line in the right place. To achieve this, it is necessary to possess the appropriate cultural values. The nature of these values, and their influence on the political constitution, is explored in Part Three.

Explanation of long term change. The final part (Part Four) illustrates how the conceptual framework can be applied to the interpretation of long-term change. Cultural change and economic growth are linked to technological change. Over the centuries, advances in carpentry, metallurgy, and elementary mechanics have opened up new technological possibilities. Some cultures take a more optimistic view of science than others; these optimistic cultures have been able to innovate more successfully than others (Landes 1998). Technological innovations have been particularly significant in promoting commerce. In particular, advances in the long-distance shipping of bulk materials have provided opportunities for the development of entrepot centres. This has occurred in countries which combine a favourable geographical position with a culture that not only takes an optimistic view of science, but legitimates the decentralisation of decisions to a mercantile middle class.[1]

Part One

I. Social Groups

Culture as a public good. The essence of culture is that values and beliefs are shared. Values and beliefs are both forms of information. Values contain information about what is right and wrong, and beliefs contain information about what is true and false. (Many economists think of informa-

1 The classic case is, of course, London. See FISHER (1935) and DAVIS (1973).

tion purely in terms of factual data regarding such matters as price, quantity, date and place, but information is a much broader and richer concept than this.) It is well known that information has the properties of a public good. The fact that one person knows some information does not preclude someone else from knowing the same information too; thus a person who 'passes on' information to someone else does not thereby lose the information themselves. Since culture is a form of information, culture too has the properties of a public good.

Face-to-face communication. The public good aspect of information means that one person can share their values and beliefs with another person. The simplest way of sharing values and beliefs is to talk to other people face-to-face. People who communicate face-to-face on a regular basis constitute a social group. People who belong to the same social group tend to share the same values and beliefs because they all have access to the same information. Social groups may interlock because they have members in common. But when interlocking is limited, different groups will tend to have different cultures.

Spatial dimension of culture. Spatial agglomeration is important in the formation of social groups. People who live in the same small town are likely to meet each other regularly, and therefore have plenty of opportunity to influence one another's views. When population density is low, one town may be some distance from the next, so that people meet other people from the same town far more frequently than they meet people from other towns. Thus each town becomes a distinctive social group, and develops its own distinctive culture. The influence of communication on the spatial structure of groups is considered further in section V.

II. An Instrumental View of Culture

Culture promotes co-ordination. From an economic perspective, it is natural to interpret culture in instrumental terms, although to view it exclusively in such terms is a serious mistake because culture has intrinsic value for members of a group. However, the intrinsic value of culture is peripheral to the discussion below. From a purely instrumental point of view, culture promotes co-ordination; in other words, it enhances the efficiency with which scarce resources are utilised by a social group. Efficiency is improved by increasing both the quantity and the quality of the information at people's disposal.

Functionally useful values. Both values and beliefs contribute to co-ordination. Not all values and beliefs contribute equally, however. Some are more useful than others; indeed some values and beliefs may be useless, or even counterproductive. Thus a value such as 'honesty' encourages people to be open and transparent in their dealings with other people. People can therefore be confident that they will not be cheated. By contrast, the morality of the 'street-wise con-man' is likely to counterproductive. People will be afraid to deal with one another on the grounds that they are likely to be cheated if they do.

Functionally useful beliefs. Accurate beliefs lead to a better quality of decision-making. Sound theories supported by careful experiment make better beliefs than idle speculations. Given better theory and more information at their disposal, individuals are less likely to make mistakes. Religious beliefs, though not directly testable in the same way as scientific beliefs, may also be functionally useful. Thus fear of the supernatural, and the anticipation of heavenly reward, may encourage people to behave in a socially responsible way.

The demand for culture. From an individual perspective, culture is useful because it simplifies decisions. Values provide moral criteria which rule out certain courses of action, so that only a subset of possible actions needs to be evaluated in detail. Shared values reduce uncertainty by making other people's actions more predictable. In particular, an individual knows that other members of the group are unlikely to adopt devious strategies. This saves time and effort in devising devious counter-strategies, and in assessing the risks they involve.

The supply of culture. The production of values and beliefs is a sophisticated task. It benefits from a division of labour in which suitably qualified individuals specialise in this task. (The principle of the division of labour is fully discussed in section II of Part Two below.) These specialists exercise a leadership role, in the sense that they provide the values and beliefs used by other members of the group. Each follower derives his judgements from what his leader says. Because information can be shared, the leadership role is a unitary one. In a small group, one person may act as leader, and everyone else becomes a follower. In a larger group, several people may share the leadership role, complementing each other by performing different aspects of it.

The market for leadership. The production of values and beliefs is expensive. Leaders need time for planning and reflection. They may also incur significant expense in disseminating their values and beliefs. Followers must therefore recompense their leaders. There are several ways in which this can be done.

- The leader could charge the followers for his services by quoting a price for each element of culture that is supplied. However, culture is usually most powerful when its message is assimilated without a conscious effort, which precludes supplying it through an explicit sale. In any case, it is difficult to 'unbundle' the different aspects of culture in this way.
- The leader may be able to charge for culture along with the supply of other services, such as defence, and law and order. Charges for these services are usually exacted through taxation, for reasons discussed in section III below. An extra tax can be levied to cover the costs of leadership - such as the maintenance of a court, the patronage of art and architecture, and so on.
- Finally, the leader may request voluntary contributions to support his work. Since leaders disseminate values, it is easy for them to incorporate in the their values an obligation to support the leader's work. Thus priests typically finance their supply of religious values and beliefs by requesting donations - indeed, this method of finance is often the only method that is compatible with a traditional religious value system.

Market adjustment. The market for leaders needs to be flexible in order to maintain an equilibrium. If a social group receives an adverse shock, which threatens to undermine cohesion within the group, then only very able leadership may be able to restore stability. To attract a leader of suitable calibre, the role of leader may have to be made more rewarding. One approach is to increase the leader's material rewards by increasing taxation or voluntary contributions. But taken in isolation, a change of this kind may only succeed in attracting a mercenary type of leader. Better results are likely to be achieved by attracting the kind of leader who is driven by a sense of mission or vocation to serve the group. This type of leader is likely to come forward only if they believe that the followers are willing to make the kind of sacrifices required to resolve the problem. The leader also needs a high degree of status in order to demand the kind of sacrifice required. Whilst excessive status can also attract the wrong sort of leader, too little status can discourage any honest person from taking the job. Thus a flexible market for leaders is most likely to operate through a mixture of adjustments, involving the leader's income, the leader's status, and the followers' willingness to make a sacrifice.

III. Defence

Proximity creates shared interests. The importance of face-to-face communication in the dissemination of culture helps to explain why for most of human history culture has been a localised phenomenon. Proximity has bound neighbours together not only culturally, but in terms of their economic interests as well. There are two specific economic interests where the influence of proximity is particularly strong - namely in the provision of defence, and of law and order (see Chapter 8).

Economies of scale in defence. Proximity affects defence because an external threat to one person usually forms an external threat to their neighbours as well. Hence neighbours have a common interest in security. Collective provision of security afford economies of scale. A single perimeter fence around a large area is more efficient than multiple perimeters round several smaller areas. It therefore pays to collaborate in security provision.

The free rider problem. There is a snag, however. This concerns the well-known 'free rider' problem. If everyone is asked to contribute to the building of the perimeter fence, then each person has an incentive to decline to pay, on the grounds that everyone else will pay instead. It is hardly practical to divert the perimeter route specifically to exclude non-payers from the benefits of the fence. But if everyone declines to pay on these grounds, then no fence can be built (Olson 1965). There are two main kinds of solution.

The strong man. The first is for someone to come forward as an enforcer. They undertake to build the fence, and in return require exactions from everyone who benefits from it. They finance the fence out of taxes levied on the beneficiaries. Everyone has to pay the tax whether they want to or not. Individuals have a choice - but only whether to leave or stay. If they stay then they commit themselves to paying the tax. If they refuse to pay then the tax will be exacted by force. For the enforcer to succeed in extracting taxes, he needs to have a reputation as a 'strong man' - someone who is likely to win in the event of a fight.

Moral leadership. The alternative is for a leader to inspire the members of the group with an ethic of social duty. Members are encouraged to perceive themselves as citizens who have a moral duty to support collective action. Their reward is an emotional one - a sense of satisfaction at having done their duty. This private self-administered reward may be supplemented by public recognition. The leader may personally thank each citizen for their contribution. Alternatively, the leader may create an ethos in which citizens express approval for each other's efforts. Each citizen who desires approval therefore makes a contribution.

Morals versus coercion. The more reliable is the moral mechanism, the less is the need for a strong man to enforce contributions. The more that people are willing to discipline themselves, under the influence of a moral leader, they less need they have to submit to the power of the strong man instead. Thus collective submission to a moral system facilitates freedom from coercion, because coercion is unnecessary when people can be relied upon to discipline themselves.

IV. Law and Morals

Arbitrating disputes. Even in a highly moral society, neighbourly relations are not always friendly. People are often inconsiderate in the way they behave. A defended space is usually a confined space, because of the need for economy in the provision of defence. Where people share a confined space, unintended interactions can cause annoyance. Disputes arise and arbitration is required. Arbitration must be seen to be fair if it is to be acceptable to all the parties. An arbitrator needs to be someone with a reputation for integrity and sound judgement. The settlement must also be enforceable. This suggests that the 'strong man' who organises the defences should also be involved in the enforcement of settlements. He may, however, choose to delegate the role of arbitrator to some other individual instead.

Reducing the incidence of disputes through private property rights. A simple way of co-ordinating spatial interactions is to give everyone a right to hold property. For example, individuals may be given exclusive rights to occupy certain portions of land. As private occupiers, they can regulate access to their land, and may exclude other people whenever they wish. It is important to note that a right is essentially a moral construct. A right is of little value unless other people accept an obligation to respect it. In order to be fully enforceable, a right needs to be endorsed by a powerful person, such as the strong man referred to above.

The abstract concept of a right. Because it is a moral construct, the concept of right does not have to be confined to a tangible asset such as land. It can be extended, not only to other tangible assets, such as durable goods, but to intangible goods and services as well. Individuals can claim a right to peace and quiet, for example. In many cases intangible rights are far more important than tangible ones. Thus no one may have a right to exclusive occupation of a perimeter fence. The asset may be held in common instead. However, everyone may have a right to be consulted about its upkeep and maintenance. In very poor societies there may be little private property other than the clothes and ornaments that people wear. This does not mean that people have no rights, however. They may well have quite important intangible rights, such as the right to participate in a village meeting at which matters of common concern are resolved.

Honest trade. The existence of rights does not obviate the need for morals. It has already been noted, indeed, that rights are themselves a moral construct. There are certain occasions on which rights become particularly vulnerable, and on these occasions morals are especially valuable. These occasions arise most frequently in a private enterprise economy. One occasion is when rights are traded. A seller of a right may part with it in anticipation of a payment which is not forthcoming, and conversely, a buyer may pay for a right which is not supplied. It is normally far easier to cheat someone over a transaction than actually to steal his or her property outright. Thus luring people into a bogus transaction is often a cost-effective way of acquiring other people's property. The risk to an honest trader of meeting dishonest traders of this kind is a serious disincentive to trade. An ethic of integrity in very useful in controlling this problem, as it discourages people from seeking to gain from trade in this dishonest way.

Honest stewardship. Another time when rights become vulnerable is when people die. People often care a great deal about how their property is used after they die. They write wills to determine the disposal of their property, and create trusts to administer their property after they are dead. The expectation of controlling property from beyond the grave appears to be an important motivator of achievement in certain cultures. Thus many political leaders choose to bequeath a legacy in the form of some prestigious building before they quit their office, whilst ordinary people may endow charities which commemorate their name. There are substantial opportunities for corruption in the administration of trusts, however. Thus expectations about the integrity of trustees can be an important influence on people's willingness to achieve and to save. Economic development depends on people being motivated to achieve and maintaining high rates of saving. A moral system that encourages trustees to behave as honest stewards of the property they hold in trust is therefore important in sustaining economic growth.

V. The Nature of Leadership and the Size of Group

Different aspects of leadership. Leadership was introduced in section II in the context of creating and sustaining culture. Section III introduced the strong man, and section IV the arbitrator. These additional roles may also be seen as aspects of leadership. Whilst the maintenance of culture depends on what may be called moral leadership, the provision of defence by the strong man calls for military leadership, and the provision of law and order by the arbitrator requires administrative leadership.

Functional specialisation within leadership. In a small group of people, these three aspects of leadership may all be combined in the same person. None of the roles is sufficiently onerous to keep a separate person fully occupied. In this case the leader needs to be a strong man, with a conscience, and a sensitivity to popular notions of what is fair. This is certainly a 'tall order', but fortunately in a small group it is unnecessary for the leader to excel in any of these characteristics. In a large group, by contrast, different people may take responsibility for different roles. Each role will be occupied by a specialist. Because the group is larger, and the roles are consequently more demanding, each specialist needs to excel in the relevant characteristics. The specialists also need to work well together. Thus the moral leader legitimates the strong man's tactics, whilst the strong man protects the moral leader in return, and the administrative leader arbitrates between them. In a large group, therefore, as exemplified by the modern nation state, there is a leadership team. Each member of the team has a specific role, and the success of the group depends to a significant extent upon how well members of the team work together.

Communication skills. Leaders need to be good communicators. The public good nature of culture means that a moral leader needs to be skilled in disseminating values and beliefs. A military leader, for example, needs to be able to inspire his troops by addressing them before battle, whilst an administrative leader needs to be able to justify his decisions as fair. If leaders are poor communicators then they need to be supported by professional spokespersons and advisors. The leaders and their support staff constitute the social elite of the group.

Communication strategies. The size of the group is limited by the ability of the leader and his elite to communicate with the followers. It has already been noted that leadership is best effected face-to-face. If leadership also has to be exercised on a one-to-one basis then the number of followers that a leader can support is very limited. It is sometimes possible, however, for a leader to extend his communication with his followers to a one-to-many basis, using large assemblies or festivals in which he addresses his followers as a group.

The technology of communication. The scope of leadership is widened further when the principle of face-to-face communication is extended using the media (see Chapter 9). A simple medium is the poster in which the leader, portrayed in heroic pose, endorses a simple slogan. A more sophisticated approach is possible using television. This is a particularly powerful medium because the leader can adopt an intimate manner and address people who are sitting in comfort in their homes. He therefore enjoys the status, not only of a leader, but of a guest. The technology of communication exercises a significant influence on the scope of leadership, and hence upon the economic size of a social group. As communication costs fall, and the capacity to mimic face-to-face communication increases, so the size of the social group that a leader can support expands.

The dispersion of social groups. It is not only the size of a social group which is affected by new communication technology, however, but also its geographical pattern. With modern telecommunications, the distance metric is fundamentally altered, because the cost penalty incurred by long-distance communication is dramatically reduced. With the distance factor reduced in importance, other factors become more important in the formation of groups. Groups develop around business and professional activities, shared political and religious commitments, and the pursuit of hobbies and leisure interests. Because these affiliations are largely independent of spatial agglomeration, they transcend the boundaries of the territorially-based nation state.

Impersonal communication. Impersonal methods of communication are also useful to leaders. Unlike face-to-face communication, impersonal communication relies purely on language, without the help of facial expression, gesture and tone of voice. Being relatively devoid of emotion, impersonal communication is useful mainly for logical arguments and straightforward facts. Until the development of telephone, radio and television, all remote communication had to be conducted in an impersonal way.

Military intelligence. Impersonal communication is useful mainly to military leaders and administrative leaders - it is less useful to moral leaders because their message must have emotional appeal. Military leaders require intelligence about the enemy's plans, and the effectiveness of military strategy depends crucially on this intelligence being up-to-date. Until the nineteenth century the only viable means of remote communication were visual signals such as lighted bonfires, smoke, and flags. The advent of the telegraph was a breakthrough, even though it was quickly superseded by the telephone. It enabled military strategy to be implemented over a wider front, and so allowed the scale of warfare to be increased. This in turn encouraged the development of bigger armies, and indirectly promoted the growth of the large nation state.

Administrative communication. Administrative leaders handle detailed information about property rights, often supported by the evidence of witnesses. Remote communication of this sort of information requires a high standard of literacy, and depends on the ability to transmit documents by post. In this context, the quality of road and rail systems is an important constraint because it governs the speed with which mail can be transported. Improvements in road and rail systems were important in the nineteenth century in enlarging the territorial area that could be administered successfully by a nation state.

Part Two

I. Entrepreneurial Leadership

The allocation of resources. There is another aspect of leadership which has not been mentioned so far. This is entrepreneurship. It involves making judgements about the allocation of scarce resources. Optimising the allocation of resources is fundamental to the performance of the economy. Entrepreneurship differs from the other forms of leadership because it is usually more decentralised. The modern nation state normally has only one moral leader, one military leader and one administrative leader, but many entrepreneurs. Naturally, there are many potential leaders in the moral, military and administrative domains, but at any one time there is only one official position in each domain to be filled. Competition in these domains takes the form of competing for a given office, and not of replicating the offices. By contrast, in a private enterprise economy there may be nearly as many different entrepreneurial roles to be filled as are there are people willing to fill them.

Pluralism. The unitary nature of culture, defence and law should not be overstated, of course. A large society comprises many sub-groups, each of which may have its own ethnic identity, and associated sub-culture. The military establishment may comprise different regiments, each with its own traditions, and so on. Thus there is a degree of pluralism in all domains of society. But the degree of pluralism amongst entrepreneurs is far greater, and the following sections explain why this is so.

II. The Division of Labour in Production

The division of labour in production. Although the concept of co-ordination was introduced in section I of Part One, little has been said so far about what needs to be co-ordinated, apart from interactions between neighbours, and the provision of defence. The need for co-ordination in an advanced economy stems from the application of the division of labour to production. The key ideas underlying the division of labour were first set out systematically by Adam Smith (1776); they are simplification, repetition, specialisation and mechanisation.

- *Simplification*. Production can involve quite complicated tasks. The division of labour breaks down a complex task into a set of simple tasks. Each of these simple tasks is connected to others by flows of intermediate product. Some simple tasks are best carried out by a single person, and others by a team of people.
- *Repetition*. Simple tasks are easier to learn than complex tasks, and so productivity is increased by simplification. People are most productive when they concentrate their attention on the same task. By repeating the same task they learn it more quickly.
- *Specialisation*. People also differ in the their natural aptitudes, and in their capacity to benefit from training. It therefore pays to allocate people between tasks according to where their personal comparative advantage lies.
- *Mechanisation*. A talented person allocated to the repetition of a simple task may think of ways to mechanise the task. Mechanisation is well suited to the continuous uninterrupted repetition of a sequence of physical operations. Unlike people, machines can be designed with the performance of a particular task in mind. Machines tend to be faster and more reliable, but more specialised and much less flexible, than people.

Trade. The advance of the division of labour is inextricably linked with the growth of trade. When different activities are specialised in different hands, they will take place at different locations. In some cases the locations may be very near, since this minimises the cost of transporting semi-finished products between them. In other cases, though, it may be advantageous to place the different activities far apart. Thus a mineral may be mined at a location that is very short of energy for refining, so the metal refinery needs to be established elsewhere. It may be advantageous to mine in territory controlled by one leader, and to refine in territory controlled by another. This may be difficult to arrange unless both people recognise the benefits of trade. The important point, from a conceptual point of view, is for the parties to recognise that trade is a 'positive sum' rather than a 'zero sum' game. In a positive sum gain it is possible for both parties to benefit: the role of bargaining is to share the surplus, rather than to determine which of the parties is going to 'exploit' the other. Cultural attitudes are important in determining whether people perceive trade as a positive sum or zero sum game.

The geography of the division of labour. The wider the area over which economic activity is distributed, the greater the opportunities for specialisation on account of differences in geology, climate and population. When enlightened leadership sustains free trade, it is mainly transport costs that constrain the geographical scope of the division of labour. In this connection, the application of the division of labour to improve productivity in long-distance transport - for example, through specialisation in shipbuilding - has proved particularly crucial.

III. Information and Organisation

Volatility. If economic conditions were totally static then production could be almost totally mechanised, and the economic system could be kept running on a sort of 'automatic pilot'. Production in each period would be exactly the same as in the previous one. Co-ordination would be required only at the set-up stage; thereafter it would be confined to identifying breakdowns in machinery and carrying out the necessary repairs. In practice, however, the economic environment is highly volatile. The division of labour constantly needs to be adjusted to changing conditions. Co-ordination is a continuous activity which involves monitoring the principal sources of volatility, interpreting the symptoms, taking appropriate decisions, and communicating the results to different parts of the system. In a highly volatile environment, co-ordination involves intensive information flow.

The cost of information. In many respects, information can be thought of as a product, just like ordinary materials. It is certainly costly to produce and transport. A lot of factual information is produced by observation, for example, and observation can be very time-consuming. Similarly the transport of information from one person to another is costly. Face-to-face communication is time-consuming, and long-distance communication, for example by post, incurs energy costs as well. The handling of information, like the handling of materials, therefore benefits from a division of labour.

The logic of organisation. Some kinds of information are handled on a routine basis. Every period a vast range of small transitory changes occur -

for example, if someone falls ill then they will switch from consuming food to consuming medicines instead. The need to handle information of this kind can be anticipated in advance, and an organisation can be set up for this purpose (Casson 1997). There is a routine procedure for dealing with each type of shock, which is activated each time a transitory change occurs. Several people may be involved in the implementation of a given procedure: for example, one person may collect the information, another may synthesise it, and a third may implement the decision. This creates an organisation. Within the organisation, people are allocated to tasks in accordance with their personal comparative advantage. The principle is exactly the same as in the case of ordinary production, although the personal skills involved are rather different, because it is intellectual rather than manual work that is involved.

Centralisation versus decentralisation. The question arises as to whether a single large organisation should be established to deal with such problems on an economy-wide basis. This strategy is superficially appealing, but suffers from the fact that the information costs incurred would be very high. Large amounts of relatively trivial information would have to be communicated over considerable distances. A lot of people's time would be tied up, and the process of decision-making would be slowed down, so that problems would get much worse before they were solved. It is usually advantageous to deal with problems 'on the spot' wherever possible. This means creating local organisations which are empowered to take local decisions without consulting organisations elsewhere. The delegation of decision-making responsibility to smaller autonomous organisations can create problems, but these can usually be resolved by building various kinds of 'redundancy' or 'slack' into the system. For example, the problem of accommodating a switch in demand from food to medicine is resolved by establishing a local food store and a local pharmacy, both of which keep stocks of the relevant products. A sick person simply decides not to go shopping for food, and asks a friend to buy them some medicine from the pharmacy instead. Information costs are reduced, at the expense of a modest increase in inventory-holding costs.

Markets. When co-ordination of production is decentralised, a mechanism is required to co-ordinate the activities of the different local organisations. Co-ordination between organisations is effected by negotiations between them. In a private enterprise economy negotiations relate to the exchange of property rights through a market process (see Chapter 6). The rights relate to money and goods. Sellers offer goods in return for money, and buyers offer money in return for goods. Sellers compete against other sellers, driving prices down, whilst buyers compete against other buyers, driving prices up. Competition creates an 'invisible hand' that balances demand and supply at an equilibrium price. To sustain a complex division of labour, a large number of different product markets are required. These product markets constitute an interdependent system, in which a change in one market spills over to affect all the other markets too.

Markets and memory. The organisation of markets requires considerable amounts of information. When property rights are routinely traded, records of ownership need to be updated on a regular basis. When trade takes place over long distances, it is difficult to synchronise payment and delivery, unless the seller travels everywhere with his goods. Credit relationships are created when a transaction is completed in stages, and not all at once. These credits need to be witnessed and recorded, because the incentive to default is high (see below). Written records are extremely useful for this purpose. But with so many details to record, filing systems are required as well. Information storage needs to be organised in a systematic way. The evolution of information storage systems is more or less a prerequisite for the geographical expansion of the division of labour described above.

IV. Flexible Configuration

Organisational births and deaths. So long as the pattern of transitory shocks remains unchanged, the same set of local organisations can be employed all the time. But if the pattern of transitory volatility changes, then a new pattern of organisation will be required. When new types of co-ordination problems emerge, then either existing organisations must be restructured, or new organisations set up in their place. Because organisations are based on routine, their structures and procedures are often difficult to change. Hence the optimal response to a persistent change in the pattern of volatility is often for new organisations to emerge, and for some existing organisations to close down.

Entrepreneurial start-ups. But who is to decide what the new configuration of organisations should be? Two main approaches are possible. One is to vest responsibility in a single organisation, whose role is to plan the structure of local organisations; this centralises the power to create new organisations and close existing organisations down. The other is to empower ordinary individuals to take decisions of this kind. Individual entrepreneurs can come forward to propose new organisations - namely private firms - whilst entrepreneurs who control existing organisations can decide, if they wish, to close down (Jones 1988).

The venture capital market. For entrepreneurship to be effective, individuals must have access to the resources required to set up new firms. This implies some measure of private ownership of resources in the economy. For otherwise individuals would have to apply to a central authority for permission to set up a firm, and this central authority would then determine, by its decision, whether new firms were set up or not. By contrast, when property is privately owned, entrepreneurs can apply to wealthy individuals for backing. In some cases the set up costs may be so large that they exceed the resources that any individual can safely risk in a single venture. In such cases a group of wealthy individuals may partner one another as shareholders, backing the judgement of some entrepreneur that an opportunity exists to establish a new firm.

The equilibrium rate of interest. In a wealthy economy, entrepreneurs compete to borrow funds, whilst shareholders compete to invest them. This creates a capital market, which complements the product markets mentioned above. The capital market is a natural extension of the short-term credit arrangements used for financing trade, as described above. Because of the long-term nature of capital loans, and the larger sums involved, information management based on written records is even more important than before. The capital market prices loans at an equilibrium rate of interest. The interest rate reflects the expected profitability of business ventures, the risks involved, and the investors' attitudes to these risks.

Competition versus monopoly. Entrepreneurs' discretion to found new businesses is particularly controversial when they propose new businesses which compete with existing ones. Such competition may be deemed to be wasteful, because it duplicates the activities of existing firms. This argument is almost invariably accepted in the case of defence and policing, as discussed above, where private competition is not normally allowed. It is often accepted in the case of utility industries too, where it is believed that there are major economies of scale - for example, in water, sewage, energy and public transport. But historically there have been major differences of opinion over the advisability of promoting competition in primary industries and manufacturing, although current opinion strongly favours it.

Differences of judgement. The advantages of promoting competition are two-fold. First, competition allows individuals to back their own judgements of whether the situation calls for new organisations or not. No one has a complete and fully up-to-date overview of the state of the economy, and hence no one is in a position to be certain that their own judgement is right (Hayek 1937). Competition prevents any one individual, or group of individuals, from imposing their judgements on others. It allows anyone who is sufficiently confident, and who can win the confidence of others, to put their judgement to the 'market test' (Harper 1995). They set up their organisation and invite the public to switch their patronage to them, on the grounds that their organisation offers better services than existing ones. If their judgement is correct than they will prosper, and if it wrong then they will fail. The more difficult it is for anyone to judge the situation, the greater the advantage of having a plurality of opinion brought to bear upon it. Since no one knows in advance what the best form of organisation is, a pragmatic test of commercial survival is the most direct way of finding out.

Reducing monopolistic distortion. When entrepreneurs put their own resources at risk, they do so mainly because of the material advantage they expect to reap. The private enterprise system is a profit-driven system which appeals to self-interest. This does not mean that entrepreneurs are wholly selfish, because they may plan to put their profits to charitable use. But because entrepreneurs know that they bear the full loss of any misjudgement, they consider it perfectly fair that they should reap the full gain as well. Thus in the absence of any threat of competition, a successful entrepreneur would exploit his monopoly power to the full. The prices he charged for his services could be much higher than the costs of providing them, and this would distort his customers' purchasing decisions. The continual threat of competitive entry leads entrepreneurs to price closer to cost, and thus minimises the distortion of customers' spending patterns.

The trend to decentralisation. To summarise, as the division of labour in ordinary production becomes more sophisticated, and the complexity of the economic system increases, it becomes increasingly important to decentralise decision-making in order to cope with the large amount of information flow This includes the decentralisation, not only of routine information processing, but of entrepreneurial information processing too. It becomes increasingly important, not merely to delegate information processing to small organisations, but also to allow ordinary individuals to decide what configuration of such organisations is best suited to society's needs. This arrangement provides considerable flexibility in adjusting the structure of an economy to changes in the pattern of volatility.

Part Three

I. Problems of the Private Enterprise System

Legitimisation of private property. Decentralisation works well only when each individual clearly understands the scope of their responsibilities. It is also necessary for other people to know each person's responsibilities, so that they know whom to get in touch with when they need to harmonise decisions. The establishment of private rights and responsibilities effects a major change in society. Many individuals stand to lose from the introduction of private property into a hitherto collectivist system - particularly those who lack the confidence or the skill to take important decisions for themselves. To maintain social cohesion, these individuals must accept the moral legitimacy of the new institutional system. But this legitimacy can be questioned on a number of grounds. It is not only that private property may appear unjust; it can also be argued that in certain respects it is inefficient too. The case for private property depends to an important extent upon the argument that these deficiencies can be overcome.

Transaction costs. As noted earlier, markets provide an excellent opportunity for cheating. Entrepreneurs who are focused on the pursuit of profit may not prove to be particularly trustworthy when it comes to trade. Ordinary consumers may not be trustworthy either, especially if they believe that market forces are weighted in favour of firms. An ethic of integrity, though useful, may need to be supplemented by a sophisticated system of commercial law, as an additional deterrent to cheating by those whose conscience is particularly weak.

Market-making firms. Where ethics and law are both ineffective, a reputation for honest dealing can prove very valuable. One of the advantages of a market system is that, up to a point, reputation can be established out of pure self-interest. Reputation is particularly valuable to a firm because a firm is more heavily engaged in trade than is an ordinary consumer. Firms may set out to build a reputation by guaranteeing the quality of the goods they supply. They use their reputation to intermediate between consumers who do not trust producers, and producers who do not trust consumers. They buy from producers and re-sell to consumers, setting a margin through which they make a profit for themselves. The firm's reputation is encapsulated in its name, or the brand name of the products it supplies. Firms that specialise in intermediating trade are 'market-making' firms, as distinct from firms which simply organise production.

Vertical integration. The problem of distrust also arises in trade between one firm and another. Consider, for example, a multi-stage production process which involves several entrepreneurs, each of whom controls a different stage of production. Self-interest may encourage each entrepreneur to bargain aggressively with the other entrepreneurs, and to try to cheat them by lowering quality in order to reduce his costs. If reputation effects are weak, then vertical integration may be the answer here (Coase 1937). All the different stages of production are brought under the control of the same firm. Once a single firm owns every stage of production, the incentive to haggle and cheat within the production process disappears.

The hierarchical structure of organisations. Vertically integrated firms tend to be large, and this leads to another problem. It is concerned with the legitimacy of hierarchical authority. The 'pyramid of authority' tends to be very tall in large organisations. Now it is often suggested that private enterprise promotes the individual at the expense of the hierarchy, but this is true only in relative, and not absolute terms. Private enterprise certainly gives people the freedom to found their own organisations if they do not like working in organisations run by other people. But private organisations still retain a hierarchical nature. In any organisation, whether private or not, the most important decisions are usually taken at the top. They are translated into specific actions by those lower down. People lower down feed information up, but otherwise they may not be consulted at all. They may be given no justification for the decisions that they are told to carry out. There can be sound economic reasons for this. It may be too complicated and time-consuming for each decision-maker to explain to each subordinate why each decision was made. But it can be very demeaning for subordinates when they are simply told what it is they have to do, and not why they are expected to do it.

Absentee ownership. The motivation of subordinates is further undermined when they know that the business is simply being run for the owner's profit. Feelings of alienation are likely to be increased if the owner is an absentee. If, in addition, the business is regularly bought and sold as a going concern, or the threat of closure or redundancy is ever-present, then loyalty amongst employees is likely to be very low indeed.

Inspiring loyalty. Alienated employees can be a serious problem for the owner of a firm because employees have plenty of opportunity to cheat. Not only can they shirk; they can also supply misinformation to the decision-makers in the firm. Lazy employees always have an incentive to cheat, however they feel towards their employer, but alienated employees have an even stronger incentive to cheat because they will feel better about having taken advantage of an employer they dislike. The performance of a firm can usually be improved substantially by inspiring loyalty rather than disaffection amongst employees. In this respect, a culture that emphasises the responsibilities of employers to their employees is likely to promote a more enlightened style of management. These values can be linked, through the principle of reciprocity, to the employee's obligation to work hard for a responsible employer.

Non-profit organisation. One of the advantages of a decentralised system is that individuals who recognise these problems can seek to address them on their own initiative. In a free society individuals can associate together for purposes other than the pursuit of their own profit. They can form organisations whose output consists of emotional rather than material rewards - for example, discussion groups whose primary objective is fellowship. People can also form organisations for altruistic purposes, such as charities. They can set up production organisations that differ from ordinary firms by embodying social principles such as co-operation and worker's control (see Chapter 3). All sorts of organisations can be formed with the aim of correcting one or more of the perceived deficiencies in the competitive system.

Efficiency versus collusion. These corrective organisations have two main kinds of purpose. The first is to improve co-ordination in cases where the competitive system is liable to fail. For example, unrestricted entry into certain industries could seriously damage the reputation of the product, by allowing incompetent producers to market output that is superficially indistinguishable from the output of competent producers. The competent producers may form a guild or trade association, and adopt a brand mark to identify their output. This improves the information on which consumers base their choice, and thereby sustains quality production which might otherwise disappear (see Chapter 7). The guild may seek to go further, however, and establish control of the industry by regulating entry. It may seek statutory support for a compulsory training scheme for new producers, and then restrict entry to the training programme. This reduces future supply artificially, and so pushes prices up. The drive for market efficiency becomes perverted into collusion against consumers instead.

Equity. Justification for collusion may be sought on grounds of equity. It may be said that the producers are poor, and are victims of socially undesirable change, such as a new technology which has undermined the traditional craftsmen's skills. The higher price is a legitimate tax on wealthy consumers, which redistributes income from the rich to the poor. This is a common defence of the craft trade union. More generally, it may be claimed that the entire working class is a victim of exploitation, and that the trade union movement as a whole must use its strike-threat power to increase workers' incomes, quite independently of efficiency issues. While it is obvious that disruption of production through strikes reduces efficiency, and that the effort devoted to organising collusion is normally wasteful from a social point of view, the role of non-profit organisation in maintaining social cohesion should not be ignored. They are, to some extent, a natural corrective to the potential excesses of the competitive system described above. From the perspective of the losers in the 'competitive game,' their freedom to belong to corrective organisations helps to legitimate the freedoms which successful entrepreneurs enjoy.

II. Culture and Organisation

The legitimisation of authority. Organisation is very closely linked with culture. Culture is concerned with some very fundamental issues, and one of the most fundamental issues concerns the legitimacy of different forms of organisation. Most cultures identify certain types of organisation as normal or natural (Hofstede 1984, Laurent 1983, Trompenaars 1993). For example, in some cultures authority is expected to be strong, and obedience automatic, whereas other cultures favour weaker authority, and allow it to be questioned from time to time, as in the case discussed above.

Beliefs about human nature as an influence on organisational forms. Organisations are composed of people, and so beliefs about people are very important in legitimating organisations. 'What are people really like?' is a fundamental question to which different cultures may give very different answers. To legitimate authority within an organisation, it is useful to show that people would behave more badly without the prevailing form of authority than they will when subjected to it.

Optimistic and pessimistic views of human nature. A pessimistic view of human nature tends to support authority. It suggests that without the element of fear engendered by authority, people would behave in an irresponsible way. It suggests that appeals to conscience will normally fail. By contrast, a more optimistic view of human nature asserts that people can be persuaded to behave responsibly without subjection to authority, because they are susceptible to moral influence. On this view people can be trusted provided that they are given appropriate guidance. Religious beliefs will have a strong influence on the view of human nature. Moral optimism, for instance, is likely to be correlated with beliefs in salvation and sanctification.

Scientific optimism. Another aspect of optimism concerns people's ability to control their environment. An optimist believes that people are able to control nature, and make it do their bidding. If they cannot control, then at least they can forecast or predict, so that evasive actions can be taken when appropriate. This means that risks are low. A related attitude is that the unknown can be scientifically researched - it can be explored by experiment, and possibly modelled by mathematics. Thus what is unknown today may be known tomorrow. The optimist visualises people as professional curiosity-driven researchers, confident in their ability to ultimately subdue natural forces and harness them for the social good. This attitude may be termed scientific optimism, to distinguish it from the moral optimism described above.

Scientific pessimism. While the scientific optimist believes that people are competent, once suitably educated, the scientific pessimist believes that they are incompetent instead. The scientific pessimist perceives nature as a maverick: its behaviour cannot be forecast except by 'reading the stars', and it cannot be controlled except through prayer and sacrifice. It is necessary to accept one's destiny, and hope that one is marked out as lucky, and has not been placed under a jinx. The pessimist believes that it is important for everyone to conform to tradition, because breaking with tradition invites disaster. New forms of organisation that may be suggested by the evolution of the division of labour, and by the emergence of competition, should be resisted.

Rules versus principles. The scientific optimist believes that natural events are governed by timeless and universal principles. These principles imply that there is usually a 'universally best way of doing things'. People who understand these principles can solve problems successfully by improvising solutions, but those who do not understand the principles cannot. People who do not understand the principles need to follow rules. These rules may have been designed by people who understand the principles, or they may have been evolved by trial and error. The scientific pessimist, on the other hand, does not believe in universal principles, or considers that they are known only to the gods. He believes that everyone should simply follow the methods used in the past - the fact that no one knows exactly where they come from, or why they seem to work (though poorly) is no reason to question them.

Interactions between fundamental beliefs. The interaction of fundamental beliefs about human nature is summarised in Table 1. The degree of moral optimism, as reflected in trust in other people's integrity, is indicated in the columns, whilst the degree of scientific optimism, as reflected in confidence in other people's competence, is indicated along the rows. It might be thought that optimism or pessimism about other people's integrity would also reflected in the view that is taken of their competence, so that the only relevant cells were those along the diagonal in the table. This is not the case, however.

Competitive professionalism. Contemporary Anglo-Saxon economies - notably the US - combine a pessimistic attitude to moral behaviour with an optimistic view of competence, seeing people as clever, calculating and devious opportunists. For example, belief in scientific progress, achieved by competent professional researchers, is coupled with distrust of professionals' ethics. Thus there is a strong belief in the need for competition to keep researchers 'on their toes'. This attitude is a reaction against the utopian aspirations that underlay the Post-war European Welfare State.

Culture of the Welfare State. The Welfare State placed a high level of trust in the integrity of professionals - particularly those in health, education and social services. The 'fiscal crisis' of the 1970s undermined this trust, whilst, conversely, trade union militancy undermined the professionals' trust in the integrity of the 'working class'.

Table 1: Effects of moral and scientific optimism on the organisation of a society, with examples

Scientific optimism	Moral optimism: Low	Moral optimism: High
Low	Tyranny Military dictatorship in a peasant society	Family Victorian paternalism
High	Economic liberalism Contemporary Anglo-Saxon economies: Competitive professionalism	Collegiality Post-war European Welfare State

The culture of paternalism. The Welfare State was in its turn a refinement of the late-Victorian concept of the paternalistic state. The Victorian elite in Britain sought to justify its privileged position through organised charity aimed at a poorly educated industrial working class. The same paternalistic approach was reflected in the management of firms, and in domestic life. Victorian culture was the mirror image of contemporary British culture, in the sense that it was optimistic in respect of morals, but pessimistic in its assessment of the competencies of the working class. The difference should not be exaggerated, though. The Victorians were optimistic about the capabilities of their professional engineers, whilst remaining pessimistic about the competencies of the ordinary worker.

Use of procedures to discourage dishonesty. There is an important practical consideration, however, which suggests a link between the two dimensions in the table. It is easier check up on whether someone has ignored a precise instruction, or failed to conform to a specific rule, than it is check whether they have failed to exercise their judgement in a responsible way. There is a subjective element in judgement, which means that one person may reasonably hold one opinion, whilst another person may reasonably hold a different one. A dishonest person can exploit this subjectivity to justify their behaviour. To exercise authority over dishonest people, therefore, it is best to give explicit instructions or to lay down formal rules. This means that a pessimistic moral attitude encourages practices that suggest (though do not imply) a pessimistic scientific attitude as well.

III. The Morality of the Leader

A pessimistic view of leadership. Cultural attitudes towards other people take on a slightly different character where attitudes to leadership are concerned, however. This is particularly true of the moral dimension, which is the focus of attention here. A pessimistic moral view that favours strong leadership on the grounds that people cannot be trusted may suggest that a leader cannot be trusted either. This leads to the well-known dilemma regarding the Leviathan of the state: 'Who will police the policeman?'

An optimistic view of leadership. The optimistic moral view of people faces fewer problems where leadership is concerned. To begin with, the need for leadership is less, because people are more likely to honest anyway, and secondly, the leader is likely to be more honest too. The leader faces greater temptations, however, because the material rewards to dishonesty are much greater where he is concerned. It is therefore necessary to recruit someone of exceptional honesty, but according to the optimistic view, this is not an impossible task.

Democrats and leadership. It is useful to make a further distinction, namely between democratic and elitist attitudes. The democrat asserts that everyone is basically the same, so that leaders are no different from anyone else. The dilemma that is generated by a pessimistic moral view is very real from this perspective. The democrat wishes to constrain the leader's power as far as possible, without undermining defence and law and order in the process (Scully 1992). But it is difficult, in practice, to constrain the leader's power without weakening the exercise of leadership in the process.

Elitists and leadership. The elitist view suggests that personal talents are unequally distributed, so that leaders, if suitably chosen, may be free of the limitations of their followers. On this view, there is not a serious problem.

For example, a pessimistic elitist may be happy to support an authoritarian leader on the grounds that the leader's sanctions will be directed solely against dishonest members of society whom the elitist fears.

Transparency and opacity. The democratic view suggests that leaders should be accessible and subject to scrutiny, whilst the elitist view suggests that leaders can keep themselves aloof, and be allowed to operate in secrecy if necessary. The democrat requires the leader's policies to be transparent, whereas the elitist is content if they are somewhat opaque.

Democracy and economic organisation. Democrats welcome the decentralisation of power associated with the private enterprise economy, since this constrains the leader. They recognise, however, that a political leader who monopolises coercion has still has the opportunity to re-centralise the economy if he does not like the way that private entrepreneurs behave. He can also regulate markets by fixing prices, and restrict competition by conferring monopoly power on certain enterprises. Democrats favour the use of constitutional checks and balances to prevent interference of this kind. Elitists are more content with centralisation because they believe that decisions will be more ethical if they are taken by the leader himself than if they are delegated to ordinary people instead.

IV. The Competence of the Leader

Obstacles to progress. It is not only the leader's morality, but the leader's competence, that is a source of concern to the democrat. The scientific pessimist's view that people are incompetent, when coupled with the democratic perspective, suggests that leaders will be incompetent too. This implies a highly conservative attitude, in which the *status quo* needs to be maintained at all costs. Any new initiative launched by the leader is likely to fail. The leader's role is to block change, and to legitimate this strategy through promoting tradition - for example, through the veneration of heroic ancestors.

Militarism. When scientific pessimism is combined with an elitist attitude, it supports autocratic leadership. The leader knows best because everyone else is stupid. This attitude tends to predominate when popular access to education is limited. Decentralisation of power is deemed to be dangerous because when ordinary people are allowed discretion they will put others at risk through their rash decisions. On the other hand, the leader may well put the whole society at risk though his own misguided actions. Autocratic leadership has its advantages, however; an autocratic style can sometimes improve co-ordination - for example, in a military campaign led by a charismatic warrior. Autocratic leadership therefore generates economic instability, in which great military victories lead to the acquisition of land and tribute, and subsequent defeat results in its loss again.

Social engineering. A scientific optimist who takes an elitist view will tend to favour radical reforms based upon the latest thinking. New technological insights acquired by the elite provide opportunities which are not to be missed. Theory alone justifies the elite's reforms, because supporting evidence is a foregone conclusion, and waiting for it will lead to unnecessary delays. With Platonic arrogance, the elite therefore pushes ahead with great experiments, confident that the results will turn out to be good. In the twentieth century, this approach was applied to both natural science and social science, with disappointing results. Experiments in low-cost nuclear energy, and child-centred education, for example, have both been deemed failures. Social science theory in particular has proved a poor basis for the radical reforms of optimistic elites.

Pragmatism. Scientific optimism combined with a democratic attitude suggests, by contrast, a far more incremental approach to progress, based upon pragmatism rather than theory. It is ordinary individuals who are expected to initiate change. Experiments are small and localised. Differences in judgement are accommodated by allowing people to explore different methods of tackling the same problem. There is no attempt to eliminate duplication of research, on the grounds that no two research programmes are ever quite the same, however similar they may appear to the outsider. The role of the leader is to provide the incentives which optimise the rate of innovation. This involves a trade-off between economic progress and social security which is very difficult to get right (Fisher 1945).

Sustained innovation. Once innovation has been decentralised, it is difficult to stop the process building momentum. All new initiatives, whether they succeed or fail, generate new information as a by-product. Because of the public good nature of information, noted at the outset, many people can learn from a single person's success or failure. Each person synthesises the new information with what they already know, and so arrives at a distinctive synthesis of their own. A new synthesis of this kind may lead to a further advance. Even greater momentum is built up when the leader places the onus on those who oppose an innovation to block it, instead of placing the onus on those who propose it to obtain permission to carry it out. This may explain why scientific optimism, when coupled with a democratic attitude, seems to have proven most successful in stimulating long run economic growth.

Combining moral and scientific optimism. Innovation raises problems of its own, however. In a modern decentralised economy, major innovations require co-operation between many different people - scientists, bankers, entrepreneurs, government ministers, and so on. A high level of trust is required, because of the considerable risks involved to each party. More generally, because modern economies are so complex, and their co-ordination depends so heavily on information flow, there are ample opportunities for stealing information, or for cheating people by supplying them with false information. These problems are often tackled by confining the flow of sensitive information to a small group of people. But this is potentially inefficient, because there may be others outside the group who could make an important contribution to it. By widening the level of trust, and expanding the innovative group, economic performance will be improved. Thus effective moral leadership is particularly important in an innovative economy. Moral optimism therefore complements scientific optimism and a democratic outlook, as a key cultural factor promoting economic growth.

V. Inter-group Relations

Trade or raid? Technological innovation and material progress are both important factors in sustaining military strength. Military strength offers a further strategy of economic advancement, namely war and conquest (see Chapter 8). If people refuse to trade, then it may pay to raid them instead. Indeed, why pay for goods that you can get for nothing by the use of force?

Competition for prime sites. In the long run, trade offers significant advantages over raids, because raids demotivate people from production, whereas trade offers the anticipation of reward. Raids nevertheless have a useful role in obtaining permanent control over immobile resources such as land. Displacing other groups from prime sites may prove advantageous even in the long run. Some land is much more valuable than the rest. Valleys with fertile soils, natural harbours and islands with entrepot potential, intersections of rivers and highways that can be used as defensible trading posts - all are attractive sites for which different groups may compete. The group with the greatest military strength is likely to be the one that secures occupation. Once it is entrenched it can set about acquiring the technological and commercial skills needed to exploit the site to the full. Groups that already have these skills, but lack the military strength to back them up, may find themselves in a subordinate position. They are employed at the centres run by the stronger groups - as free aliens, or possibly as slaves. They may achieve entrepreneurial success, but they cannot attain the power of leadership.

Investing in military strength. The moral is clear: the economic benefits that are generated by optimism and democracy need to be channelled into defence as well as private consumption if the territory occupied by a successful group is to defended against others. It was noted above that autocratic groups may well prove effective in the military domain. Although their technology may be weaker, the power of sacrifice that their leader commands is much greater, and this may tip the military balance in favour of the less sophisticated group.

Migration. Another aspect of inter-group relations is migration. It has so far been implicitly assumed that membership of the national group is fixed. Yet dispossessed people need to find some territory in which to live, and this induces 'push' migration (see Chapter 5) Rational search by dispossessed groups will tend to identify the most prosperous sites for settlement (see Chapter 4). It is not, of course, only the dispossessed who have an incentive to migrate. 'Economic' motives draw people from poorer territories to richer ones. Young people, in particular, will emigrate voluntarily in order to improve the lifetime prospects.

Selective migration. The leader of a group can either attempt to restrict migration, to promote it selectively, or allow it to be free. Democrats tend to favour free migration because it constrains the leader to respect citizen's rights. Abuse of power will lead to an exodus of members. Emigration involves an element of self-selection: the most enterprising people tend to leave because they have the best economic opportunities elsewhere, and are most alert to these opportunities. This leaves the abusive leader with a smaller and less productive population, and hence a smaller tax base from which to support himself. Conversely a successful leader can expect to attract able immigrants. Democrats are less concerned about controls on immigration because they recognise the economic advantage to the host country of restricting immigration to highly productive people. This process of migration is the analogue, at the international level, of competition between firms in the national labour market. Historically, advances in transport technology, notably the steamship, have increased geographical mobility, and thereby promoted greater choice of national allegiance. This has encouraged national leaders to be tolerant of ethnic diversity in order to attract and retain the most able people.

Part Four

I. Long Term Economic Change

Scope of this book. The contributors to this book range widely in terms of level of analysis, function, time and space. Some authors focus on intellectual movements, such as economic liberalism, and co-operation, which have influenced many different countries. Others focus on the cultures of particular countries and regions, or on specific urban areas. Some writers emphasise the political dimension, whilst others emphasise the media, the legal system, or specific types of institution, such as the firm or the guild. Some writers delve back into pre-history, whilst others concentrate on the twentieth century. Some focus on England, or Europe as a whole, whilst others offer a global perspective on their subject.

Growth of scientific optimism. All the writers appear to agree on a few key points however. The first is that scientific optimism has slowly gained ground throughout the last millennium. This began with the increasing use of writing for administrative work. Mathematics was applied to accounting, and then to the interpretation of astronomical observations, leading to improvements in time-keeping and in navigation. The design of tools was improved, permitting greater precision in the construction of capital goods. Advances in carpentry and metallurgy facilitated the building of larger, faster and safer ships. By increasing the dimensions of cargo-carrying vessels, and reducing the risks of loss at sea, the costs of international shipping were dramatically reduced. This increased the potential market area for producers, encouraging producers in different regions to specialise more heavily in terms of their comparative advantage. In agriculture, for example, specialised cash crops for export replaced the traditional mixed farming geared to the farm household and the local economy.

Industrialisation. The extension of the market had its most profound impact on nascent industries such as textile manufacture. A better understanding of mechanical principles, allied to the natural ingenuity of production workers, enabled the principles of rotary motion to be applied in numerous ways to the mechanisation of continuous flow processes. Initially this advance was based on water power. Subsequently, the harnessing of steam gave greater speed and reliability, not only to production, but also to transport, through the railway and the steam-ship. The development of electricity provided a new and more flexible method of distributing power, allowing mechanised production to be used even in remote rural sites.

Growth of decentralisation. The growth of scientific confidence went hand in hand with a growing decentralisation of economic power. As the division of labour was progressively extended, the structure of the economic system became increasingly complex. As already noted, improvements in long-distance transport promoted continual advances in the division of labour on an inter-regional and international basis. The problems of coordinating the international division of labour through centralised planning would have been insuperable, even if centralisation had been politically possible. As it was, different sovereign states participating in the division of labour learned about the gains from trade in a pragmatic way. Those leaders that refrained from restricting trade, or from taxing it too heavily, were the ones who derived the greatest advantage from it.

Growth of democracy. Along with the decentralisation of economic power went the development of new curbs on absolute political power. The autocratic sovereign and the warrior leader were increasingly subjected to pressures from local princes and lords to reduce their exactions and permit greater local autonomy. These princes and lords behaved to begin with as though they were natural aristocrats, but gradually they too faced increasing pressure from an emergent commercial elite (Jones 1982). This was particular true of the major entrepot - the great urban centres of import, export, and intermediate product processing that developed along with the growth of international trade in bulk commodities. Urban merchants, organised on a voluntary collective basis through companies and guilds, were very much in favour of more democratic forms of government, because this permitted them to share power with the landed aristocracy. The rising economic power of large groups of urban craftsmen and artisans created further pressure for a widening of the franchise, though it was not, of course, until the twentieth century that a universal franchise became the norm in advanced economies.

II. Cycles of Moral Optimism and Moral Pessimism

Advances in the division of labour increase the demand for moral commitment. Because scientific optimism, coupled with the decentralisation of power, advances the division of labour, it means that people spend more time producing goods that other people will consume, and less time producing goods that they will consume themselves. It has already been noted, for example, that farmers will devote more land to cash crops for export, and less to subsistence crops. With the evolution of manufacturing industries, such as textiles, workers spend all their time producing goods that others will consume; it is only when they return home that they produce goods and services, such as meals and domestic entertainment, that they consume themselves. Producing goods for other people increases the incentive to cheat. This is not just a question of default on delivery - taking customers' money and offering nothing in return - but of default on quality. The easiest way for a seller to cheat and get away with it is often to cheat on quality. Quality is easier for a seller to assess than a buyer, because the seller has possession of the good before the buyer does, and so can inspect it more easily; he may also know more about the way in which it was produced The incentive for the seller to cheat is particularly great when he collaborates with many other people in the production of the good. This means that responsibility for defect in the finished product is very difficult for the buyer to isolate. The seller may be a worker, selling his labour, who forms part of a large production team, in which the contribution of any individual worker to the quality of the finished product is difficult to assess. Alternatively, the seller may be involved in just many separate stages of production through which the product passes. The more advanced the division of labour, and the more complex the pattern of teamwork, the more difficult the imputation of responsibility becomes. As the division of labour advances, therefore, the scope for cheating increases too.

Responses to increased cheating. To sustain the production system, therefore, the incentive to cheat must be controlled more rigorously as complexity increases This means that the intensity of moral commitment must advance in step with the division with the division of labour. Other factors can alleviate the problem of cheating, but none of them can solve it entirely. Thus reducing 'outwork' by agglomerating workers into factories may improve the quality of supervision. Advances in technology may also help: for example, closed-circuit television surveillance, metering of machine performance, and the electronic tagging of components can all assist in monitoring of worker performance. Specialised intermediators may emerge at various points in the production process to assure the quality of products passed on to the next stage. But all these responses add to the overall cost of production. Moreover, these changes only occur on an intermittent basis, and there is no guarantee that better solutions will emerge as soon as the problem gets worse.

Value shocks. The historical record suggests that advances in moral commitment have only just kept pace with these demands. The intensity of moral commitment reflects the degree of moral optimism at the time, and the degree of moral optimism has fluctuated around a rather modest upward trend. Oscillations in moral optimism are caused by value shocks - new ideas and ideologies which arise at particular times. Positive shocks increase moral commitment - such as the emergence of Calvinistic Protestantism, as described by Max Weber (1930). The declining reputation of the Roman Catholic church in Northern Europe, caused by the sale of indulgencies, stimulated the rise of new religious force that was well adapted to increasing ethical standards in private enterprise. Negative shocks decrease moral conviction - such as the challenge to Victorian religiosity posed first by Darwin and later by Freud. This undermined the shared convictions on which many successful Victorian business networks were based.

Scientific advance as a cause of value shocks. These value shocks are often the by-products of scientific endeavour, in the sense that they reflect a popular reaction to scientific advances. Negative shocks arise from advances which are perceived to undermine the traditional beliefs on which the existing moral code is based. Positive shocks occur when new knowledge offers new hope by replacing a moral view which is already discredited with another view which is more credible. Since scientific optimism promotes scientific advances, the volatility caused by value shocks is likely to increase when scientific optimism is gaining ground.

Commitment and complexity in equilibrium. A positive value shock allows the division of labour to advance further, because more complex forms of organisation can be sustained without a serious risk of cheating. By contrast, a negative value shock requires the division of labour to be retarded, so that complexity can reduced and cheating contained at tolerable levels. This retardation involves reverting to a situation where more people work at directly producing goods that they consume themselves, and where individual responsibility for faults can therefore be more readily ascertained. If the division of labour continues to advance following a negative value shock the society is endangered by collapse. Cheating increases to the level where the risks of participation in trade suddenly become so unacceptably high that people withdraw from trade, and the division of labour breaks down altogether.

III. Leadership Succession and Inter-group Relations as a Source of Volatility

Leadership succession as a cause of military shocks. Another threat to the division of labour comes from military action. Military shocks can usually be traced back to changes in the leadership of a group. Following the retirement, forcible removal or death of a leader, a successor with a very different outlook may come to power. The succession mechanism may install in power a leader who perceives greater advantage in raids than they do in trade. The threat they pose to neighbouring groups encourages these groups to re-arm for defensive reasons. In this climate of tension, no group wishes to be dependent on other groups for supplies of strategic materials. The production systems of the groups are therefore de-coupled, and each groups adjusts towards self-sufficiency. The leaders may actually benefit from this situation. They can strengthen the internal cohesion of their groups by appealing to loyalty and solidarity. They can blame the decline in consumption standards on the switch from civilian to military output, rather than on the decline in the efficiency of the inter-group production system caused by the switch to autarky.

Effects of war on moral and scientific optimism. Wars can be either ‘hot’ or ‘cold’, depending upon whether the groups merely threaten each other or decide to fight. A 'cold war' may heighten scientific optimism, in the sense that it focuses research on military technology, and intensifies researchers' efforts because their own security is at stake. A 'hot war' can be bad for moral optimism, however. Fighting creates losers, and losers can be come demoralised. Even the victor may feel disheartened by the loss of life - the First World War being an obvious case in point. A loser may not remain demoralised for long, however - in the aftermath of defeat, a new leader may come to power who offer a stimulating vision of what can be achieved if the group makes a 'fresh start'. The stimulating effects of change of leadership were evident in several European countries after the Second World War.

The degree of moral optimism as a constraint on progress. Over time, therefore, value shocks and military shocks, rooted in scientific optimism and leadership change, have generated considerable instability in moral optimism. The failure of moral optimism to sustain itself at adequate levels has constrained the ability of the international system to realise the full potential that a progressive combination of scientific optimism and democracy affords.

IV. Summary and Conclusion

Summary. The broad historical picture is summarised in Tables 2-4. These tables are, of course, extremely crude, given the long time span they cover. The focus is on Western Europe, and on Britain in particular. It is desirable to focus on a specific country when dating historical movements, because movements began at different times in different countries. Britain has been chosen because the documentary evidence is well preserved, and there is a wealth of secondary literature to draw upon - indeed, far too much to be summarised here. It is quite natural that, in a book devoted to as broad a subject as cultural factors in economic growth, generalisation should be made at the highest level, and detailed qualifications ignored for reasons of space.

Conclusion. A cursory examination of these tables supports the view that there is some convergence over time towards the kind of culture which the analytical framework developed above indicates is the one most conducive to economic growth. Convergence is neither steady nor uniform, however. There are cycles superimposed upon the trends, and in respect of one of the key dimensions - moral optimism - the upward trend is very small. There has been progress, therefore, but only to a limited extent. Whether further progress is possible depends upon future intellectual trends, and the capability of future leaders to tap into new intellectual developments and put them to productive use. The readers may draw their own conclusions as to whether this constitutes a basis for optimism or not.

Table 2: Summary of organisational change in Britain 600-2000

	Government	**Market**	**Firm**	**Entre-preneur**	**Key non-profit organi-sation**
Tribalism 600-900	Tribal elders	Reciprocal gifts	Household	Chief	Clan
Feudalism 900-1100	Kingdom supported by local barons	Stable customary prices	Manor	Knight, lord of the manor	Local court
Urbanism 1100-1300	Monarchy sustaining municipality	Local monopoly prices	Self-employed artisan, shopkeeper	Burgher	Craft guild
Mercantil-ism 1300-1700	Autocratic developmen-tal state	Chartered monopoly	Trading company	Merchant banker	Company of merchant adventurers
Commer-cialism & early industrial-ism 1700-1900	Democratic parsimonious state	International competition in wholesale markets	Partnership family firm	'Self-made' man	Regional business elite
Corpora-tism & late industrial-ism 1900-2000	Welfare state	Oligopolistic rivalry	Large joint-stock managerial firm	Salaried CEO	Professional association
Information society 2000-	Autonomous federated regions	International com-petition	SME embedded in network	Every-one	Special interest group

Table 3: Principal technological changes in Britain and Western Europe and their effect on the division of labour in production

	Transport	Communi-cation	Energy	Key industries	Key raw materials
Tribalism 600-900	Foot, back-pack	Oral	Human power (including slaves)	Hunting, husbandry, pottery	Animal skins, wood, clay
Feudalism 900-1100	Waggon	Oral	Animal power	Arable farming textiles	Wool, alum
Urbanism 1100-1500	Coastal & river shipping	Letter	Windmills & watermills	Building, metal working, brewing	Stone, Gold, silver, tin ores
Mercantil-ism 1500-1700	Ocean-going shipping	Letter	Sail-power	Ship-building, armaments	Oak, iron ore
Commer-cialism & early indus-trialism 1700-1900	Railways	Letter, mail services	Steam power	Civil & mechanical engineering	Coal
Corpora-tism & late industrialism 1900-2000	Aircraft	Telephone, radio & TV	Electricity	Chemicals & pharmaceutical	Oil, copper ore, bauxite
Information society 2000-	Aircraft	Internet	Electricity	Electronics	Silicon ore

Table 4: Evolution of inter-group relations: UK and Western Europe

	Political unit	Relations between units	Principles of trade
Tribalism 600-900	Tribal elders	Tribal warfare	Raiding, enslavement, bride-sale
Feudalism 900-1100	Kingdom supported by local barons	Knightly warfare	Tribute
Urbanism 1100-1300	Monarchy sustaining municipalities or chartered boroughs	Warfare between kings' armies disputing both territory and religion	Inter-urban trade, with market taxes
Mercantilism 1300-1700	Autocratic developmental state	National naval warfare, piracy	Rival entrepot seeking to monopolise certain trades. Shipping subsidies
Commercialism & early industrialism 1700-1900	Democratic parsimonious state	Trade rivalry	Free trade plus infant industry protection
Corporatism & late industrialism 1900-2000	Welfare state	Industrial rivalry	Multilateral trade agreements
Information society 2000-	Autonomous federated regions	Regulation by international organizations	Global free trade

References

BUCKLEY, PETER J., CASSON, MARK: "Economics as an Imperialist Social Science", *Human Relations*, 46 (1993), pp.1035-52.

CASSON, MARK: *The Economics of Business Culture*, Oxford (Clarendon Press) 1991.

CASSON, MARK: *Information and Organization*, Oxford (Clarendon Press) 1997.

COASE, RONALD H.: "The Nature of the Firm", *Economica*, New series, 4 (1937), pp. 386-405.

DAVIS, RALPH: *The Rise of the Atlantic Economies*, Ithaca (Cornell University Press) 1973.

FISHER, ALLAN G. B.: *The Clash of Progress and Security*, London (Macmillan) 1945.

FISHER, F. J.: "The Development of the London Food Market, 1540-1640", *Economic History Review*, 5 (1935).

GODLEY, A. C.: *Enterprise and Culture: Jewish Immigrant Entrepreneurship in New York and London, 1880-1914*, Cambridge and New York (Cambridge University Press) 1999.

HARPER, DAVID A.: *Entrepeneurship and the Market Process*, London (Routledge) 1996.

HAYEK, FRIEDRICH A. VON: "Economics and Knowledge", *Economica*, New series, 4 (1937), pp. 33-54.

HOFSTEDE, G.: *Culture's Consequence* Beverley Hills (Sage Publications) 1984.

JONES, ERIC L.: *The European Miracle*, Cambridge (Cambridge University Press) 1982.

JONES, ERIC L.: *Growth Recurring*, Oxford (Clarendon Press) 1988.

KNIGHT, FRANK H.: *The Ethics of Competition and Other Essays*, London (George Allen & Unwin) 1935.

LANDES, DAVID S.: *The Wealth and Poverty of Nations*, New York (Little Brown) 1998.

LAURENT, A.: "The Cultural Diversity of Western Conceptions of Management", *International Studies of Management and Organization*, 13 (1983).

OLSON, MANCUR: *The Logic of Collective Action*, Cambridge, MA (Harvard University Press) 1965.

SCULLY, GERALD W.: *Constitutional Environments and Economic Growth*, Princeton, NJ (Princeton University Press) 1992.

SMITH, ADAM: *The Nature and Causes of the Wealth of Nations* (Glasgow edition, 1976), Oxford (Oxford University Press) 1776.

TROMPENAARS, F.: *Riding the Waves of Culture*, London (Nicholas Brearley) 1993.

Chapter 2

Trust as a Governance Device

BART NOOTEBOOM

I. Introduction

In spite of its importance, and in contrast with the literatures in sociology and management, trust has been neglected in the economic literature, with some exceptions (Arrow 1974, Buckley and Casson 1988). One reason for this neglect probably is that while economists strive for analytical precision, trust appears to be an irredeemably imprecise notion. And indeed it is a complex and slippery concept; a minefield of potential misunderstanding. Different people can mean different things by it, and this can lead to disaster. We need to answer the question what precisely its meaning, sources and limits are. A second, more substantive reason for its neglect in economics follows from an argument proposed by Williamson (1993).

In his earlier work, Williamson (1975) employed the notion of "atmosphere", which appears to be closely related to the notion of trust. That notion was left imprecise, and Williamson did not return to it in his later work. Williamson (1985, 1991) did recognise the effect on transaction costs of "the larger context in which transactions are embedded", but the nature and workings of this context were not elaborated. In his 1993 article he explicitly faced the notion of trust, and developed the following argument. If trust does not go beyond calculative self-interest, it has nothing to add to what is already offered in (transaction cost) economics. If it does go beyond calculative self-interest it is blind, and blind trust is unwise; it will not survive in the struggle for survival in markets. It has its place only in personal relations with close friends and family. Hence trust is redundant.

This article will counter that argument to show that trust is not redundant and is indeed indispensable for all economic action. It proposes that trust plays an important role in the relation between culture and economic growth. By 'culture' we can mean a number of things. The broadest concept is that of culture as opposed to nature: everything made by man. This includes art, law, customs and ethics, but also science and technology and also pollution, persecution and warfare. A second concept is culture as heritage: the stock of documented or otherwise embodied achievements from the history of civilisation: arts, artifacts and documents. The anthropological concept of culture denotes the totality of norms and values developed in a certain group. This is the idea we have when talking about 'multicultural communities'. The sociological concept of culture denotes the habits and life styles that distinguish a group. Here one can talk, for example, of 'youth culture'. And finally, there is culture as art. When someone claims that the young lack culture, he can mean that the young have insufficient knowledge of our heritage, or that they lack the values and norms he is accustomed to, or that he objects to their life style, or that the young are insufficiently interested in art (or that he does not like their art). The relation between trust and culture lies primarily in the anthropological and sociological meanings of culture. Trust is related to norms and values of conduct, and to habits and life styles; to normativity and habituation.

By economic growth we usually mean the increase of prosperity as measured, say, by gross national product. But we could refer to broader notions of performance, in terms of well-being or the quality of life. Trust relates to both. Trust is an instrument for the governance of relations which contributes to prosperity by reducing transaction costs. That may be called its extrinsic value. Many authors have pointed this out (Arrow 1974, Jarillo 1988, Bradach & Eccles 1989, Powell 1990, Casson 1991, 1995, Helper 1990, Sako 1992, Gulati 1995, Berger, Noorderhaven & Nooteboom 1995, Chiles & MacMackin 1996, Nooteboom 1996, Nooteboom, Berger & Noorderhaven 1997). Trust can also have intrinsic value, as part of a broader notion of well-being or quality of life. People may prefer, as an end in itself, to deal with each other on the basis of trust (Blau 1964). Most economists tend to think of value in exchange as something that exists independently from the transaction. As formulated by Murakami & Rohlen (1992, p. 70): "The value of the relationship itself is typically ignored and the impersonality of the transaction is assumed". In intrinsic utility, the exchange process itself matters, as does the economic surplus and its sharing that the exchange yields. This was also recognised by Buckley and Casson (1988). It also seems to be what Williamson (1975) had in mind with his notion of 'atmosphere'. People may prefer to transact on the basis of trust and its sources: ethics, kinship, friendship, or empathy. Social exchange relies more on unspecified, implicit obligations, which depend on shared systems of meaning, belief, and ethics. The idea that exchange includes non-contractual elements goes back (at least) to Durkheim. Let us next look more closely at the role of trust in exchange.

II. Trust as a Governance Device

As indicated, trust has intrinsic value: many of us prefer to have trust-based rather than opportunistic relations. But none of us could live without trust. To trust is to accept risk, vulnerability, uncertainty; at some point to stop questioning meaning, quality, competence, intentions, outcomes. One cannot mistrust everything because that would yield an infinite regress which precludes all action. One cannot keep on demanding definitions of the terms of definitions and guarantees for the terms of guarantees. The less trust there is, the further questioning will proceed, thus accumulating effort of exchange.

> *In some states of the US one needs to deposit money or a credit card at the counter of a gas station before taking gas, and then return to conclude the transaction. In Europe the first trip to the counter is not required.*

In other words: mistrust raises transaction costs. Transaction costs are costs that arise in processes of exchange, which can be divided into three stages: Contact, Contract and Control. The transaction is an event at the transition from contract to control. In the stage of contact there are costs of search for demand and supply. In the stage of contract there are costs of evaluating quality and reliability, negotiation and the preparation of an agreement (possibly a contract), including measures to reduce costs and problems in the final stage of control. These are: costs and limitations of monitoring performance, interpreting the agreement, haggling, adapting the agreement to changed circumstances, enforcing the terms of a contract, loss of specific assets when the exchange relation breaks, loss of hostages.

In transaction cost economics (TCE), given bounded rationality and potential opportunism, 'specific assets' are crucial: assets that are sunk in the transaction relation; have less or no value in alternative relations. These form switching costs and hence part of an exit barrier, which creates dependence and hence vulnerability to 'hold-up'. Another component of the exit barrier is the value that the partner offers in excess of the next best alternative. Thus one is captive, and thereby subject to the risk of hold-up, in proportion to the sum of switching costs and relative value of the partner (Nooteboom 1996).

There are four basic classes of instruments to govern relational risk: decrease captiveness, increase control by means of contracting, increase incentives from self-interest, decrease propensity towards opportunism (Nooteboom 1996).

One can decrease captiveness by not engaging in specific investments and by keeping options open for alternative partners in the focal activity. Here one solves the problem by evading it. But specific investments are often needed to increase joint added value, to achieve product differentiation (in order to increase profit by evading pure price competition), and to achieve the mutual understanding and adjustment that is needed for pooling competencies for innovation. Such mutual adjustment and close interaction is needed, in particular, when the knowledge to be shared is tacit, as is especially the case in early stages of innovation. Limiting the number of partners may be needed to evade the multiplication of set-up costs of governance, and to limit spill-over risks for the partner, which may be needed for him to open up his knowledge for co-operation and joint development.

The risk imposed by captiveness cannot be eliminated completely by legal contracting, since even legal language does not yield full closure of conditions, even if they were foreseeable, which they are not. There is uncertainty concerning the capabilities and intentions (opportunism) of the partner and uncertainty concerning novel conditions that might arise and that might create novel 'opportunities for opportunism' (Nooteboom 1996) not covered in the agreement or contract. Novel, more attractive partners may appear on the scene. Objectives may change. Technology may change. Furthermore, contracting can itself be expensive in money and time. It yields a straightjacket for action which can be very constraining especially when the goal of the relation is innovation: the development or implementation of novelty. Furthermore it can set a relation off on a foot of mistrust which inhibits the development of trust, and may yield a vicious circle of regulation and mutual constraint.

Next, one can try to govern by self-interest: see to it that it is not in the interest of the transaction partner to 'utilize opportunities for opportunism'. This can be because he is himself sufficiently captive, because of the high relative value that he receives, or because of a high share of ownership in extensive and highly specific investments. It can be because he has surrendered hostages, in the form of resources whose value declines or disappears if he reneges on his commitment. This can be the surrender of some resource that is of great value to him and not or less to the party holding the hostage[1] (patents, key personnel, other forms of knowledge), or in the form of taking a minority participation in the partner firm. It can be because he risks his reputation in breaking the relationship.

Perhaps nothing works better than self-interest, but is there anything beyond it? It will be argued below that trust does go beyond self-interest, and thereby has something to add which economic science lacks. The point here is that whatever its sources, trust reduces transaction costs. It does so by lowering costs of search (Casson 1995), in the stage of contact, and costs of monitoring, in the stage of control, because trusting people are less secretive and more readily supply information (Zand 1972). In other words: trust reduces uncertainty and risk. Trust further reduces costs of contracting and control because it lowers fears of opportunism (Bradach & Eccles 1989) and accepts more influence from the partner (Zand 1972).

However, we should not forget that trust involves surrender to vulnerability, and can have disastrous consequences. And as argued by Zucker (1986) trust does not always enhance efficiency. Its production can be very costly, and when it is embedded in institutions it can limit flexibility and obstruct innovation. Once it becomes a 'rule of the game' it may have to be followed even where it is detrimental to efficiency. This raises the question

---

1 For a historical discussion of hostages, see DE LAAT (1996).

whether perhaps a trust-based economy meets obstacles in radical innovation (Nooteboom 1997a). On the other hand, Hill (1990) argued that since trust economises on transaction costs, trust-based societies have a competitive advantage, and will prevail in the evolution of global competition. But this presumes that such society can prevent entry of opportunists that may break down the domestic ethic of trust, but if one does not open one's borders in that way one may be ostracised from world trade (Nooteboom 1998). Perhaps this is what is happening to Japan.

Different institutional environments and arrangements provide for different relations between firms, and hence different structures of capitalist economies (Nooteboom 1997b). In the 'Rhineland' economies of continental Europe (Albert 1993), there is a tendency towards 'network economies', with more or less durable ties between organisations. In Anglo-American economies firms tend to be more autonomous. In the Dutch policy debate much attention has been given to the role of 'clusters' of complementary firms and industries (Jacobs 1996), inspired by the work of Michael Porter (1990). Recently, the present minister of economic affairs has elaborated the view of his predecessor by proposing that his ministry has a brokerage role to play in stimulating the development of such clusters. In these matters, a thorough understanding of trust and its meaning, sources, production and limitations is crucial.

III. The Meaning of Trust

When someone assures you that he can be trusted, what could it mean? When the mafia boss says: 'Trust me my son', this could just be a threat that you should obey or else. Alternatively, it could be a mere ploy to prevent you from covering yourself against the risks of his opportunism. When the assurance is honest, it could mean that he sees himself contractually bound to honour his commitments: he has no 'opportunities for opportunism' (Nooteboom 1996). Or it could mean that although he has opportunity, he has no motive: it would not be in his interest to utilize them, since he is dependent on you and would not want to antagonize. Or it could mean that even if he has both opportunity and motive he will not defect because he feels that would be unethical, or because he does not want to harm you out of friendship. But how far would this go? How can we untangle this mess of meaning?

Consider the following broad and simple definition of trust:

> (1) To trust is to accept or neglect the possibility that things will go wrong.

This definition is based on scrutiny of the many definitions given in the literature. It ties trust closely to the notion of risk in the sense of the possibility that things go wrong, as is customary in the literature (Luhmann 1988, Chiles & McMackin 1996, Nooteboom 1996)[2]. Note that the definition leaves open for whom things go wrong: the bearer of trust or someone for whom he has concern. I can trust that things do not go wrong for you. The definition also leaves open a wide range for the object of trust: that to which trust is extended: goods, people (including oneself), social systems (such as firms, economies, legal systems, governments), nature or God. Thus we can speak of consumer confidence in the economy, for example. When extended to people it is usually called *behavioral trust*. The definition also leaves open the cause of things going wrong: by accident or by design.

By including both 'acceptance' and 'neglect' of the possibility of things going wrong, the definition also includes *cognitive and affect based trust* (McAllister 1995) as well as *routine* based trust. To 'accept' risk is to conduct an explicit, rational evaluation of the probability of things going wrong, and the implications of it. 'Neglect' of the possibility of things going wrong may be based on habit or routine: certain actions in certain contexts never went wrong, and we lose awareness of the possibility (Parkhe 1993, Gulati 1995, Nooteboom, Berger & Noorderhaven 1997). Trustworthiness is often taken for granted until violated. Such non-rational routine behaviour is rational when the capacity for rational evaluation is limited, as Herbert Simon explained long ago. Neglect may also be based on naivety, or on unwillingness to face risks due to fear. It may be based on cognitive dissonance related to friendship or kinship: one does not want to contemplate the possibility of opportunism on the part of friends or family. Particularly in the latter case trust is to a greater or lesser extent based on affect. But also ethics based trust can be related to affect: emotions connected with the no-

2 Note that this is not the economist's definition of risk as the variance of a probability distribution of returns. There is evidence that in practice actors see risk rather as the probability of things going wrong.

tion of justice or decency. Emotional closure to reason, while not rational in its operation, is rational in its consequences to the extent that it yields credible commitments that lift people from prisoner's dilemma's (cf. Frank 1988).

Another definition of trust is given by Deutsch (1962, quoted in Zand 1972):

> (2) Trusting behaviour consists of actions that (1) increase one's vulnerability (2) to another whose behaviour is not under one's control (3) in a situation where the penalty one suffers if the other abuses that vulnerability is greater than the benefit one gains if the other does not abuse that vulnerability.

This definition limits damage to the bearer of trust, limits the object of trust to people one deals with, and assumes that possible damage exceeds possible gains. But for the purpose of studying transaction relations this is a very useful definition.

A distinction has been made between trust and confidence (Luhmann 1988). This distinction does not exist in all languages; e.g. not in Dutch. Trust is associated with choice, and confidence with the inevitable. Trust refers to relations we choose to engage in, and when it goes wrong we can blame our judgement. Confidence refers to the continuity of the natural and moral order: nature, God, the government, the legal system. If things go wrong we cannot blame our judgement. The distinction seems related to Douglass North's distinction between institutional environment ('the system') and institutional arrangements for specific circumstances (North & Thomas 1973). To the extent that one is inevitable to oneself, one can speak only of self-confidence. But if there is no unitary identity of the self, and there are several selves that can oppose each other, as in problems of 'weakness of the will', one may be able to speak of trusting or mistrusting oneself. Confidence can be taken as a special case of the more general notion of trust. Note that confidence in social systems and behavioral trust in people can connect: behavioral trust may be based on the expectation that the trusted person is susceptible to norms and values that are part of the 'institutional environment', and this is at the same time confidence in the robustness and 'tightness' of the social system.

Trust has been defined as a subjective probability that something will not go wrong (Dasgupta 1988, Gambetta 1988, Mayer, Davis & Schoorman 1995). This is an appealing idea, and ties in well with the idea that trust is intimately related to risk (in the sense indicated above). But it seems to imply that trust is always calculative, if subjective probabilities are seen to be conscious and as obeying the customary axioms and calculation rules of ordinary probabilities. As indicated above, trust can also be based on routine, lack of awareness, naivety or emotional or ethical commitment. Or in other words: the basis for trust can be implicit, or tacit. And it is doubtful that tacit subjective probabilities make sense.

Summing up: the general notion of trust, according to definition (1), has many ramifications and forms. We have so far seen the following: behavioral trust (the object is individual people), confidence (the object is an encompassing, inevitable social or natural system), explicit/rational trust (in terms of subjective probabilities), tacit affect- or routine- based trust. But there are more ramifications.

What is the object of trust: to what can it be extended? The difference was mentioned between trust in people (behavioral trust) and trust in social or natural systems (confidence). How about trust on an intermediate level: organizational trust? How can a firm be the object of trust, and how would that relate to behavioral (personal) trust? How is it produced? One might think that trust in organizations is always built upon personal trust in people from the organization that one deals with. But personal trust is conditioned (limited, enhanced) by the organizational role of the person: how important is the trusted person; what is his position with respect to organizational rules, procedures and competencies; will he be backed up by his boss, etc. And trust in persons will depend on personnel turnover across roles: how long will the person be incumbent in the relevant role. There is 'system trust' in terms of ethical or other restrictions and guidelines of behaviour to which people are bound. Here organizational culture and even industrial culture come in, in both the anthropological and sociological sense: the values, norms, habits and styles of conduct that prevail in the firm and in the industry. These in turn are conditioned by the circumstances that the organization or the industry face, such as the effectiveness and importance of reputation mechanisms, and the intensity of competition. When competition is lax, a firm can afford to be more altruistic than when competition forces it to utilize every opportunity to obtain short term profit (Nooteboom 1996).

Summing up: the relation between organizational and personal trust lies in the assignment of people to roles, and the conditions and directions given for playing these roles, in the form of organizational and industrial structure, procedures and culture. Particularly important for the perception of trust are the public conduct of the firm's leadership and roles that connect with partners: 'boundary spanners and gatekeepers' such as purchasers, marketers, negotiators, staff exchanged or combined in joint teams. Thus organizational trust is a constellation of behavioral trust, with organizational structure and culture acting as institutions that limit and guide the behaviour of staff. Thus it goes beyond any simple 'aggregate' of behavioral trust.

A crucially important distinction in behavioral and organizational trust is that between competence trust and intentional or goodwill trust (Barber 1983, Nooteboom 1996). If I say that I do not trust someone with my car, I may mean that I doubt his driving abilities (competence), or I may mean that I expect him to be careless or to steal my car (intentions). I someone does not honour his commitment, it may be from incompetence or force majeure or from opportunism, and what action is appropriate depends on that. If someone cannot do something, one may help. But if someone does not want to do something that would be a waste of time, and one should improve his motivation or exert control. The complication is, of course, that if someone defects by opportunism he will claim force majeure, and one may often be incapable to establish which is the case: force majeure, incompetence, neglect, opportunism. Thus limits in competence and in intention demand different actions but cannot always be distinguished.

Note that behavioral trust is more encompassing than intentional trust. Behavioral trust can be based on intentional trust, but also on other factors (such as a failure to recognize unilateral dependence), and the existence of intentional trust cannot be inferred from the presence of behavioral trust alone (Craswell 1993, Kee & Knox 1970, Noorderhaven 1996).

IV. Sources of Trust

What are the sources of trust? Williams (1988) proposed a scheme for the determinants of co-operation, which is reproduced in Table 1. These may also be seen as sources of trust. The macro sources, which apply beyond any specific exchange relation, relate to North's 'institutional environment': ethics, god, the law. The micro sources relate to 'institutional arrangements': sources that one might use in specific relations.

Williams argued that none of these sources by itself suffices and that, in co-operation, some mix will always be operative, while no universally best mix, regardless of specific conditions, can be specified. Often, trust based on friend- or kinship will not suffice as a basis for co-operation. Conversely, material self-interest and coercion are seldom sufficient as a basis for co-operation: one needs trust on the basis of non-egotistic sources to the extent that one cannot fully control the partner's conduct by threat and reward (cf. Deutsch 1962, quoted in Zand, 1972); to make this fragile basis for co-operation more resilient (Ring and van de Ven 1992).

Table 1: Sources of cooperation[3]

	macro	**micro**
egotistic	coercion or fear of sanctions from some authority (god/ law)	material advantage or 'interest'
non-egotistic	ethics: values, norms of proper conduct	bonds of friendship, kinship or empathy

If we consider the conscious, explicit and rational (rather than the tacit, habitual) side of intentional trust, and identify that with a subjective probability that the partner will not behave opportunistically, without further qualification, then anything that contributes to such subjective probability would belong to trust; anything that restrains the partner in his opportunistic conduct. That would include the direct control that one may exercise over his conduct by contract, monitoring or threat (coercion). It would also include motives of self-interest that restrain the partner, such as the preservation of his reputation (Weigelt & Camerer 1988), expectation of future rewards from co-operative conduct in the present (Telser 1980), or the desire to protect 'hostages' (Williamson 1985).

Thus it is useful to distinguish between a wide and a narrow concept of trust. The wide concept includes all sources of trust, as in definition (1). The narrow concept would go beyond self-interest. We trust someone in the narrow sense if we believe that he is likely to co-operate even if he is not

3 WILLIAMS (1988).

coerced to do so and has no direct material interest in doing so. Following Nooteboom (1996) I define it as follows:

> (3) To have trust in the narrow sense, or 'real' intentional trust, is to accept or neglect the possibility that a partner will utilize opportunities for opportunism even if it is in his interest to do so.

There are two arguments for using this narrow or 'strong' notion of trust. One is that it corresponds more closely to common sense intuitions of trust: is it really a matter of trust when you expect someone to conform to agreements out of self-interest or coercion? It is proposed here that you 'really' trust someone when you are willing to *forego* guarantees on the basis of coercion or self-interest. Only then does trust economize on transaction costs. This yields the second reason why in this article trust is taken in this way: the purpose here is to see how trust can economize on transaction costs.

As noted before, especially the non-egotistic sources of trust are to a greater or lesser extent affect based: this is clear for the micro sources of friendship and kinship, but also the macro source of ethics has an emotional loading: it is connected with emotions concerning justice, fairness and decency. Trust in this narrow sense is based on commitment to mutual interest; to taking care about the partner's interest. If something goes wrong in the relation, the first impulse is not to run away ('exit') but to discuss and try and solve the problem ('voice') (Hirschman 1984, Helper 1990, Nooteboom 1997a). But this does not mean that such commitment is boundless and that trust can be blind.

Table 2: Modes of trust production[4]

basis	**examples**	**connection with Table 1**
characteristics	membership of family, community, culture, religion	all sources
institutions	certification, professional standards, benchmarking, intermediaries	macro
process	loyalty, commitment, friendship, habituation	micro

4 adapted from ZUCKER (1986).

Zucker (1986) made a distinction between different modes of trust 'production', which is complementary to the different sources in table 1. They are given in table 2. Zucker (1986) argued that in the US increasingly characteristics based related to family and (local, ethnic or religious) community and process based trust in ongoing relations have eroded. Communitarianism was replaced by individualism, and the vacuum had to be filled by means of institutional based trust. A similar argument was later presented by Fukuyama (1995).

But in what sense can trust be 'produced'? Institutions in the form of values, norms and standards of conduct can be part of the macro sources of co-operation: the institutional environment. But they may also be built up in specific relations, on the micro level, as part of institutional arrangements. And the two interact: institutional arrangements build upon the institutional environment and in due course may shift it (Sydow 1996). Some institutions, such as technical standards or systems of certification, can be developed on the basis of some rational design, although this may take quite some time, since they tend to affect established interests and may require a political process. One can select a partner on the basis of his characteristics, such as being a member of a family or community. But one cannot simply buy into characteristics based trust: one can marry into a family and one can become a member of some communities, but entry selection can be strict and it can take considerable time. Process trust can only grow. Such growth can be facilitated, by creating favorable conditions, but it cannot be purchased and installed by the pound. To 'produce' process trust is as paradoxical as to order spontaneity: if it worked it would not be real. Process trust is as much the outcome of a relation as the basis for it. Sydow (1996) approached this from the perspective of Giddens' structuration theory: to the extent that process trust is already available it provides the basis for a relationship, it is reproduced in the relation, if it goes well, and may be further deepened to provide the basis for further extending the relationship.

In the attempt to create conditions for process trust to develop, detailed contracts can be destructive: they demonstrate mistrust which engenders mistrust, so that mistrust becomes a self-fulfilling prophecy (Macauley 1963, Zand 1972). But how then does one begin a relation if there is no prior basis for trust in the institutional environment, or in selection on the basis of characteristics, while self-interest does not suffice to prevent risks of opportunism? Between strangers a relation will tend to start gingerly, with small steps that do not demand detailed contracts and whose success generates more trust.

Process based trust moves through several stages. Generally, for people who are not acquainted ex ante, at the beginning of the process calculativeness will tend to prevail: the focus is on the generation of material value. The greater this value or its urgency, the more risk one may be willing to take. Partners are given the benefit of the doubt, within certain margins of risk left by incomplete contracts, accepted on the basis of some heuristic that takes into account prevailing ethics, customs, experience, urgency and the intrinsic value attached to trust. As the relation begins to generate value, trust in both competence and intention may deepen due to understanding of the sources of both. Next, bonds of friendship and identification with each others' interests may develop to deepen trust further, and routinization may weaken the awareness of risk.

In the development of trust relations intermediaries can perform important roles (Sydow 1996, Nooteboom 1999): If X has competence as well as intentional trust in Y and Y has intentional trust in Z, then X may rationally give intentional trust in Z a chance. X needs to feel that Y is able to judge well and has no intention to lie about his judgement. This can speed up the building of trust between strangers, which might otherwise take too long. The intermediary can also perform valuable services in protecting trust when it is still fragile: to eliminate misunderstanding and allay suspicions when errors or mishaps are mistaken for opportunism.

V. How Far Does Trust Go?

As indicated before, there is no trust in economics. Williamson came close to accepting the notion of trust with the notion of 'atmosphere' in his earlier work (Williamson 1975), but this did not reappear in his later work. Williamson (1985, 1991) did recognize the effect on transaction costs of 'the larger context in which transactions are embedded', which seems similar to the 'institutional environment' indicated above. But the underlying assumption is that it applies equally to all actors in a given context or culture. It does not serve to distinguish between alternatives of governance structure ('institutional arrangements') within that context. This is not acceptable, for two reasons (Nooteboom, Berger & Noorderhaven 1997). First, the susceptibility to values and norms (which are part of the institutional environment) is likely to differ between individuals within a national culture and between organizations, as part of organizational culture, so that their impact may vary within national boundaries (cf. Noorderhaven 1995). Second, institutions in the sense of norms and values (the anthropological dimension of culture) and habituation in the sense of customs, routines and styles of conduct (the sociological dimension of culture) may not be exogenous to a transaction relationship and may partly develop within it, as part of process based trust (Ford 1980).

There is a patent inconsistency in Williamson's argument concerning opportunism. His argument is explicitly not that everybody is opportunistic all the time, but that people are more or less opportunistic more or less of the time, and since prior to transaction one does not know how much and how often, one should take into account the *possibility* of opportunistic conduct. But the argument implies variation in opportunism between people, which is subsequently ignored. There is also an anomaly of time. On the one hand, time is of the essence for the problem of specific investments: the problem is that in order to recoup an investment made now, one needs repeated transactions in the future. On the other hand the assumption of opportunism is based on the argument that prior to transaction one does not know the extent of the partner's opportunism. One problem with that is that it negates the possibility of a reputation mechanism, which Williamson accepts elsewhere. The second problem is that if time is relevant, in ongoing transactions to recoup specific investments, it is relevant also for learning about the partner's inclination towards opportunism.

As indicated before, Williamson (1993) the issue of trust in institutional arrangements is confronted squarely. Williamson proposes that if trust does not go beyond calculative self-interest, it adds nothing to conventional economic analysis, and should be discarded as superfluous and confusing. That is a reasonable and useful comment. But if trust does go beyond calculative self-interest, Williamson argues, then it is blind trust, and that is ill-advised and will tend not to survive. It should be reserved for family or other loved ones only. There are two problems with this.

Firstly, action can be non-calculative without being blind. One can and does, and in view of limited cognitive capacity has to, act partly on the basis of routines. Here, this is called 'habituation'. Such action is non-calculative, because it is non-reflective. But it is not blind, in the sense that it has a rational basis: it is based on experience that it works, before it becomes a routine. In other words: it is inevitable that we take certain aspects of the behaviour of others for granted. One reason was given before: to question everything is to get bogged down in an infinite regress of suspicion and questioning. The second reason is that reliance on routine is rationally warranted in view of persistent success and lack of disaster in the past.

Secondly, to go beyond calculative self-interest logically one can go beyond calculativeness, which is the option that Williamson considers, or one can go beyond self-interest, and this option Williamson ignores. To go beyond self interest is to take into account the interests of others, even if this may to some extent damage one's own interests. People are willing to do this to some extent, which varies between people, and this is based on the non-egotistic sources of cooperation recognised by Williams (table 2): the institutional environment of norms and values, and institutional arrangements based on bonds of friendship or kinship, or habituation.

But indeed: trust should not be blind, because there are limits to trustworthiness. To say that to a greater or lesser extent people will remain loyal to a relationship even if there are opportunities for opportunism and it is advantageous to utilize those opportunities, does not imply that this resistance to temptation is boundless. Perhaps the cynic is right who says that everyone has his price. After all there are degrees of temptation: from small advantage to sheer survival. Firms in more competitive markets will succumb to temptation sooner than firms in markets with lesser pressures of competition.

The deeper trust and trustworthiness are, the greater this resistance to temptation is, but even the strongest may succumb to a 'golden opportunity'. When relying on trust, the art is to find out how far one can go; to assess when the partner's resilience to temptation is tested too much. How far will partners go in trying to solve problems that affect their interests before they defect? Some will go further than others, and this will depend on the wider culture (institutional environment), bonds of kinship, habits and routines or bonds of friendship built up in a relationship (institutional arrangements; characteristics and process based trust). People develop heuristics to assess all this.

So, the fact that trust is limited does not eliminate that it allows for limited contracts and monitoring, thereby yielding cheap governance, flexibility in relations and a basis for further developing trust.

If blind trust is unwise, trust often is a step by step process of building mutual trust, and one can observe little more than people's actions, how does one assess the intentional trustworthiness of a partner from his actions? It shows itself best in loyalty under adversity. It is especially important to assess whether it is intrinsic or extrinsic, because in the first case loyalty is an internal goal, while in the second case it is a means to pursue self-interest. The first does not require monitoring, and the second does. The first is based on ethics and conscience, based on norms and values, or on emotions of friendship or kinship, or on the enjoyment of trusting relations. The latter is based on quid pro quo, lack of opportunity for opportunism, dependence or fear of reputational loss (Deutsch 1973). Connected with this, Deutsch also recognised the notion of 'focus', with three possibilities: focus on results for the other, on warrantable effort (is one seen to be doing one's reasonable best?), or on doing as one is told. Is one genuinely trying to co-operate or is one intent only on legitimizing one's actions?

So, when a supportive action by X is observed, how does one judge what lies behind it? The following sequence of questions can be an aid to assessment (adapted from Deutsch 1993):

1. Was the outcome intended by X, or was it an unintended result of his action?
2. Did the action entail significant risk to X?
3. Was X aware of the risk, and was it not neglected out of impulsiveness?
4. Did X attach a *positive* value to this risk, out of masochism, sensation, (self) image?
5. Did X have a choice, or was the action dictated by compulsion or conformity?
6. Was it out of confidence in the system rather than a positive evaluation of the situation?
7. Was it out of enlightened self-interest?
8. Was it out of enjoyment of trust relations?
9. Was it out of ethics, friend- or kinship, habituation?

Deutsch noted that, as can be seen from the above, power can have an adverse effect on trust: if one is very powerful, there is more suspicion that people subjected to one's power are trustworthy only because they have no choice[5]. In case of absolute power, the hypothesis that this is the case can never be rejected. This is how the powerful become suspicious. And the problem with that is that mistrust tends to feed upon itself even more than trust does. (Mis)trust by X tends to engender (mis)trust on the part of Y, which justifies and deepens X's (mis)trust. But while trust can be falsified because it leads to reliance on others which can be disappointed, mistrust cannot, because it blocks trusting action that might disprove it.

VI. Measurement

Contrary to common opinion, trust can be measured, and can then be fed into an econometric equation to test its effect. The methodology is that of factor analysis, as used in psychometrics. Different dimensions of trust are identified, which are not themselves directly measurable ('latent variables'), but for which indicator variables can be hypothesized to reflect or 'span' the latent variable. Confirmatory factor analysis is used to construct an underlying variable from the indicators, and to test whether it is indeed a significant variable (on the basis of the Cronbach alpha test: alpha should exceed 0.7). The significance of the contribution of each of the indicator variables can be tested on the basis of the significance of its correlation with the constructed variable. If it is not, it is discarded, and the procedure is repeated until either the hypothesis of an underlying variable is rejected or all indicators have a significant 'loading' and the variable satisfies the Cronbach test.

For a demonstration how this works, see Nooteboom et al (1997). This was a study of ten companies supplying components and sub-assemblies to producers of electrical/electronic apparatus, with ten customer relations each. Two dimensions of trust were hypothesized: institutionalization and habitualization. By the first is meant the emergence of common norms to regulate behaviour within a relationship. The second means the development of habits, routines and a shared style of conduct. The two dimensions of trust relate directly to the anthropological and sociological dimensions of

5 Here I take power in the usual definition of the ability to affect the alternatives of choice for the object of power.

culture. The indicator variables (five-point Likert scales) are specified below. Cronbach's alpha for the constructs is also given.

HAB: Habitualization (á=0.75)

- Because we have been doing business so long with this customer, all kinds of procedures have become self-evident
- Because we have been doing business for so long with this customer, we can understand each other well and quickly
- In our contacts with this customer we have never had the feeling of being misled

INST: Institutionalization (á=0.73)

- In this relation, both sides are expected not to make demands that can seriously damage the interests of the other
- In this relation the strongest side is expected not to pursue its interest at all costs

HI: Habitualization/institutionalization (á=0.77) = Habitualization + institutionalization + item:

- In this relation informal agreements have the same significance as formal contracts

The last item is kept apart from HAB and INST because it could with equal theoretical and empirical justification be added to either of them; in both cases Cronbach's alpha increases with ten percentage points. The resulting variables were included in an econometric model to explain perceived relational risk, with two dimensions: the probability that the relation goes wrong, and the penalty involved if it does. The trust variables competed for explanation with more traditional explanatory variables, derived from transaction cost economics. The potential size of loss is hypothesized to depend on switching costs (due primarily to ownership of specific assets) and the value of the partner (relative to the next best alternative). Continuity of the relation (measured as growth and future perspectives) also contributes to the perceived value of the relation and hence the potential size of loss. The probability that such loss arises is hypothesized to depend on trust next to a range of other variables. One covers the restrictions of opportunities for opportunism faced by the partner, as determined by the closeness and detail of legal and private ordering. Another explanatory variable is the perceived dependence of the partner, determined by the value that the respondent perceives himself to have for the partner, which reduces partner's incentives to utilize opportunities for opportunism. A further variable is the continuity of the relation: in ongoing relations risk is perceived to be less. Control variables were added to control for firm-specific attributes such as firm size and the degree to which the firm tends to avoid risk. The latter was expected to have a positive effect on perceived probability of loss: risk-averse firms take a dimmer view of risks of dependence.

The empirical results showed that indeed trust has a significant effect on perceived probability of incurring a loss due to opportunism, next to the effects of other variables that one would expect from transaction cost economics. One disconfirmation of hypotheses was that instead of the expected positive effect of uncertainty avoidance on probability of loss there was a negative effect. But this can be interpreted very well: risk averse suppliers make sure they have low-risk partners. The second disconfirmation was that a high perceived value offered to the partner did not have the expected negative effect on the perceived probability of loss. Our interpretation of this is that firms are not sophisticated enough in their assessment of the situation: they did not take into account the motivations of the partner; did not ask the question what they would do if they stood in his shoes.

VII. Conclusion

Trust is a complex and slippery concept, but it can be rigorously defined, analyzed and tested empirically. The object of trust can be objects, people and organizations. It can apply to wider social and natural systems and God, and then it is called confidence. When applied to people it is called behavioral trust. Trust in organizations is based on a combination of behavioral trust concerning people with whom one interacts and 'system' trust in organizational structure, culture and external conditions of the firm's survival. Organizational structure includes roles assigned to people and the manner in which they are controlled. Culture and survival conditions restrict and guide people in their organizational roles. Behavioral and organizational trust can concern competence or intentions. Intentional trust can have several sources: coercion, incentives from self-interest, ethics and norms/values, and habituation and bonds of kinship or friendship. It can be based on the wider social environment (institutional environment) and on specific institutional arrangements, which build on the institutional environment. To have trust in a wide sense is to accept or neglect possibilities of things going wrong. This can be based on any of the sources indicated. To have trust in a narrow sense is to accept or neglect the possibility that someone might utilize opportunities for opportunism even if it is in his interest to do so. This is based on the sources of ethics, norms/values, and habituation and bonds of kinship and friendship: the anthropological and sociological dimensions of culture.

Governance of relations has four basic classes of instruments: evasion of dependence, control by contracting, incentives from self-interest and propensity towards opportunism. The latter is the region of trust in the narrow sense.

Trust is a governance device, in the sense that it helps to reduce transaction costs, and has the advantages of low cost and flexibility due to lesser need of detailed contracts. However, it cannot be purchased and installed at will. It can be present ex ante, prior to the development of a specific relation, in the form of an institutional environment, or by selection of partners on the basis of characteristics such as membership of a family or clan. It can be built up in a specific relation ('process based trust'), by the development of institutional arrangements such as habituation, development of shared norms and values and bonding by friendship. This builds on the ex ante institutional environment. But institutions supporting trust can also inhibit flexibility and innovation. Occasional breaks of trust, or its underlying institutions, may be needed to allow for Schumpeterian innovative novel combinations or, if that does not obtain, to demonstrate and reconfirm the benefits of trust.

Trust can be measured on the basis of behavioral indicators, and on the basis of this its effect next to other governance devices can be tested econometrically. Its effect is then confirmed empirically.

References

ALBERT, M.: *Capitalism against Capitalism* (translated from French), London (Whurr Publishers) 1993.

ARROW, K. J.: *The Limits of Organization*, New York (W.W. Norton) 1974.

BARBER, B.: *The Logic and Limits of Trust*, New Brunswick NJ (Rutgers University Press) 1983.

BERGER, J., NOORDERHAVEN, N. G., NOOTEBOOM, B.: "The Determinants of Supplier Dependence: An Empirical Study", in: J. GROENEWEGEN, C. PITELIS, S. E. SJÖSTRAND (Eds.): *On Economic Institutions; Theory and Applications*, Aldershot (Edward Elgar) 1995, pp. 195-212.

BRADACH, J., ECCLES, R.: "Price, Authority and Trust: From Ideal Types to Plural Forms", *Annual Review of Sociology*, 15 (1989), pp. 97-118.

CASSON, M.: *The Organization of International Business: Studies in the Economics of Trust*, Aldershot (Edward Elgar) 1995.

CASSON, M.: *The Economics of Business Culture*, Oxford (Clarendon Press) 1991.

CHILES, T. H., MCMACKIN, J. F.: "Integrating Variable Risk Preferences, Trust, and Transaction Cost Economics", *Academy of Management Review*, 21/7 (1996), pp. 73-99.

CRASWELL, R.: "On the Uses of 'Trust': Comment on Williamson, 'Calculativeness, Trust, and Economic Organization'", *Journal of Law & Economics*, 36 (1993), pp. 487-500.

DASGUPTA, P.: "Trust as a Commodity", in: D. GAMBETTA (Ed.): *Trust; Making and Breaking of Cooperative Relations*, Oxford (Blackwell) 1988, pp. 49-72.

DEUTSCH, M.: "Cooperation and Trust: Some Theoretical Notes", in: M. R. JONES (Ed.): *Nebraska Symposium on Motivation*, Lincoln, Nebraska (University of Nebraska Press) 1962, pp. 275-319.

DEUTSCH, M.: *The Resolution of Conflict: Constructive and Destructive Processes*, New Haven (Yale University Press) 1973.

FORD, D.: "The Development of Buyer-Seller Relationships in Industrial Markets", *European Journal of Marketing*, 14 (1980), pp. 339-353.

FOSS, N. J., KNUDSEN, C.: *Towards a Competence Theory of the Firm*, London (Routledge) 1996.

FRANK, R. H.: *Emotions Within Reason, the Strategic Role of the Emotions*, New York (Norton) 1988.

FUKUYAMA, F.: *Trust, the Social Virtues and the Creation of Prosperity*, New York (Free Press) 1995.

GAMBETTA, D.: "Can We Trust Trust?", in: D. GAMBETTA (Ed.): *Trust; Making and Breaking of Cooperative Relations*, Oxford (Blackwell) 1988, pp. 213-237.

GAMBETTA, D.: "The Price of Distrust", in: D. GAMBETTA (Ed.): *Trust, Making and Breaking of Cooperative Relations*, Oxford (Blackwell) 1988, pp. 158-176.

GULATI, R.: "Does Familiarity Breed Trust? The Implications of Repeated Ties for Contractual Choice in Alliances", *Academy of Management Journal*, 30/1 (1995), pp. 85-112.

HELPER, S.: "Comparative Supplier Relations in the U.S. and Japanese Auto Industries: An Exit/Voice Approach", *Business and Economic History*, 19 (1990), pp. 1-10.

HILL, C. W. L.: "Cooperation, Opportunism and the Invisible Hand: Implications for Transaction Cost Theory", *Academy of Management Review*, 15 (1990), pp. 500-513.

HIRSCHMAN, A. O.: "Against Parsimony: Three Easy Ways of Complicating Some Categories of Economic Discourse", *American Economic Review*, 74 (1984), pp. 88-96.

JACOBS, D., DE MAN, A. P.: "Clusters, Industrial Policy and Firm Strategy: A Menu Approach", *Technology Analysis & Strategic management*, 8/4 (1996), pp. 425-437.

JARILLO, J. C.: "On Strategic Networks", *Strategic Management Journal*, 9 (1988), pp. 31-41.

KEE, H. W., KNOX, R. E.: "Conceptual and Methodological Considerations in the Study of Trust and Suspicion", *Journal of Conflict Resolution* 14 (1970), pp. 357-366.

KOHNNSTAMM, R.: in a column in *NRC-Handelsblad*, 1998.

LUHMANN, N.: "Familiarity, Confidence, Trust", in: D. GAMBETTA (Ed.): *Trust; Making and Breaking of Cooperative Relations*, Oxford (Blackwell) 1988 pp. 94-108.

MACAULEY, S.: "Non-contractual Relations in Business: A Preliminary Study", *American Sociological Review*, 28 (1963), pp. 55-67.

MCALLISTER, D. J.: "Affect- and Cognition Based Trust as Foundations for Interpersonal Cooperation in Organizations", *Academy of Management Journal*, 38/1 (1995), pp. 24-59.

MAYER, R. C., DAVIS, J. H., SCHOORMAN, F. D.: "An Integrative Model of Organizational Trust", *Academy of Management Review* 20 (1995), pp. 709-734.

NOORDERHAVEN, N. G.: "Opportunism and Trust in Transaction Cost Economics", in: J. GROENEWEGEN (Ed.): *Transaction Cost Economics and Beyond*, Boston (Kluwer) 1995, pp. 105-128.

NOOTEBOOM, B.: *Will Opportunism Go away?,* research report, Faculty of Management & Organization, Groningen University 1998.

NOOTEBOOM, B.: "Roles of the Go-between", in: S. M. GABBAY, R. LEENDERS (Eds.): *Corporate social capital*, Deventer (Kluwer) 1999.

NOOTEBOOM, B. (1997a): *Voice and Exit Based Forms of Corporate Control: Anglo-American, European and Japanese*, paper for the EAEPE conference, Athens, 6-9 November 1997.

NOOTEBOOM, B. (1997b): "Sources of Trust and Prosperity", in: *Institutions, Values, Norms and Growth* (in Dutch), NYFER Special Studies, 9, Breukelen, September 1997.

NOOTEBOOM, B.: "Trust, Opportunism and Governance: A Process and Control Model", *Organization Studies*, 17/6 (1996), pp. 985-1010.

NOOTEBOOM, B., BERGER, J., NOORDERHAVEN, N. G.: "Effects of Trust and Governance on Relational Risk", *Academy of Management Journal*, 40/2 (1997), pp. 308-338

NORTH, D., THOMAS, R.: *The Rise of the New World: A New Economic History*, Cambridge (Cambridge University Press) 1973.

PARKHE, A.: "Strategic Alliance Structuring: A Game Theoretic and Transaction Cost Examination of Inter-firm Cooperation", *Academy of Management Journal*, 36 (1993), pp. 794-829.

PORTER, M. E.: *The Competitive Advantage of Nations*, London (Macmillan Press) 1990.

POWELL, W. W.: "Neither Market nor Hierarchy: Network Forms of Organization", in: B. M. STAW, L. L. CUMMINGS (Eds.): *Research in Organizational Behavior* 12 (1990), Greenwich, Conn, pp. 295-336.

RING, P. S., VAN DE VEN, A.: "Structuring Cooperative Relations Between Organizations", *Strategic Management Journal*, 13 (1992), pp. 483-498.

RING, P. S., VAN DE VEN, A. : "Developmental Processes of Cooperative Interorganizational Relationships", *Academy of Management Review*, 19/1 (1994), pp. 90-118.

SAKO, M.: *Prices, Quality and Trust: Inter-firm Relations in Britain and Japan*, Cambridge 1992.

SYDOW, J.: *Understanding the Constitution of Inter-organizational Trust*, paper SASE conference, University of Geneva, 12-14 July, 1996.

TELSER, L. G.: "A Theory of Self-enforcing Agreements", *Journal of Business*, 53 (1980), pp. 27-44.

WEIGELT, K., CAMERER, C.: "Reputation and Corporate Strategy: A Review of Recent Theory and Applications", *Strategic Management Journal*, 9 (1988), pp. 443-454.

WILLIAMS, B.: "Formal Structures and Social Reality", in: D. GAMBETTA (Ed.): *Trust; Making and Breaking of Cooperative Relations*, Oxford (Blackwell) 1988, pp. 3-13.

WILLIAMSON, O. E.: "Calculativeness, Trust, and Economic Organization", *Journal of Law & Economics*, 36 (1993), pp. 453-486.

WILLIAMSON, O. E.: "Comparative Economic Organization: The Analysis of Discrete Structural Alternatives", *Administrative Science Quarterly*, 36 (1991), pp. 269-296.

WILLIAMSON, O. E.: *The Economic Institutions of Capitalism; Firms Markets, Relational Contracting*, New York (The Free Press) 1985.

WILLIAMSON, O. E.: *Markets and Hierarchies*, New York (The Free Press) 1975.

ZAND, D. E.: "Trust and Managerial Problem Solving", *Administrative Science Quarterly*, 17/2 (1972), pp. 229-239.

ZUCKER, L. G.: "Production of Trust: Institutional Sources of Economic Structure 1840-1920", in: B. M. STAW, L. L. CUMMINGS (Eds.): *Research in Organisational Behaviour*, vol. 8 (1986), pp. 53-111.

Chapter 3

A Measure of Culture: Trust and Defection in Southern Italy

FRANCESCO L. GALASSI

I. Introduction

Saying that efficient institutions are essential to economic development may be a commonplace, and yet the point is still worth making because behind its triteness lie a large number of important connections between social, historical and cultural factors to which economists have turned their attention in the last twenty years. If we look at development as a process of redistributing resources across sectors and across space, we can argue that unless there is a well known and efficient mechanism by which property rights can be established and protected, resources will remain 'locked away' in under-productive uses or wholly unproductive hoards.[1] Not to belabour

1 The accumulation of precious metals is in this sense no different from unemployed labourers: in both cases, a factor input which has cost resources to produce, is 'withdrawn' from productive uses because property rights to the stream of income it could potentially produce are unclear or mis-specified or non-

the point too much, it seems reasonable for owners of factors inputs to be hesitant about engaging their resources in production unless they have a reasonable assurance that they will capture most, if not all, of the income resulting streams. Because this mostly involves trading current for future claims upon resources, and because these future claims are almost inevitably contingent upon third party behaviour, confidence in a reasonable degree of predictability plays a major role in what Abramovitz (1986) has called 'social capability'.

Yet seeing the issue in terms of predictability underestimates its full complexity, because actors may be predictably dis-honest, meaning they may consistently seek to seize streams of income to which they are not entitled. Leaving aside for the moment how entitlements are determined, one implication is that economic development depends on the successful resolution of many Prisoner's Dilemmas. This in turn demands not only that actors have correct expectations about others' behaviour (predictability) but these expectations must also be 'positive', in the sense that actors have to be reasonably (and correctly) certain that their entitlement to future income streams will not be infringed upon. The expectation that entitlements will be respected I will refer to as 'trust' (Gambetta 1988). To make the concept analytically insightful, trust can be seen as the probability individuals attach to other individuals' or groups' respecting one's entitlements, and in this paper I will develop one approach to measuring trust in the particular historical setting of Italy's South, an area noted for its traditions of low trust, in the early 1900s.

The issue is of interest both in a development context and historically because recent work (Putnam 1993) has strongly suggested that Southern Italy, the poor and underdeveloped part of the country, was plagued by a lack of 'civil culture', a term used to suggest that Southern Italians were, to put it roughly, unwilling or unable to co-operate. One consequence of this may have been the very backwardness of the area. Without even attempting the review the massive literature on the 'Southern Question', still it is worth noting that in 1911 the South had a per capita output barely 3/4 of the national average and personal income one half of the industrial North (Zamagni 1993, p. 39). Literacy, infant mortality, life expectancy equally lagged behind the national norm. Explanations range from some form of

---

enforceable. A saver who does not invest accumulated capital is equivalent to an unemployed worker who does not move to where jobs can be found.

geographic determinism to a marxian 'development of under-development,' with cultural accounts taking an intermediate position. The underlying idea of most cultural explanations, first discussed in Banfield (1958), is that networks of mutual engagement are necessary to ensure that decision makers feel they can commit their resources without fear that the income deriving from their commitment will be appropriated by other parties. Because this is a feature of most economic transactions, i.e., it is extremely difficult to define contractually all contingencies and enforce all property rights through contracts or the legal system, and because monitoring is costly if, as is mostly the case, the margins on which cheating may occur are numerous, networks function by providing a public good (trust) under conditions where incentives to defect are high. In a society dominated by mistrust, this 'social capital' is low and collective action will not take place outside of narrowly restricted circles. "When your neighbour's house is on fire," admonishes a Southern Italian proverb, "bring water to your own."

The approach is appealing, and has been explored empirically with encouraging results: A'Hearn (1997) found that southern depositors' diffidence played a significant part in explaining the different success of Schultze-Delitsch co-ops (*Banche popolari*) in Northern and Southern Italy, though other factors unrelated to culture seem just as important. Focussing on the fate of institutions which very clearly depend on mutual engagement (such as co-operatives) helps put into stark relief the question of culture and economic growth in areas such as Italy's South. And yet cultural explanations such as Putnam's suffer inevitably from a serious shortcoming. The problem is that expectations seldom leave behind well documented records, so that there is always the danger of circularity in the reasoning. A hypothesis (poor traditions of social engagement) is proposed to explain an observation (an under-developed, patron-client based society). Because the hypothesis relies on unobservable variables (culture, expectations), it cannot be tested independently of the observation. Thus the observation may end up being taken as evidence in favour of the hypothesis. It is this circularity that this paper tries to break, offering a measure of the trust Southern Italians had for one another.

To that end, I will examine another set of institutions relying on co-operative behaviour, the *casse rurali*, small-scale farmers' lending co-ops designed on the Raiffeisen lines (Marschalk 1984; Bonus and Schmidt 1990), which were introduced in Italy in the early 1880s and grew rapidly to the First World War. Because these co-ops by law had unlimited liability, they provide an excellent testing ground for the cultural explanation of the Southern problem. If I can show that the *casse*'s less than brilliant performance in the South was linked to the local low trust culture, Putnam's thesis will be supported by my research.

In the next Section I will define such concepts as 'trust' and 'culture'. In Section III I will provide the historical context, sketching a brief history of agricultural co-operative lenders in Italy and emphasising the role played by the Catholic clergy in providing an 'honest broker' to assist setting up the co-ops. Section IV will present a simple model to estimate 'trust' in this context, and some numerical exercises will be carried in Section V.

II. Trust and Culture

This section makes two points. First, following Dasgupta (1988), I argue that trust is interconnected, depends on credible sanctions and correct incentives. This allows me to define the expression 'culture of trust'. Secondly, I define the concept of entitlement. Both definitions are necessary to approach the cultural explanation of the poor performance of rural co-operative banks in Southern Italy.

The first point relates to the motivational aspects of trust. It would seem that others may be trusted either because they are believed to be intrinsically honest, or because honesty is believed to be in their interest. The former case is in a way a dead end, in that intrinsic characteristics are unobservable, while observable behaviour may be motivated by opportunism, strategic considerations, and the like (Dasgupta 1988). In the latter case trust derives from knowledge of others' awareness that future benefits depend upon current honesty, or on efficient enforcement mechanisms. In a deep sense, therefore, trust is cumulative, meaning that A's trust in B's respecting A's entitlements depends on B's trust in A's respecting B's entitlements, and both A and B know this. Alternatively, A's trust in B depends on A's trust in an external enforcing agency, and again both A and B know this.[2] Trust therefore has a number of the characteristics of a public good, in that

2 The biological and evolutionary bases of co-operative behaviour are discussed in RIDLEY (1997).

it is extremely difficult, and probably downright impossible, for a supplier of trust to capture all, or even many, externalities, and it does not diminish with use.[3] In addition, trust implies unobservability in a complex world. If all actions could be costlessly observed, and if all outcomes could be known, trust (a probabilistic extimation of behaviour) would have no role to play. Unobservability and complexity mean that individuals routinely come into contact with others of whom they have scant or no previous knowledge but whose co-operation must be engaged if the actor is to benefit from some aspect of his/her entitlements. Reliance on an enforcement agency may play a role here, but it hardly needs stressing that enlisting the help of this agency or agencies is not costless, so that if third party enforcement were the only assurance of co-operative engagement, one or the other of the parties could always seek to appropriate a portion of the other's entitlement as long as this was smaller than the cost of litigation.[4] It follows that besides being cumulative, trust is also general, meaning that for it to work effectively (that is, to solve multiple prisoner's dilemmas), there has to be a 'culture of trust'. This expression may sound disturbingly woolly, so it has to be given analytical incisiveness. A culture of trust exists when the overwhelming majority of people expect that in the overwhelming majority of transactions they enter into other parties whose behaviour cannot be fully monitored will not seek to seize a share of the cumulative benefits of the transaction greater than their entitlement. A culture of trust is a group's systemic bias in favour of co-operative resolutions to multiple prisoner's dilemmas (Rubinstein's contribution in this volume offers a valuable insight into the problems of defining what constitutes a 'group' in this context).

The second point refers to the definition of entitlement. What is 'an honest day's wage for an honest day's work'? While it is evident that moral codes, traditional values, religious beliefs and other non tangibles enter the fray here, I will take an unabashedly Paretian approach and suggest that we may consider an entitlement as the stream of income received by a non-defecting player from a successful co-operative game such that the expected value of all possible outcomes leaves the player at least as well off as if s/he

---

3 In fact, as GAMBETTA (1988) has pointed out, trust may increase with use.

4 Note that this opens both parties up to the threat of blackmail in that A can threaten to claim that B has seized part of A's entitlement and thereby ruin B's reputation, in order to seize part of B's entitlement. In other words, enforcement must not be exclusively thought of as linked to formal courts or police.

had chosen not to play in the first place. To make this clearer, suppose that individual I has a resource that yields income y per period of time. Suppose that I can choose to join a game in which the resource will yield income stream b with probability t (co-operative outcome) and loss L with probability (1-t). Suppose further that $L > s$. Then I's expected income from participating in this game is $E = tb-(1-t)L$. As long as $E \geq y$, it will pay a risk neutral player to enter the game.[5] The player's entitlement is b, the benefit from a co-operative outcome, which at the margin is at least equal to $[y+(1-t)L]/t$. Note that even if $L=0$, b would still be greater than y (the non-participating income) by a factor of 1/t. So an entitlement is the realized benefit of the co-operative solution of a game in which $E \geq y$.

A culture of trust, based on expected respect for entitlements deriving from successful engagements, may seem like an analytically useful tool, but one that will be empirically difficult to measure. In Section IV I will propose a functional form that will allow me to make quantitative statements about relative trust in different areas. Before turning to that, however, a brief overview of the historical setting must be provided.

III. Rural Credit Co-operatives in Italy, 1883-1926

The salient facts relating to rural co-operative credit in Italy are easily stated. The first *cassa rurale* was founded in June 1883 near Padua. By December 1899 over 6,000 farmers had joined similar co-ops, and loans financed by these banks had grown in real terms by more than 2,800% (Agostini 1985, p. 133; Zalin 1985, p. 37). At the same time, after the encyclical *Rerum Novarum* in 1891 in which the Vatican signalled an easing of its rejection of anything smacking of modernity and social activism, a number of Catholic credit co-ops were started thanks to the initiative of several parish priests. Seven years after the founding of the first Catholic *cassa* (August 1892), Catholic co-operatives in Italy numbered 779 and loans financed by them went from less than 40,000 lire per year to over 10 million (Cooperazione 4.11.1894, p. 44; Tramontin 1974; Tamagnini 1952,

5 This can be re-specified to take into account risk aversion, but nothing of substance will change in the argument.

p. 101). While no census of co-ops was undertaken before the interwar years, it appears that by December 1916, some 2100 *casse rurali* operated in Italy, with a total membership of 115,000 (Tamagnini 1952, p. 105). Though aggregate data are poor, loans and deposits seem to have risen by more than 1,000% in the years up to the First World War (Caputo 1989, Galassi 1998). The evidence, limited though it is, also strongly suggests that rapid growth was not bought at the expense of solvency: few *casse* ever failed and borrowers seldom defaulted (Tamagnini 1952, p. 100; Bresolin 1980, p. 138)

This success is all the more remarkable because there were good reasons to expect that few people would join. Legally, a credit co-operative was constituted when no less than three individuals - all of whom had to be able to 'read, and write their own name' - signed the articles of incorporation, the main feature of which was that members were 'jointly and severally responsible with all their property' for the co-op's liabilities. Co-operatives raised funds either by accepting deposits from the public, or by obtaining backing from another financial institution in the form of a 'collective IOU', which in effect was a loan note secured on the property of members. Lending was restricted to members of the co-op residing in the commune in which the incorporation had been registered. In addition, shares in the co-op were not tradable, no dividends could be distributed, and each member only had one vote regardless of the number of shares held. Finally, the co-op required a significant commitment in time and effort for members, which by law could not be remunerated.

In spite of the risks and drawbacks associated with these legal requirements, the co-ops soon attracted a large membership. A complete sociological investigation into the backgrounds of members is still to be carried out, yet some data published by the Federation of credit co-ops in the late 1890s give the following cross section: in 1898, 57.7% of co-op members were small landowners; 29.2% were fixed rent tenants or sharecroppers; 9.1% were artisans, shopkeepers or small merchants; 4% were farm hands. In the same year, 30.4% of co-op loans were used to buy livestock; 19.1% financed trade or small scale manufacturing activity; 16.3% were used to purchase fertilisers, herbicides, or fungicides: 13.3% went into land improvement projects; 11.8% to buy food; 6.1% to buy fodder; 1.7% financed seasonal migrants; and 1.3% to buy farm tools (Caputo 1989, pp. 28-29).

These data are interesting, if vague. It is not clear, for example, what is meant by 'small landowner', or 'small scale manufacturing', yet the flavour of the information points definitely to localised, short term micro credit. This is confirmed by one of the few instances of recorded collateral accepted by a cassa, that in Treviglio (40 km east of Milan). From 29 March to 12 September 1899, this co-op extended credit on the following security: cows (110 heads in 56 transactions), oxen (6 in 3 transactions), calves (4 in 3 transactions), horses (12 in 10 transactions), donkeys (15 in 15 transactions), carts (3 in 3 transactions), and even a borrower's garlic crop (Treviglio 1899).

This local character was never compensated by a strong federal structure, unlike the Crédit Agricole in France or the Raiffeisen in Germany. At a reasonably early stage, inter-bank lending appeared as co-ops that had grown faster than others acted both as clearing houses and as providers of discount facilities (Bermond 1996, pp. 15-16; Lanzavecchia 1986, p. 171; Ristorto 1971, p. 80). In most cases, however, the local Savings Banks, which were predominantly urban in character, acted in the secondary market for co-ops (Saguatti 1989, pp. 234-254; Veneruso 1982, pp. 575-576; Cafaro 1996, pp. 96-97).

The portfolio of the *casse* appears to have consisted mostly of loans, secured and unsecured, and deposits with larger banks. Only very occasionally did they invest in government securities or commercial paper: each of these accounted for less than 1% of assets in 1905 (Ruggieri 1964). Important regional differences existed, however, in their liabilities, which were mostly current and savings accounts in Northern Italy (less commonly term or time deposits), while they included a significant portion of loans from banks of issue[6] in the South, particularly in Sicily (Sannucci 1990).

A number of federations of *casse rurali* were founded from the mid-1890s onward, but they were almost always local affairs, at times consisting of no more than half a dozen co-ops. These organisations never became large enough to act as discounters or lenders of last resort for the co-ops, which, outside of a few privileged areas such as Sicily, did not have easy access to the banks of issue for liquidity. Several national conventions resolved set up a nation-wide bank to provide better rediscount and secondary market facilities, but in practice fewer than 20 % of existing *casse* ever

6 This was a general policy by Italian banks of issue in this period: see POLSI (1996).

bothered to join the initiatives (Cafaro 1985, pp. 53-72). In fact, the *casse* appear to have been either actively opposed to, or at least suspicious of, any attempts to tie them to a wider network (Pessina 1987, pp. 294-295; Cooperazione 25.10.1914), often precisely because their strong local character made them uneasy with organisations based in other parts of the country (Di Taranto 1996, p. 512; Lo Giudice 1996, pp. 572-573). This disintegrated structure and the extreme reliance of the co-ops on the local economy did not cause important liquidity problems in the years before the First World War. The 1907 financial crisis (Bonelli 1971) did bring about a decline in the number of co-ops, but what took place was that the co-ops that failed did so because of losses suffered when larger financial institutions closed their doors. In any event, the loss in numbers was reasonably quickly made up. However, except for 1907, when their financial support simply vanished, failures were rare among co-ops, even in crisis years such as 1898 (Cafaro 1985, p. 34), and those that did occur appear to be related to individual mismanagement or fraud (Pretelli 1990; Di Fazio 1985, p. 378). The inflationary experience of the war years changed this situation dramatically.

The fragmented structure of co-operative credit in post-1918 Italy meant that as a rule co-ops used a few larger intermediaries (at times only one) as providers of rediscount facilities or as placement for excess liquidity. Wartime inflation and rationing from 1915 onward brought about a rapid rise in the *casse*'s liabilities, the proceeds from which were often simply placed on term with larger local banks with which co-ops already had long standing relationships. In fact, what the co-ops lacked was a diversified investment strategy, which left them open to important, often critical, losses when the larger institutions found themselves in difficulties in the post war deflation (Zamagni 1993, p. 217; Caroleo 1986). In a repetition on a grander scale of the 1907 problem, the early 1920s saw a sharp decline in the number of co-ops operating in the country (Cafaro 1996, p. 86).

The financial difficulties of many casse in the early to mid-1920s gave the Fascist régime the excuse to intervene, bringing them under direct supervision by the Ministry of Finance and the central bank, forcing a number of co-ops to merge, and setting up a federation to which all credit co-ops had to belong. The *casse* were thereby removed from the influence of the Catholic clergy, which had been instrumental in setting them up, and brought under the control of the Fascist party (Caputo 1989, pp. 47-53; Caroleo 1986; Roggi 1982, pp. 34-35). From that point on the *casse* lost their purely rural character, as a number of legislative measures merged them with urban co-operative and mutual aid societies, forming larger bodies whose operations were still geographically restricted, though on a somewhat wider scale than before. The effect of these reforms was to reduce the number of banking co-operatives, and the intervening depression, though less acute in the heavily protected Italian economy than elsewhere, further weakened their position. The 2263 *casse* active in 1926 had by 1937 declined to 1748 (-22.8%), while total liabilities fell by 43.4% in the same period, and the value of their portfolio declined by over 2/3 (Caputo 1989, p. 53). In fact, it was only with the Italian 'economic miracle' in the 1950s that co-operative banks experienced renewed growth (Gigliobianco 1996).

If these were the broad national trends, regionally the co-ops underwent widely varied experiences. In Northern Italy (the 30 provinces constituting the regions of Piedmont, Liguria, Lombardy, Venetia, Emilia) their growth was extremely rapid, and the area came to have a disproportionate number of *casse*. The only region outside of the North where these co-ops were common was Sicily which, with 9% of Italy's farm labour force, accounted for 17.6% of credit co-ops in 1910. Excluding Northern Italy and the anomaly of Sicily, the rest of the country had fully half the farm labour force but less than 20 % of all co-operative lenders, and only 13.3 % of their assets (Caputo 1989, p. 38; Galassi and Cohen 1994, p. 594). The casse thus mirrored the North-South gradient that characterizes the Italian economy.

Sicily appears anomalous, but the higher concentration of rural co-op lenders there is somewhat deceiving. From the start, the Bank of Sicily, which was a bank of issue, subsidised co-operative banks in rural areas by assisting in setting them up and extending credit over the years (La Loggia 1914; Lorenzoni 1909, pp. 708ff; Lo Giudice 1966; Muzzioli 1983, pp. 175-178). In most cases these banks remained dependent on loans from the Bank of Sicily to raise capital, and few developed into active financial intermediaries of their own (Lo Giudice 1966).

The regional distribution of rural credit co-ops on 31 December 1910 is presented in Maps 1 to 4. A number of different considerations determined the choice of the year. In the first place, since reporting absolute numbers would mean little, the observations had to refer to a year near enough other information for Italian agriculture to allow the data to be standardised. The agricultural census of 1911 (Galassi and Cohen 1994 for discussion) offers the necessary benchmark to do so. Secondly, the year had to be away from financial crises (1892-1893, 1898, 1907) and sufficiently removed from the beginnings of the co-operative movement to pick up a situation that was in some way already in equilibrium. 1910 is not ideal in this sense, as the contraction in the number of co-ops in operation following the 1907 financial panic had not yet been made good. However, in later years the number of co-ops returning information to the Ministry was considerably smaller than in 1910, and in the post-war years conditions were too unsettled to give a meaningful portrait. Finally, since these were farmers' banks, data had to be available in large enough volume for a date in the agricultural year when the harvest and sowing cycle in different regions would not interfere differentially with the numbers (hence the choice of the end of December).

The co-ops were required to send their balance sheet to the Ministry of Agriculture which published them in its bulletin (MAIC 1911) reporting the total number registered with its office in each province, the number that its records showed were in fact active, and giving highlights from the balance sheets it received. In practice, only about 2 in 3 co-ops sent in their balance sheet, and even then what they sent often did not conform to Ministry guidelines. Interestingly, the areas with the highest density of *casse* were also most prone to under-reporting: for Northern Italy and Sicily fewer than 60% of *casse* sent their balance sheet in, compared to three quarters from other areas.

Inconsistencies in the published data mean that the only category that can be usefully employed in analysis is the total assets reported by each co-op. Even there, it is unfortunately mostly unclear how the assets were distributed between reserves, capital, loans and other investments, so that only the roughest kind of image can be drawn. The under-reporting problem is serious, but it is probably reasonable to estimate total co-op assets in each province through an adjustment by the factor of under-reporting[7]. The farm labour data used in preparing Maps 1 and 2 were derived from MAIC (1912). Data on savings accounts in Map 4 are from MAIC (1911).

The basic pattern that emerges from these maps is of a wide gap between the North, especially the North-East, of Italy, and the South. South-

7 Thus if information is available for only 2 of 3 banks in one province, the estimate used in preparing the maps is the sum of co-op assets for that province as published in MAIC (1911) multiplied by 3/2. Provided both reported and unreported co-ops are distributed around the same mean, this adjustment should leave relative provincial positions unchanged. In any event, the results are consistent with available qualitative information (ZANINELLI 1996).

ern *casse* were smaller and less common, which may reflect either an unwillingness of local farmers to join, presumably related to the unlimited liability clause, or an unwillingness to deposit, and possibly both. If so, this is a reasonably typical case of co-ordination failure in a prisoner's dilemma: the obstacle lies in setting up clear ground rules and enforcement mechanisms that will ensure that no-one's entitlements will be appropriated by defectors in the future. If actors do not believe that entitlements will be safe, if, in other words, they live in a low trust culture, the co-ordination failure will constitute a stable, if sub-optimal equilibrium. Before I can put flesh on these bones, however, the situation on the ground has to be outlined.

Were Southerners unwilling to join or unwilling to deposit? Or both? Map 1 suggests the former: the number of co-ops per 100,000 farm workers by province in December 1910 forms a gradient falling from Italy's North East (Venetia) to the South. From an average of one bank per 2,033 farm workers in the former, we reach a low of one every 66,700 near Naples. Overall, the 30 provinces of Northern Italy had one *cassa* every 4,115 workers (σ=4,160), as opposed to one every 14,700 (σ=13,550) in the other 32 (excluding Sicily's 7 provinces, where the figure was on 'Northern' levels, one every 3,800, σ=5,423). The standard deviations are in all cases extremely high, reflecting widely varying provincial density of these banks. More importantly, the means are almost 4 standard errors away from each other. Southerners were significantly less likely to join.

A similar story emerges from Map 2, where assets of all rural cooperative banks are standardised by farm worker for each province. The picture is slightly different here, in that not all co-ops were 'active' according to the Ministry, which reported no assets for a number of *casse*. The gradient is visually less clear: while high figures are registered in the North/North East, low points are found both in the North and outside it.

Map 1
Casse Rurali per 100,000 Farm Workers by Province, 1910.

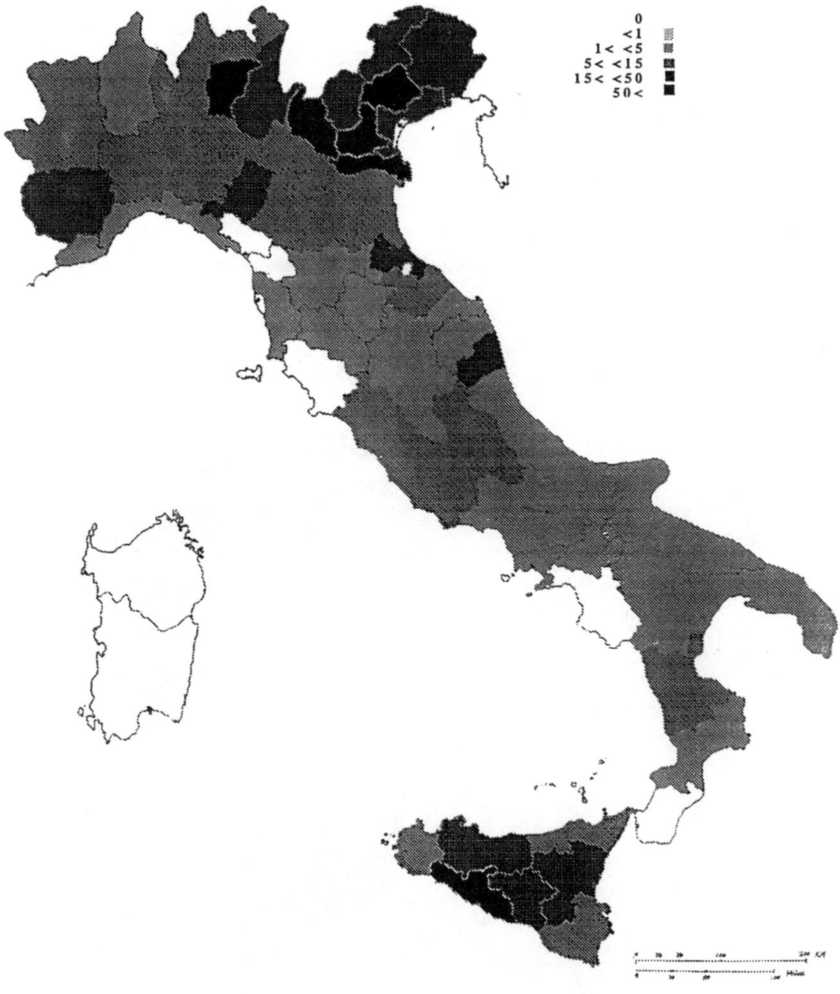

Map 2
Casse Rurali Assets per Farm Worker, by Province, 1910.

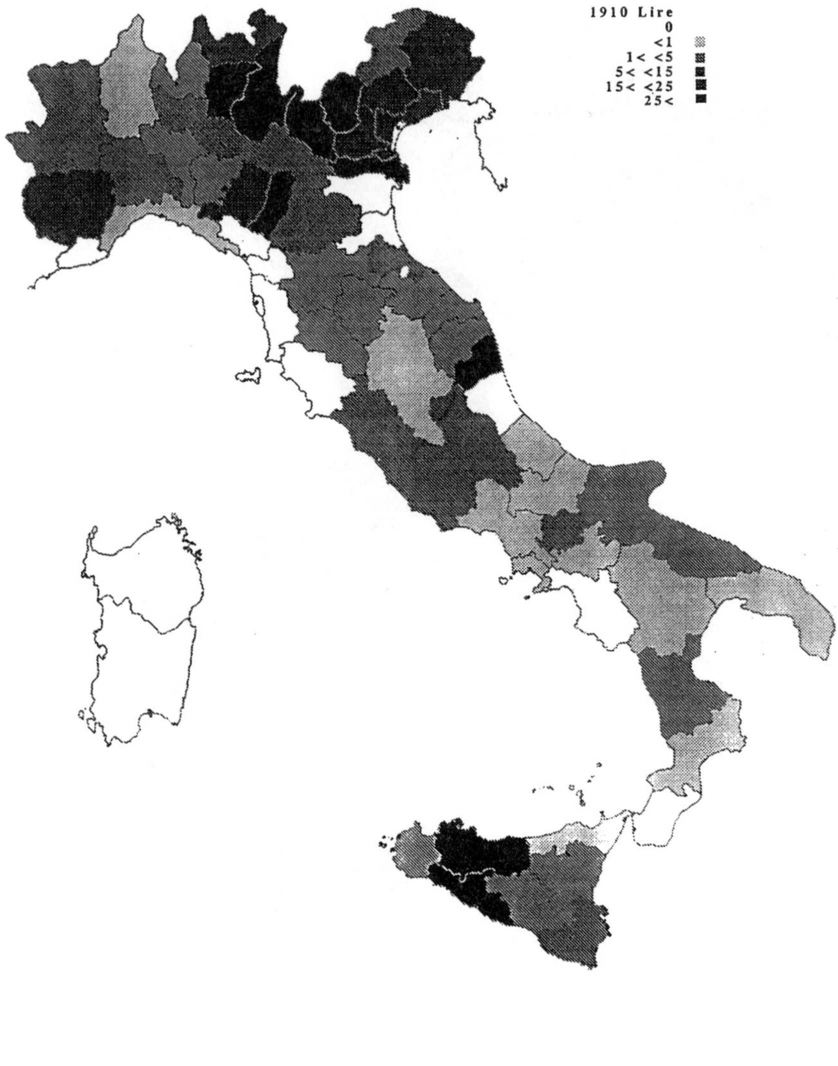

Map 3
Assets per Cassa Rurale
by Province, 1910.

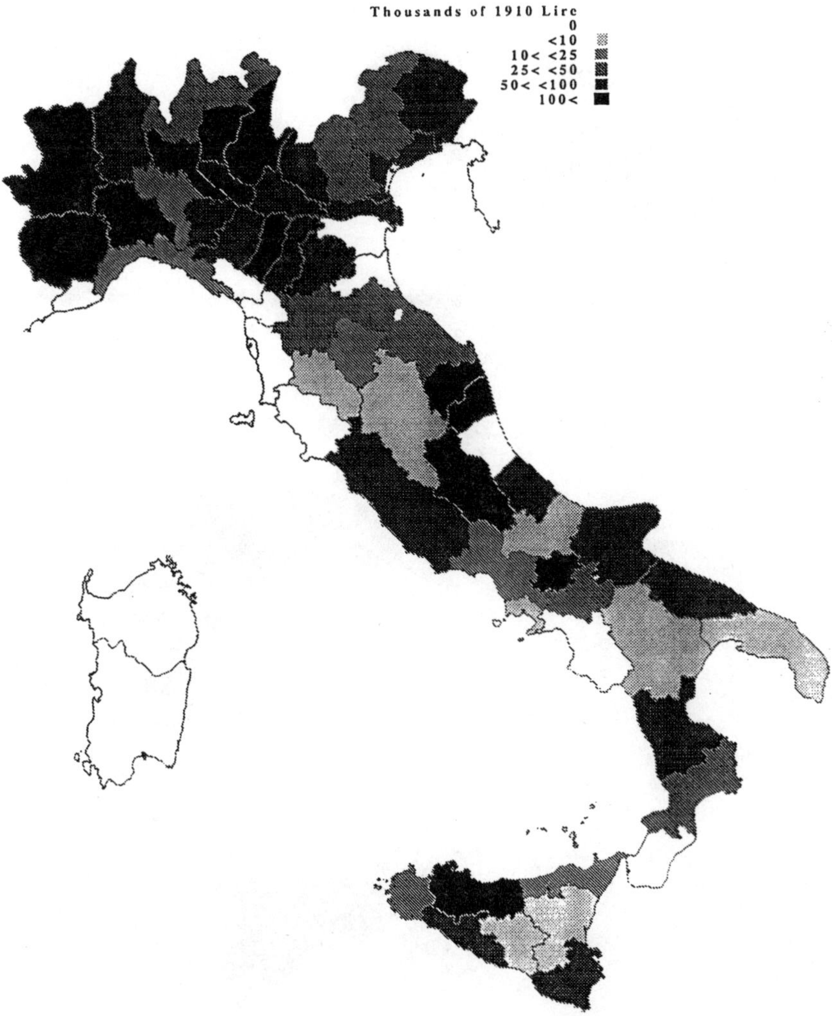

Map 4
Casse Rurali Assets per 1000 Lire of Savings Bank Assets, By Province, 1910.

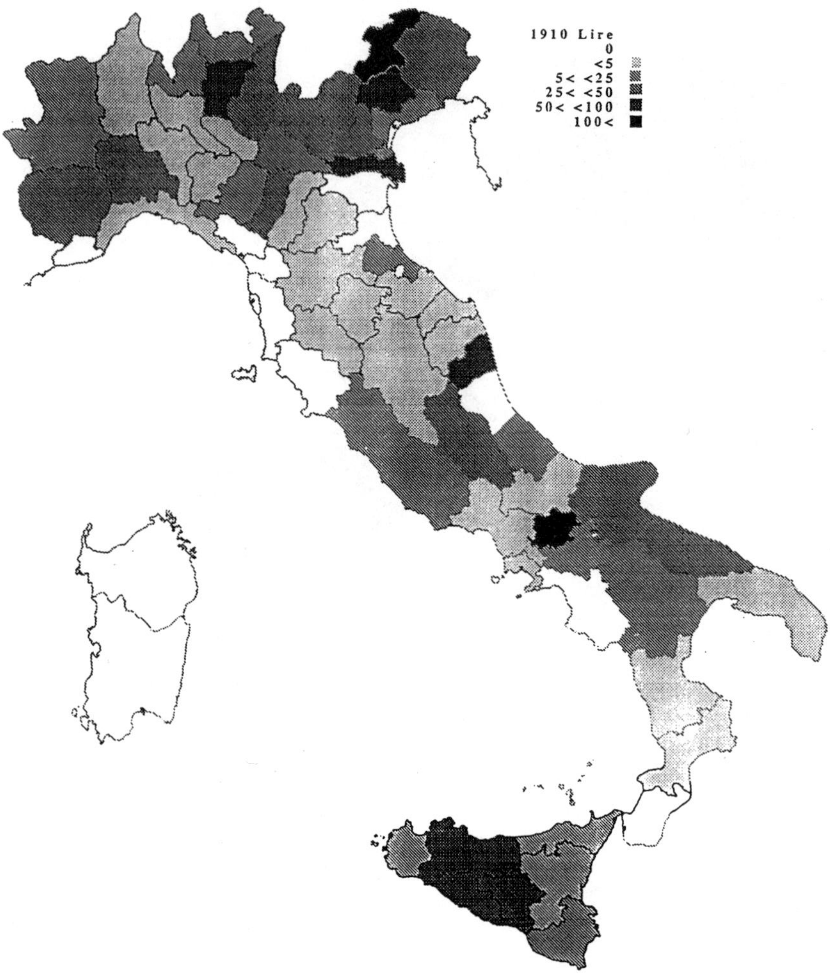

Differences remain high, however: on average, Northern farm workers had five times more assets in *casse rurali* than their compatriots elsewhere. Putting this differently, the Northern and Southern means (respectively 18.52 and 3.66 lire), excluding Sicily, are 3.3 standard errors away from each other, and even including the anomaly of Sicily remain 2.6 standard errors apart.

This raises the important question of whether these differences are really no more than a reflection of differing labour productivity in the two areas. Poor workers save less. Are there any reasons to believe that this is the source of the gap?

The answer is, no. As a crude but effective way of testing this, the correlation coefficient between co-op assets per worker, number of active *casse*, and labour productivity in agriculture by province (Cohen and Galassi 1990 for methodology) can be calculated. A high and positive r would support the idea that the North-South gap was caused by regional productivity differences. For the entire country, the r for co-op assets and output per worker by province is -0.023. For the number of active co-ops and labour productivity, $r=0.091$. The former is negative. The latter has the 'right' sign, but is rather weak: productivity differences 'explain' less than 10% of the North-South gap in numbers of co-ops. If we exclude Sicily, because the subsidies given by the local bank of issue to the co-ops create a disturbing element, for the remainder of Italy (62 provinces out of 69) $r=0.035$ for co-op assets and output per worker, and 0.066 for number of co-ops and output per worker. While these are at least both positive, they both are also almost surprisingly small. There is no escaping the conclusion that something other than the productivity gap was at work.

The North-South gradient breaks up further in Map 3, which reports assets per *cassa* by province. While more high points are found in the North than outside it (in 8 provinces out of 30 in the North the average is over 100,000 lire in assets, as against only 5 out of 39 in the rest of the country), the difference has narrowed. The average asset value of a co-operative bank in the North was 71,410 lire ($\sigma=66,395$) as against 37,660 ($\sigma=50,722$) in the South excluding Sicily (43,972 including Sicily, $\sigma=66,364$). Note that the two means are now just two and a quarter standard errors away from one another (the inclusion of Sicily puts the difference of the means just a shade outside $2s_{(n-s)}$), which was definitely not the case when assets were divided by the agricultural labour force. It would seem that, once established, Southern *casse* were significantly less effective at attracting funds than Northern ones in absolute terms (assets), but the gap is markedly smaller by this measure than when numbers and assets of co-ops are related to the labour force. The question remains whether there is a significant difference between North and South when co-op size is related to the size of other financial intermediaries province by province.

Map 4 relates the assets of co-ops by province to the assets of savings banks and urban co-operative banks (*banche popolari*, in effect Schulze-Delitzsch co-ops, see A'Hearn 1997), the other main forms of savings mobilisation in pre 1914 Italy[8]. If the problem in the South was that local co-ops were less successful at attracting deposits than the *casse* in the North, they should account for a smaller proportion of provincial assets of banks accepting saving deposits. The North South gradient has, on the contrary, disappeared. The means are revealing: for the thirty provinces in the North, casse assets were 27.5 lire per every 1000 of total assets of banks with saving deposits ($\sigma=45.37$). For the rest of the country, the proportion was 24.16 per 1000 ($\sigma=71.98$). Excluding Sicily, it fell to 20.75 ($\sigma=80.67$). The observed means are in this case less than one standard error apart, whether or not Sicily is included. Southern co-operative lenders were smaller than Northern ones in absolute terms. They were virtually the same in relation to the market where they operated (though their scatter was greater).

One way to interpret the evidence contained in the maps is that Southerners were no less willing to entrust their savings to co-ops, but were less willing to set them up, than Northerners. Putting this differently, once a

8 Another form of savings mobilisation were post office accounts. However, there are methodological difficulties in using post office data because it makes little sense to compare bank assets with savings accounts, which is what the post office collected. A direct comparison of savings accounts in both banks and the post office is made impossible by the way in which the Ministry published the bank data, lumping different kinds of deposits together. However, it has to be noted that post office savings deposits were higher in Northern Italy than in the South, so that by excluding them I am in fact over-estimating the share of the savings market the co-ops had in the North by a greater margin than elsewhere. The relative ability to attract savings of Southern co-ops is therefore under-represented, and my argument would receive even stronger support if postal savings were included. The large commercial banks such as the Banca Commerciale or Credito Italiano were excluded as not being saving mobilising institutions.

cassa was in operation and demonstrated its reliability, savings were forthcoming. This strongly suggests that the co-ordination failure in the South lay in the initial set up. The stumbling block was finding people willing to sign the original incorporation and manage the co-op in the early stages of its existence. Is there any other evidence to support this interpretation?

Some telling information does in fact exist. In the 1890s, a number of Catholic newspapers, observing the growing gap between the diffusion of rural co-ops in different areas, suggested setting up a number of 'demonstration' co-ops in Southern Italy whose incorporation would last for only one year, at the end of which the co-op would be dissolved and any assets distributed among members. It was hoped that this would convince others of the workability of the idea and subsequently join 'real' co-ops (Tosti 1996, p. 416). The idea was never tried in practice because of the high set up costs associated with incorporation[9], yet the very fact that the proposal was made at all supports the interpretation emerging from the cross sectional data for 1910.

Other evidence also confirms that Southern co-ops' less than brilliant performance stemmed from the initial co-ordination problem. In 1897 the first *cassa* in Southern Italy completed its first year of operation. In its report, the management committee reviewing the events of the previous twelve months thought them "highly satisfactory ... considering local conditions, [people being] still unfamiliar with the functioning of these institutions, still in the grip of mistrust, while at the same time [there is] a great fear after so many bankruptcies, so many frauds, suffered at the hands of dishonest folks" (Di Taranto 1996, p. 529)[10]. Elsewhere in the South, it was difficult to find people who both possessed the skills to manage an undertaking of this sort and who enjoyed the trust of the community: in many areas it was commonly believed that the managers of a co-op would inevitably use it for their own personal advantage, either to enrich themselves and their families, or by using it as a step to further a political career (Di Taranto 1996, pp. 516-517; Rossi 1977, pp. 332-333; Gallo 1996, pp. 502-503).

---

9 In an example of bureaucratic folly, the articles of incorporation had to be registered with each of 4 different offices and published in 5 different official bulletins, all at the signatories' expense. The process took months.

10 The bankruptcies referred to are those of the 1893 crisis, which did not involve coops.

Such suspicions just do not appear to have surfaced in the North. A number of authors have explained this difference by arguing that historical events, such as long periods of subordination to foreign powers and elites, created a cultural context in Southern Italy in which all relations, not just credit relations, were "based on family and kinship lines" (Sinisi 1989, p. 407). As I have already outlined a number of authors have argued that Southern Italy is a 'vertical' society, where relations of personal dependence and clientelism prevail. Low trust outside such relations makes co-ordination virtually impossible from the very outset. The co-ops would, in this perspective, be just another victim of low 'social capital'. Lacking credible mutual engagements, Southerners expect others to defect. In order to protect their own entitlements, they therefore are the first ones to defect, and in the case of the co-ops such initial co-ordination failure creates an insurmountable obstacle.[11] In the case of the co-ops, this is broadly confirmed by the regional distributions discussed in this section. Southerners did not easily agree to collaborate, thus fewer co-ops existed in the South, but when they did they were not significantly less successful than co-ops elsewhere.

Before concluding this section, some attention has to be paid to the role of the Catholic clergy in setting up co-operatives. Since over 90% of co-ops existing before the First World War were Catholic (MAIC 1911), this aspect cannot be overlooked if we are attempting to understand how they were established in the first place. I have already stressed that co-ordination is public good, and thus likely to be undersupplied unless a credible agent can provide it. Ireland's experience strongly suggests that co-operatives failed there in part because the Catholic church did not put its imprimatur on these banks (Guinnane 1994, p. 55). As an anonymous contemporary commentator wrote of the Italian *casse*, the co-ops had "to be Catholic ... because only thus can they offer the assurance that deposits will be entrusted to people with clean hands" (cited in Lo Giudice 1996, p. 560).

The role of the co-ordinator has to be made clear, because it may have some bearing on why co-ops did well in Northern Italy and poorly in the South. Effective co-ordination means reducing the probability of defection and sending out clear signals to that effect. For co-operative lenders, this

11 The initial co-ordination problem was a problem everywhere, of course, and explains why the Church was so important in their success in Northern Italy. For a discussion of the Church as an 'honest broker' see GALASSI (1998).

involves three functions: establishment of homogeneous selection criteria, consistent application of these criteria, and provision of effective sanctions. The first is aimed at defining a clear benchmark of 'social collateral' for members. The second establishes the credibility of the first: stringent rules that are not applied are of little value in guarding against defection. The third guarantees against individuals behaving strategically to meet the benchmark, only to defect later.

Fulfilling these functions, especially the first two, will be difficult for any group that does not have a clear set of shared values defining acceptable behaviour for the specific task at hand (again Rubinstein's typology in this volume enters into the discussion). In particular, defining a benchmark through debate is likely to generate an unstable outcome because participants in the game can never be sure that a given criterion actually serves a collaborative purpose rather than private interests of other players (i.e., other games). Putting this differently, significant savings can be obtained by 'buying in' a set of criteria ready made. Beside reassuring players on the impartiality of the contents, participants can 'shop around' and select sets that have proved more successful. Hence the importance of an external agency, in this case the Catholic church, first in defining and enforcing criteria (acting as a 'honest broker'), and secondly in disseminating information and experience relating to their performance. It is indicative of the advantages of 'buying in' benchmarks that fewer than 10% of co-operative lenders in Italy in 1910 were non denominational, the remainder being Catholic (MAIC 1911).

What were these criteria? The introduction to the Articles of Incorporation distributed in the 1890s by a Catholic newspaper in Milan as a model for new co-ops is worth quoting:

> In order to be accepted as a member of the Cassa Rurale of .... , individuals must
>
> i) be good practising Catholics, respect all religious feastdays, attend Mass and take Holy Communion regularly;
>
> ii) not force or ask their family members, employees, apprentices, servants, or other dependants, to work during Holy Days;
>
> iii) not gather in places of ill repute such as public houses;

iv) have never defaulted on a debt;

v) not be currently in debt;

vi) be known as good and dutiful members of the family and community, providers for their children, and respectful of authority;

vii) not have a criminal record;

viii) be known for their morality, moderation and Christian spirit.

(*Cooperazione*, 4.11.1894)

To comment briefly, the selection criteria favour individuals with a strong work ethic (vi), and low consumption habits (iii, iv, v, and viii), who participate regularly in communal activities (i and vi), and whose membership in the co-op gives a clear signal of credible commitment and reliability (ii, vii, and viii). Note that both i) and vi) describe implicitly the source of credible sanctions: people involved in communal activity to this degree could quickly disseminate adverse and credible (i, ii, vi, and viii) information about defectors. Note also that the credibility both of the membership signal and of potential sanctions derives from accepted external criteria (good Catholic, Christian spirit). Mutual trust could not exist, argued the newspaper, "unless members are of one mind in religious matters" because "only religion [can be] an absolute and truly effective safeguard of morality."

Stringent selection alone, however, does not a successful co-op make. Another Catholic periodical warned co-op managers against letting down their guard when it came to approving loans. A well run co-op, mindful of the dangers of easy credit, "which only teaches people to get deeper into debt", would finance "useful loans" only, that is, loans where

> ... the borrower intends to make a profit from the money applied for, so as to increase his wealth ... [while the bank would] reject, without yielding to misplaced feelings of sympathy, loan applications intended for consumption, that is those that [if granted] would impoverish the borrower ... such as ... using borrowed funds to improve the quality of food on his table, or to dress his family with finer clothes, or to provide the dowry for a daughter's marriage,

> thereby consuming his income before receiving it. (*Distribuzione* 1915, 19)

The intention here is guard against defection not through opportunism but through a debt trap. Rigorous application of the usefulness test (does the loan increase the borrower's wealth?) is recommended by the newspaper as the antidote to eventual defection. The emphasis is on impersonal decision rules: an individual who meets the admission standards is not thereby entitled to credit. Objective and clear criteria are needed to maintain solvency and ensure participation.

Is this the way, then, towards understanding the difference in Northern and Southern co-ops? It seems difficult to make a convincing argument in this direction, in that there is little to suggest that Southern Italians were any less Catholic than their Northern fellow countrymen. Yet if the set of values that allowed for the creation of clear benchmarks in the North existed also in the South, as it certainly did through the structure of the Catholic church, then the pattern detected in Maps 1 to 4 cannot be the result of the absence, in the South, of 'honest brokers'. Or, putting it differently, if the same set of values were potentially available to all Italian farmers regardless of the region they lived in, then the different ability to use these values to solve co-ordination problems must reflect a deeper predisposition to co-operate. The question then is, were Southern clergymen less able/willing to act as honest brokers? Again the evidence is scanty, and in any event the answer to that particular question may not matter in that if Southern priests were unwilling or unable to function as credible brokers, the issue comes back to Putnam's argument that Southerners co-operated less in general, to the idea of a 'vertical society', and 'amoral familism'.

The approach is appealing, but one may legitimately ask whether its analytical content is in the end as incisive as it appears to be. Is 'amoral familism' or 'low trust' really more than a description of the phenomenon under a different guise? Is there a way of testing the cultural explanation? The next section provides an approach to that question.

IV. An Analytical Framework

This section sketches the essential features of a simple model of the decision to join a co-operative lender of the kind described above (the complete model is discussed in Galassi (1999). I am not concerned here with the design of the co-operative, in the sense that I am trying to establish under what circumstance a rational decision maker would 'switch' from not joining to joining. In other words, I am studying how an individual with particular characteristics and subject to given forms of informational asymmetries, decides whether to participate in setting up a co-op (join) and thereby gain access to cheaper credit but also accept certain types of risk (defection by other members which would rebound against him because of the unlimited liability clause), or to forego lower borrowing costs and also avoid such potential problems. This will allow me to define a switching locus in relation to 'trust.'

Start with the elementary observation that an individual will join a co-op of this sort if he expects to benefit from it. The benefit (lower borrowing costs) has to be weighed against the non-zero probability that other members will default in such number that creditors will seize the member's assets. I have argued elsewhere (Galassi 1996) that the co-ops, not being profit maximisers, will set the interest rate they charge members at the lowest level consistent with maintaining solvency. The co-op, for its part, has to borrow at competitive rates, that is, it has to offer investors (depositors) at least the rate they would get on their best alternative investment opportunity, weighted by the probability p that the investors attach to the co-op's repaying in full and on time, net of the possible litigation costs q in case assets have to be seized to satisfy creditors upon a possible default. Treating this, for simplicity, as if it were a single investor lending an amount X to the co-op and having a riskless rate of return R, the rate the co-op has to pay can be defined as

$$r = \frac{1 + R - (1-p)(1-\theta)}{p} - 1 . \qquad [1]$$

The co-op is a price taker in the capital market, the price it pays being determined by the saver's expectations as to its solvency, but has considerable latitude in setting its interest rate because borrowers are in a sense captive, in that they cannot easily move elsewhere without incurring dramatically higher borrowing costs (indeed, that is why they are in the co-op in the first place). The difference with an ex-post monopolist, however, is that the co-op is not a profit maximizer. Its behaviour in setting prices can therefore be modelled by arguing that the co-op takes its own solvency as the constraint and maximizes the members' surplus from the investment project[12] (Galassi 1996). The co-op, that is, will choose the lowest possible interest rate i consistent with meeting its obligations (repay (1+r)X at maturity). Assuming that all inputs are provided free of charge to the co-op by its members, there still are two reasons why $i > r$. In the first place, the co-operative has an incentive to accumulate reserves, both because these represent funds that can be loaned out to members in the future without having to raise them in the capital market,[13] and because they represent a 'buffer' against default by members. Second, and related to this, the co-op has to set i in such a way that even if some members' projects do not work out and/or some members default, it will still be in a position to meet its obligations. This in effect means that the co-op must ex ante set what it expects to receive from its borrowing members to be at least equal to its obligations in the capital market. Using g to indicate the proportion of members who are expected to pay their loans in full on time and p to indicate the proportion of members' investments projects that pay a return greater than i (Galassi 1999, appendix), this means that

$$\pi\gamma(1+i)X = (1+r)X + A \qquad [2]$$

---

12 Because members are both borrowers and managers.

13 In this sense reserves may be seen as an intertemporal subsidy: choosing to keep a smaller proportion of the investment surplus today, co-op members may opt for yet lower borrowing costs in the future. The optimal time path of reserves may then be shown to depend on the reduction in borrowing costs and the co-op members' rate of time preference. It is worth pointing out that if the ratio of the reduction in future borrowing costs to the increase in current borrowing costs is greater than the rate of time preference, co-ops will tend to accumulate 'excessive' reserves in the sense that they will not take the cost of accumulated reserve funds into consideration. In other words, since accumulated reserves do not explicitly cost the co-op anything, their (discounted) effect on future borrowing costs is almost bound to be greater than their increase on current borrowing costs. Co-ops tend thus to accumulate funds. See DI SALVO and GALASSI (1997).

where A indicates the amount of reserves the co-op chooses to have at the end of the period.[14] If, ex post, the value of the expression on the left of the equal sign turns out to be greater than (1+R)+A/X, the difference is assumed to become part of reserves A. If, on the other hand, the co-op's receipts turn out to be lower than its commitment, the co-op is assumed to reduce first reserves and then, once A=0, to call upon the assets of members to make up the shortfall (note that because of the value of r given in [1] above, this is already implicit in the right-hand side of [2]).[15] The implication is that the co-op will choose i in such a way that

$$i = \frac{\dfrac{1+R-(1-p)(1-\theta)}{p} + \dfrac{A}{X}}{\pi\gamma} - 1 \qquad [3]$$

From the point of view of a perspective member, i is given by the decisions made within the co-op. In principle, a borrower wishing to join a co-op has to devote resources over time to building up a positive reputation (Dasgupta 1988). At any point in time, however, reputation is a given, and can therefore be treated as a sunk cost. The perspective borrower will therefore evaluate the expected net benefit B of joining - given that his reputation is sufficiently high - by setting the reduction in borrowing costs against, first, the value of inputs in the borrower's possession which membership will demand be provided free of charge to the co-op, and, second, against the probability that default by other co-op members lead to some (or all) of the borrower's assets being seized to repay the collective IOU. Using l for the value of inputs a member will have to devoted to the co-op and s for his share of any defaulting members' repayment, B can be written as

$$B = (r_l - i)x - \lambda - s \qquad [4]$$

The value of s has to be carefully specified. As suggested above, if the co-op's receipts fall below the value of (1+r)X by an amount greater than W (sum of members' assets), the co-op is bankrupt. Each member, there-

---

14 It will be noticed that in effect this means i = i (A), as suggested in the previous footnote. We are not here concerned with the optimising value of A, treating it instead as something set by a vote among co-op members. From the point of view of a perspective member, A is thus given at the time of the decision to join, which is what we are modelling here.

15 If i < (1 + r - q) / pg, the amount actually repaid plus members' assets cannot cover the co-op's financial commitment, and the co-operative will then simply be bankrupt.

fore, stands to pay (1-gp)(1+i)x/gp ($\equiv$ s $\geq$ w) if (1-gp)m members default.[16] This specification of s suggests that g is the same for the co-op as a whole and for individual perspective members. If the co-op, by pooling highly specific knowledge, is in a position to assess g with a high degree of accuracy, it follows that an individual who is not yet part of the co-op may have an incorrect perception of g. Which way is this error likely to bias the expected value of g? If the co-op selects for high honesty, individuals with low collateral but high g will be more frequent among co-op members than in the general population. It may therefore be reasonable to suggest that a potential borrower deciding whether to join a co-op will attribute to its members a higher degree of honesty (a higher g) than to the population at large. Even so, while membership in the co-op may in fact act as a signal, the signal is 'noisy' in the sense that the potential borrower cannot ex ante know whether the selection procedures in place are either effective or well implemented. Therefore it is likely that the perspective member's assessment of g will be lower than, or at most equal to, the co-op's estimation of the honesty of its own members (the proportion of m expected to repay). Thus, using the same value for g I am in effect using a lower bound to the value of s, the share of defaulters' debt a member has to repay, and thus an upper bound to the net benefit of joining (B).

Subsitution of [3] into [4] plus some manipulation yields the following equation in g for B = 0:

$$\gamma(B=0) = \frac{\sqrt{\dfrac{1+r+\dfrac{A}{X}}{\left(1+r_l-\dfrac{\lambda}{x}\right)}}}{\pi} \qquad [5]$$

Equation [5] defines a locus along which a rational actor will switch from wishing to remain outside the co-op and incur high borrowing costs to wishing to join. Consider what this formulation implies: the value of g, that is, the minimum proportion of co-op members expected to repay their loans necessary for a rational actor to decide in favour of joining the co-op, is a function of the inverse of the probability of success of an investment proj-

16 If gp=1 (no defaults), the amount paid by each member (other than in repayment of their own loan) will be 0.

ect, p. If projects are on the whole riskier, that is, p is smaller, g has to rise: in a riskier environment, you want more trustworthy colleagues. But while the slope of the switching locus is defined by p, its position is given by the remainder of the expression.

The ratio under the square root in [5] deserves some attention. It consists of the ratio of the interest rate co-ops have to pay in the money market plus their reserve-to-deposit ratio, to the rate a borrower would have to pay a profit maximising lender net of the cost in resources a member of the co-op has to devote to its management as a percentage of the value of his loan. Recall that by [4] the numerator of this ratio is the main component of the interest rate the co-op charges its members. Its denominator (the denominator of the expression under the square root) is the difference between the cost of not being a co-op member and paying 'market' rates, and the cost of helping run the co-op. In other words, the numerator of [5] relates the cost of membership to its benefit: the higher are (i) the rate the co-op has to pay, (ii) the co-op's reserve ratio, (iii) the cost in resources to the member of helping run the co-op, the higher will the value of the square root be. For any value of p, g will then have to be higher to make the expected net benefits of membership at least equal to zero. Conversely, the higher the rate a borrower has to pay outside the co-op (r_l), the lower the value of the numerator of [5], and the lower can g be: with very high market rates, it would pay to join a co-op even if a significant proportion of its members were believed to be dishonest.

This is illustrated in Figure 1. Since both $g,p \in (0.1)$, the function has only been drawn in (1,1)space. The values of the numerator of the function are obviously arbitrary and only serve the purpose of exposition. If the numerator of [5] equals 0.75,[17] an actor would decide to join if he estimated that the combination of 'honest' members and riskiness of investment projects placed him at a point such as A. With that value of the numerator, points B and C are below the locus: joining the co-op with these values of g and p would result in an expected net loss. If, on the other hand, the numerator of [5] is 0.5,[18] point B is a feasible combination: with these implied relative costs of membership, the net benefits from joining would be posi-

17 That is, the relation of the cost in resources of membership to the savings from not having to pay 'market' rates is about 0.56.

18 Implying that the relation of the cost in resources of membership to the savings from not having to pay 'market' rates is 0.25.

tive even if the perspective member has lower expectations about the honesty of other actors.

The area above the locus defines the set of feasible combinations of exogenous risk (p) and 'trust' (g), for a given credit market structure (the value of $\{[1+r+A/X]/[1+r_l-l/x]\}^{1/2}$), that would induce an actor to join a co-op. The greater is this area, the greater in principle is the number of feasible combinations which may give rise to a successful co-operative lender. These combinations may vary in their precise balance: in an area where exogenous risk is low (p is high), lower values of g may be tolerable.

FIGURE 1
Feasible Sets in (γ,π) Space

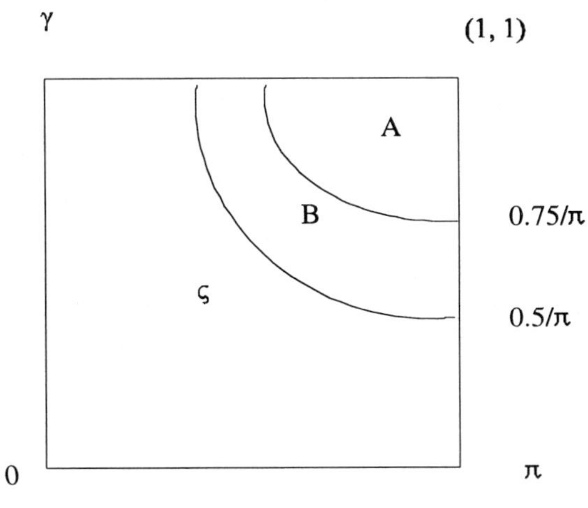

Where the capital market is very imperfect (the value of $\{[1+r+A/X]/[1+r_l-l/x]\}^{1/2}$ is low), implying that significant quasi rents are accruing to 'moneylenders', the opportunities for setting up a co-operative lender are very high[19], so that greater exogenous risk and lower trust can in principle be tolerated.

---

19 Note that if the value of the numerator of [5] is low, this implies that *r* is low relative to r_l, that is that the co-op can borrow at low rates relative to those

The simple framework outlined in this section has a number of shortcomings, first among which is that actors are depicted as engaging in a once-off game. Reputational issues, repetitive interaction, evolutionarily stable solutions, and risk aversion, are among the many issues not given their due weight. In spite of these gaps, however, the framework has one decided advantage, which is that the limited data available for Italian co-ops at the beginning of the 20th century permit the estimation of the feasible set for this kind of institutional arrangement in different parts of the country. To be more precise, the right-hand side of [5] can be estimated in a reasonable straightforward manner, which allows me to draw the g(p) locus for different areas of Italy. Comparing the feasible sets of North and South will then allow me to answer the question: were there objectively fewer opportunities for Southerners to engage in co-operative games? If the feasible sets in Northern and Southern Italy are significantly different (the South's being presumably the smaller), that is, if the structure of the credit market effectively restricted the width of the area over which co-operative behaviour would bring fruit, then the smaller number of co-ops in the South has a ready explanation: Southerners were the prisoners of circumstances beyond their control. But if the feasible sets are substantially the same, then the relatively lower incidence of co-ops in the South is the result of a different force. In effect, similar feasible sets mean that, whatever the level of exogenous risk in the South, Southerners were unable to identify a group of people who had, collectively, the level of trust necessary to deal with a low p. In other words, Southerners did not trust one another. They were prisoners of their own culture.

---

charged by profit maximising lenders (the village 'usurer'). If the cost of funds is high for the co-op, the value of other numerator of [5] will be high and the set of feasible combinations will be small.

V. Culture or Risk?

The historical record shows a considerable gap between the presence of rural co-operative lenders in Northern and Southern Italy. Northern co-ops were more numerous and larger, but were not signally more successful at attracting deposits. This probably means, I suggested earlier, that Southerners were less willing to set up co-ops, but once these were functioning they were not much less willing to deposit with them. There is little evidence that once set up Southern co-ops failed with undue frequency (Galassi 1998), so that the low numbers cannot be explained as the result of massive defections. In other words, the South seems to have suffered from an initial co-ordination failure: the problem was overcoming reticence (establishing trust) in the first place, rather than fighting defection. Of course the problem of trust arose because there was a widespread fear of defection, but what kept numbers down in the South was that first crucial step.

But there is at least another way to explain the observation that co-ops were less common in the South, and explaining it is the task of this Section. Rather than the cultural or social capital argument, whereby a low trust culture has trouble producing institutions which rely on mutual engagement, it can be argued that Southerners lived under some sort of external constraint - possibly the structure of the capital market - which made co-operatives less attractive. Which is right? If the South can be shown to have a smaller feasible set than the North, the cultural argument would be severely damaged. In that case, there simply would be less equilibria in which co-ordination was worth the trouble.

This section uses data for four provinces in pre-1914 Italy to estimate the feasible sets in the two areas of the country, the co-operative-rich North and the much poorer South. The choice of the provinces is dictated by the availability of data. While gross assets are known for about 2/3 of all existing *casse* in 1910 (see Section 3), it is not always possible to reconstruct an important element of equation [5], namely the reserve/loan ratio (A/X). The data are available at present for only four provinces (two in the North, Milan and Forlì and two in the South, Catania and Cosenza[20]). The sample can only be taken for what it is, in the sense that until reserve/loan ratios can be

20 Published in CAPUTO (1989, pp. 43-46).

estimated for all 69 provinces of pre-1914 Italy, the results obtained below have to be considered only broadly indicative. Even so, they are suggestive.

The sample suffers from several problems, first of which is its size: in the four provinces for which reserve/loan data are available, only 86 co-ops are reported, which represent 4.6% of the national total. A further problem is that these four provinces include neither any areas in the heartland of the co-op movement, the North East, nor any of the truly co-op-deprived provinces in the South. Table 1 reports the standing of these provinces in relation to their regions.

Table 1: Selected data for sample provinces in relation to regional totals, 1911.

Province or Area	Assets/ farm worker (1911 Lire) (s)	Co-ops/ 100,000 farm workers (s)	Co-op assets/ 1000 Lire of savings bank assets (s)
Entire North	18.25	24.04	27.50
	(4.5)	(24.03)	(45.37)
Milan	14.26	9.78	1,.19
Forlì	11.51	29.36	7.64
Entire South	6.11	6.8	24.16
	(8.63)	(7.38)	(71.98)
Catania	1.49	24.58	17.95
Cosenza	9.25	11.60	4.86

Sources: see Section III.

The sample is clearly biased. While the sample co-ops from the South are poorer than those from the North, they are actually more common when standardised by farm labour force than those in Milan, and more successful overall in attracting deposits from the local market. In which will this bias the estimation of the minimum value of g that would make joining an attractive proposition in the sample areas? Clearly in these two provinces of the South the initial co-ordination problem had been solved. This may mean that the feasible set for these two Southern provinces was substantially the same as for the Northern ones: if nothing else, the fact that the ratio of co-ops per 100,000 farm workers was not significantly different in the Southern and Northern provinces of this small sample (while it was very different for the country as a whole) suggests that the opportunities to benefit from co-operation were similar. If so, then the sample is biased in favour of the cultural argument, because if the feasible set was the same in Northern and Southern Italy, different responses must have derived from different local traditions of engagement and 'trust'.

Accepting that the issue cannot be finally resolved at this stage, and that more data have to be collected to compare all Northern wit all Southern provinces, it is still possible to evaluate the size of the feasible sets in these four provinces and see whether it differed significantly in the North and South. To this I now proceed.

Reserve/loan ratios for the co-ops in these four provinces are known for 1910 (Caputo 1989). While in no case are the co-ops' borrowing or lending rates reported, official data exist for rates paid by savings banks on current accounts in each of these provinces, so that these may be used as a reasonable proxy for the co-ops' own borrowing costs. Greater difficulties are encountered in estimating first, the ratio of members' resources devoted to running the co-op as a share of the loans taken out, and second, the market (profit-maximising lender's) interest rate. While the complaints about 'usurious' borrowing costs were widespread at the time (Placanica 1990), actual figures are hard to come by. Some evidence, however, suggests that 40% was a reasonably typical rate in Sicily, where one of the sample provinces - Catania - is located (Lorenzoni 1909, p. 708). This rate, which is in line with current observations from LDC money markets (Gillis et al 1988, p. 512), turns out to be exactly 6.25 times the market rate charged by savings banks in the same area at that time (MAIC 1910). Lacking other information on moneylenders' rates, I will therefore assume that moneylenders in other provinces wielded the same degree of market power and faced the same cost structure, and will therefore use the market rate in each province multiplied by 6.25 to estimate local moneylenders' rates (r_l). The estimate is crude, but should give at least an approximation of the borrowing costs faced by farmers outside the co-operatives.

The problems involved in estimating the values of p would take us too far from the immediate topic, and interested readers can be referred to the Appendix in Galassi (1999). Suffice it to say that, as calculated, p represents the probability that the average farmer in these provinces would be unable to meet repayment of the average loan at current interest rates given the (known) riskiness of crops in that area.

Taking for the time being the view that most borrowers provided little or nothing in the way of their own resources to the running of the co-op (thus $0.05 \geq 1/x \geq 0$), the values of g can be estimated (varying the 1/x allows for some simple sensitivity analysis).

Putting the results into words, it appears that for a co-op to constitute an attractive option, borrowers in the North had to count on at least 88/90% of their colleagues playing by the book. Southerners, it seems, had a more difficult task: the minimum proportion of 'honest' co-op members they needed was somewhat higher, in the neighbourhood of 92 to 97%. Is this gap sufficient to explain the geographic distribution of co-operative lenders in pre 1914 Italy?

Even in view of the likelihood that the sample is biased in favour of the cultural explanation, these results are striking. In fact, while this sample suggests that the feasible set was smaller for the South than for the North, what matters is why. The value of the numerator, the part of the expression that contains the 'behavioural' variables, is lower for the two Southern provinces than for the Northern ones. If Southern farming had been no riskier that Northern farming, if, in other words, the value of p were the same, Southerners should have had a larger feasible set than Northerners. That they did not is entirely due to the higher riskiness of farming in Southern Italy.

Table 2: Estimated values of g(B=0) in sample provinces[21]

Province	r	A/X	rl	l/x	[(1+r+A/X) /1+rl- l/x)]^1/2	p	g
Milan	0.0535	0.0214	0.334	0	0.898	1	0.898
Forlì	0.0595	0.0434	0.372	0	0.897	1	0.897
Catania	0.064	0.0145	0.4	0	0.878	0.962	0.912
Cosenza	0.0625	0.0125	0.391	0	0.879	0.905	0.971
Milan	0.0535	0.0214	0.334	0.05	0.915	1	0.915
Forlì	0.0595	0.0434	0.372	0.05	0.913	1	0.913
Catania	0.064	0.0145	0.4	0.05	0.894	0.962	0.929
Cosenza	0.0625	0.0125	0.391	0.05	0.895	0.905	0.989

These findings, preliminary and partial as they are, have to be treated with great care. In the first place, the minute size of the sample, and the level of aggregation of the data (province-wide, instead of information on individual co-ops) mean that I cannot estimate confidence intervals around these results, so that stating that the feasible sets were smaller or larger in one area or the other is in a sense arbitrary. In addition, the results are extremely sensitive to small variations in the parameters, and are therefore not 'robust' in any meaningful way. Finally, all that the estimated values of g in Table 2 indicate is that the two southern provinces in the sample appear to have been 'closer' to the g=1 line in Figure 1. This does not actually

21 Sources: r: MAIC (1910); A/X: CAPUTO (1989); rl: LORENZONI (1909), and text p: from GALASSI (1999, Appendix).

give a good portrait of the relative size of the feasible sets, because it really is the area above the p(g) function that determines the opportunities for co-operative engagement in the different provinces. The most that can be said at this juncture is therefore that limited and incomplete evidence on a restricted number of provinces is not consistent with the cultural explanation. It would seem that there were fewer opportunities for co-operation to be rewarding in the South, and it is not surprising that Southerners co-operated less. Culture may have had less impact on this than the vagaries of the climate.

VI. Conclusion

Co-operative arrangements are a good testing ground for claims about the importance of cultural variables in determining institutional choice, largely because they embody to an extraordinary degree the problems of defection/co-ordination and free riding that appear in more muted guises in other forms of economic activity. The cultural argument about differential institutional choice hinges on unspoken ceteris paribus assumptions, however: if all opportunities were the same, then cultural differences, that is, different expectations about the distribution of behaviour choice, would indeed provide an explanation of different responses. But it is extremely difficult to ensure that all else is in fact the same, so that attempts to use culture to explain institutional arrangements (and thereby ultimately performance) have to be treated with great care, lest different responses be attributed to culture rather than objective constraints. On an admittedly small sample, I have argued that all else was not to the same between the co-operative-inclined Northern Italians before the Great War, and their less co-operative brethren in the South. The sample is probably too small to allow me express strong doubts about the cultural hypothesis, but the least that can be said at this stage, pending further data collection, is that limited available evidence, and evidence that is arguably biased in favour of the cultural hypothesis at that, is not consistent with it. In a way, in fact, there is a broad hint in these numbers that causation may flow the other way: where the opportunities for co-operating were fewer, mutuality and trust did not develop.

Can this sort of framework be used to quantify cultural variables in other settings? In principle, there is no reason why not. While co-ops offer a particularly stark example of the co-ordination problems faced in most economic decisions, the fact remains that in one way or the other cultural codes underlie the range of possible tools and resources that can be brought to bear on ensuring co-ordinated solutions to complex interactions where monitoring is difficult and outcomes are contingent on third party willingness to engage co-operatively. Ultimately that is the essential link between culture and economic activity. I am here trying to argue in favour of a purely functionalist view of culture, but rather I am underscoring yet again that the codes of behaviour we are accustomed to have an impact on the range of feasible choices open in economic activity. The measure estimate in this chapter, at the same time, warns us not to attribute automatically to cultural variable elements or choices which may indeed reflect cultural choices but may also have their roots in external constraints. Culture may, in some ways, be endogenous.

References

ABRAMOVITZ, M.: “Catching up, Forging Ahead and Falling Behind”, *Journal of Economic History*, 46 (1986).

ADAMS, D. W., GRAHAM, D. H., VON PISCHKE, J. D., (Eds.): *Undermining Rural Development with Cheap Credit*, Boulder, Colorado (Westview) 1984.

AGOSTINI, F.: "Leone Wollemborg (1859-1932), pioniere del credito agrario." in: G. ZALIN (Ed.): *Un secolo di cooperazione di credito nel Veneto: le Casse rurali ed artigiane 1883-1983*, Padova (Signum) 1985.

A’HEARN, B.: “Could Southern Italians Cooperate? Banche Popolari in the Mezzogiorno”, Paper presented to the Conference on the emergence of Cooperatives in 19th and 20th century Europe, Institute of Economics, University of Copenhagen, 7-10 November 1997.

ARROW, K. J.: *The Economics of Agency, Stanford Institute for Theoretical Economics Technical Report n.451*, October 1984.

BANERJEE, A. V., BESLEY, T., GUINNAINE, T. W.: "Thy Neighbor's Keeper: The Design of a Credit Cooperative with Theory and a Test", *Quarterly Journal of Economics*, 109 (1994).

BANFIELD, E. C.: *The Moral basis of a Backward Society*, Glencoe, Illinois (Free Press) 1958.

BASU, K.: "Civil Institutions and Evolution: Concepts, Critique and Models", *Journal of Development Economics*, 46 (1995).

BELL, C.: "Credit Markets and Interlinked Transactions", in: H. CHENERY, T. N. SRINIVASAN (Eds.): *Handbook of Development Economics*, Amsterdam (Elsevier), vol. 1, 1988.

BERMOND, C.: "L'area piemontese e valdostana: un progetto di modernizzazione", in: S. ZANINELLI: *Mezzo secolo di ricerca storica sulla cooperazione bianca*, Verona (SCA) vol. 1, 1996.

BESLEY, T., COATE, S.: "Group Lending, Repayment Incentives, and Social Collateral", *Journal of Development Economics*, 46 (1995).

BESLEY, T., COATE, S., LOURY, G.: "The Economics of Rotating Savings and Credit Associations", *American Economic Review*, 83 (1993).

BHADURI, A.: "On the Formation of Usurious Interest Rates in Backward Agriculture", *Cambridge Journal of Economics*, 11 (1977).

BLOK, A.: *The Mafia of a Sicilian Village 1860-1960*, New York (Harper&Row) 1974.

BONELLI, F.: *La crisi del 1907*, Torino (Einaudi) 1971.

BONUS, H., SCHMIDT, G.: "The Co-operative Banking Group in the Federal Republic of Germany: Aspects of Institutional Change", *Journal of Institutional and Theoretical Economics*, 146 (1990).

BOF, F.: "L'area friulana e giuliana: una capillare diffusione di esperienze a supporto dell'econiomia agricolo pastorale", in S. ZANINELLI: *Mezzo secolo di ricerca storica sulla cooperazione bianca*, Verona (SCA) vol. 1, 1996.

BRAVERMAN, A., GUASCH, J. L: "Institutional Analysis of Credit Cooperatives" in: P. K. BARDHAN, (Ed.): *The Economic Theory of Agrarian Institutions*, Oxford (Clarendon) 1989.

BRESOLIN, P.: "Il contributo delle casse rurali lombarde all'agricoltura locale (1886-1926)", *Bollettino dell'Archivio per la Storia del Movimento Sociale Cattolico in Italia*, 15 (1980).

CAFARO, P.: *Per una storia della cooperazione di credito in Italia. Le casse rurali lombarde (1883-1963),* Milano (Franco Angeli) 1985.

CAFARO, P.: "L'area lombarda: l'alternativa cooperativa nella regione a più intenso sviluppo economico del paese", in: S. ZANINELLI: *Mezzo secolo di ricerca storica sulla cooperazione bianca*, Verona (SCA) vol. 1, 1996.

CAPUTO, L.: *Cento e più anni di storia e di statistica nel contesto delle Casse Rurali ed Artigiane Italiane*, Cosenza (Patitucci) 1989.

CAROLEO, A.: *Il movimento cooperativo in Italia nel primo dopoguerra 1918-1922*, Milano (Franco Angeli) 1986.

COHEN, J. S., GALASSI, F. L.: "Sharecropping and Productivity: 'Feudal Residues' in Italian Agriculture, 1911", *Economic History Review*, 43 (1990).

Cooperazione: *La cooperazione popolare. Rivista del Movimento cooperativo cattolico*, several years.

CUEVAS, C. E., GRAHAM, D. H.: "Agricultural Lending Costs in Honduras", in: ADAMS, D. W., GRAHAM, D. H., VON PISCHKE, J. D., (Eds.): *Undermining Rural Development with Cheap Credit*, Boulder, Colorado (Westview) 1984.

DARLING, M. L.: *Some aspects of Co-operation in Germany, Italy and Ireland*, Lahore (Punjabi Government Printing Office) 1922.

DASGUPTA, P.: "Trust as a Commodity", in: GAMBETTA, D.: *Trust*, Oxford (Blackwell) 1988.

DE MATTIA, R.: *I bilanci degli istituti di emissione italiani, 1845-1936*, Roma (Banca d'Italia) vol 2, part 1, 1967.

DI TARANTO, G.: "L'area del Mezzogiorno continentale", in: S. ZANINELLI: *Mezzo secolo di ricerca storica sulla cooperazione bianca*, Verona (SCA) vol. 2, 1996.

DISTRIBUZIONE: *La distribuzione del Credito nelle Casse Rurali,* 22 (1915).

DYE, A., GALASSI, F. L.: "Paternalism and Protection: the institutional response of the European periphery to industrialization", in: P. MARTÏN-ACENA, J. SIMPSON (Eds.): *The economic development of Spain since 1870*, Aldershot (E. Elgar) 1995.

FEDERICO, G.: "Il valore aggiunto dell'agricoltura", in: G. M. REY (Ed.): *I conti economici dell'Italia: Vol. 2 Una stima del valore aggiunto per il 1911*, Roma (Laterza) 1992.

FLORO S. L., YOTOPOULOS, P. A.: *Informal Credit Markets and the New Institutional Economics. The Case of Phillipine Agriculture*, Boulder, Colorado (Westview) 1991.

GAMBETTA, D.: *Trust*, Oxford (Blackwell) 1988.

GALASSI, F. L.: "Social Capability and Growth: Culture as an Explanation of Italy's Economic Dualism", *European Review of Economic History*, 4 (1999).

GALASSI, F. L.: "Co-ordination and Monitoring in Lending Co-operatives: The Italian Casse Rurali, 1883 1926", in: P. L. COTTRELL, J. REIS (Eds.): *Finance and the making of the modern capitalist world*, London (Routledge) 1998.

GALASSI, F. L.: "Screening, monitoring and incentives in co-operative banks: the case of Italy's casse rurali, 1883-1926", *Discussion Paper in Economic and Social History,* No. ESH96/2, The University of Leicester, 1996.

GALASSI, F. L., COHEN, J. S.: "The Economics of Tenancy in Early Twentieth Century Southern Italy", *Economic History Review*, 47 (1994).

GALLO, M.: "L'area laziale: tra stagnazione e nuovo protagonismo", in: S. ZANINELLI: *Mezzo secolo di ricerca storica sulla cooperazione bianca*, Verona (SCA) vol. 2, 1996.

GARELLO, G.: "Cooperazione cattolica e mondo agrocolo in provincia di Cuneo", *Quaderni del Centro Studi Carlo Trabucco*, 9 (1990).

GIGLIOBIANCO, A.: "Banche locali negli anni '50: nascita e attività", *Cooperazione di Credito*, 48 (152/3) (1996), pp.319-326.

GILLIS, M., PERKINS, D., ROEMER, M., SNODGRASS, D.: *Economics of Development*, New York (Norton) 1988.

GUESLIN, A.: *Le Crédit Agricole*, Paris (Economica) 2 vols., 1984.

GUINNAINE, T. W.: "A Failed Institutional Transplant: Raiffeisen's Credit Cooperatives in Ireland, 1894-1914", *Explorations in Economic History*, 31 (1994).

GUINNAINE, T. W.: "Cooperatives as information machines: German agricultural credit cooperatives 1883-1914", *Institute of Economics, University of Copenhagen, Discussion Paper*, 97-20, December (1997).

HULME, D., MOSLEY, P.: *Finance against poverty*, London (Routledge) 2 vols., 1996.

ISTAT: (Istituto Centrale di Statistica) *Statistiche storiche dell'Italia 1861-1975*, Roma (Istituto Poligrafico) 1976.

KISHLEV, Y., LERMAN, Z., ZUSMAN, P.: "Recent Experience with Cooperative Farm Credit in Israel", *Economic Development and Cultural Change*, 39 (1991).

LA LOGGIA, E.: *Il movimento cooperativo agricolo in Sicilia*, Agrigento (Licudi) 1914.

LADMAN, J. R.: "Loan Transaction Costs, Credit Rationing, and Market Structure: the Case of Bolivia", in: ADAMS, D. W., GRAHAM, D. H., VON PISCHKE, J. D., (Eds.): *Undermining Rural Development with Cheap Credit*, Boulder, Colorado (Westview) 1984.

LANGE, E.: "Financial Institutions and Markets in Twentieth Century Scandinavia", in: G. D. FELDMAN, U. OLSSEN, M. D. BORDO, Y. CASSIS (Eds.): *The Evolution of Modern Financial Institutions in the Twentieth Century, (B 12, Proceedings, Eleventh International Economic History Congress, Milan, September 1994),* Milano (Università Bocconi) 1994.

LANZAVECCHIA, R.: "Per una storia della cooperazione bianca nel basso Piemonte", *Quaderni del Centro Studi Carlo Trabucco*, 9 (1986).

LEONARDI, A.: "L'area trentino-tirolese: la regione a più forte sviluppo co-operativo d'Europa", in: S. ZANINELLI: *Mezzo secolo di ricerca storica sulla cooperazione bianca*, Verona (SCA) vol. 1, 1996.

LO GIUDICE, G.: *Agricoltura e credito nell'esperienza del Banco di Sicilia tra l'800 e il '900*, Catania (Fattorre) 1966.

LO GIUDICE, G.: "L'area siciliana", in: S. ZANINELLI: *Mezzo secolo di ricerca storica sulla cooperazione bianca*, Verona (SCA) vol. 2, 1996.

LORENZONI, C.: "Sicilia. Relazione del delegato tecnico", in: COMMISSIONE D'INCHIESTA PARLAMENTARE: *Relazione della Commissione d'Inchiesta Parlamentare per accertare le condizioni dei lavoratori della terra nelle provincie meridionali e in Sicilia*, Roma (Bertero), vol. 6, 1909.

MAIC: (Ministero dell'Agricoltura, Industria e Commercio, Drezione Generale Generale del Credito della Previdenza, della Cooperazione e delle Assicurazioni, Ispettorato degli Istituti di Credito e della Previdenza: *Bollettino delle Casse di Risparmio Ordinarie. Situazione al 31 dicembre 1910* , Roma (Bertero) 1910.

MAIC: (Ministero dell'Agricoltura, Industria e Commercio, Ispettorato Generale del Credito e della Previdenza) *Bollettino ufficiale delle società per azioni: situazioni mensili delle società che hanno per principale obbiettivo l'esercizio del credito*, 23 (12), Roma (Bertero) 1911.

MAIC: (Ministero dell'Agricoltura, Industria e Commercio, Direzione Generale della Statistica, Ufficio del Censimento) *Censimento 1911: relazione*, Roma (Bertero) 1911.

MARSCHALK, P.: *Bevölkerungsgeschichte Deutschlands im 19. und 20. Jahrhundert*, Frankfurt (Suhrkamp) 1984.

MATTESINI, F., COSCI, S.: "Credito e sviluppo nelle province italiane", *Cooperazione di Credito*, 48 (1996).

MUZZIOLI, G.: *Banche e agricoltura*, Bologna (Il Mulino) 1983.

PESSINA, M.: "Prime note sull'organizzazione federativa cattolica di credito", in: *Bollettino dell' Archivio per la Storia del Movimento Sociale Cattolico in Italia*, 22 (1987).

PLACANICA, A.: "Il mondo agricolo meridionale: usure, caparre, contratti", in: P. BEVILACQUA (Ed.): *Storia dell'agricoltura italiana*, Venezia (Marsilio) vol. 2, 1990.

POLSI, A.: "Financial Institutions in Nineteenth-century Italy: The Rise of a Banking System", *Financial History Review*, 3 (1996).

PRETELLI, S.: *Le Casse Rurali nelle Marche. Storia e problemi attuali*, Urbino (Sanzio) 1990.

PREZIOSI, A. M.: "Appunti sulla origine e sulla diffusione delle casse rurali nel padovano", in: G. ZALIN (Ed.): *Un secolo di cooperazione di credito nel Veneto: le Casse rurali ed artigiane 1883-1983*, Padova (Signum) 1985.

PUTNAM, R. D.: *Making Democracy Work: Civic Traditions in Modern Italy*, Princeton (Princeton: University Press) 1993.

RAHMAN, I. R.: *Impact of Grameen Bank on the Situation of Rural Poor Women* Dhaka 1986.

RIDLEY, M.,: *The Origins of Virtue. Human Insticts and the Evolution of Cooperation*, Viking (New York) 1997.

RISTORTO, M.: "Il piccolo credito e i cattolici cuneesi", *Bollettino dell' Archivio per la Storia del Movimento Sociale Cattolico in Italia*, 6 (1971).

ROGGI, P.: "Il fascino della sopravvivenza. La storia della Banca Toscana dalle origini al 1940", in *Banca Toscana: storia e collezioni*, Firenze (Sansoni) 1982.

ROSSI, M. G.: *Le origini del partito cattolico*, Roma (Editori Riuniti) 1977.

RUGGIERI, E.: *Le casse rurali e artigiane italiane ottanta anni dopo la loro nascita (1883-1963)*, Cosenza (Patitucci) 1964.

SAGUATTI, A.: "La Cassa di Risparmio di Parma negli anni della prima trasformazione dell'economia e della società", in G. L. BASINI, G. FORESTIERI (Eds.): *Banche locali e sviluppo dell'economia. La Cassa di Risparmio di Parma*, Milano (Giuffrè) 1989.

SANNUCCI, V.: "Molteplicità delle banche di emissione: ragioni economiche ed effetti sull'efficacia del controllo monetario (1860-1890)", in: *Ricerche per la storia della Banca d'Italia,* Roma (Laterza) vol. 1, 1990.

SIMPSON, J.: *Spanish Agriculture: the long Siesta 1765-1965*, Cambridge (Cambridge University Press) 1995.

SINISI, A.: *Economia, istituzioni agrarie e gruppi sociali in Basilicata (1861-1914*), Napoli (D'Onofrio) 1989.

STIGLITZ, J. E., WEISS, A.: "Credit Rationing in Markets with Imperfect Information", *American Economic Review*, 71 (1981).

STIGLITZ, J. E.: "Peer Monitoring in Credit Markets", *World Bank Economic Review*, 4 (1990).

TAMAGNINI, G.: *Le casse rurali*, Roma (Ministero del Lavoro e della Previdenza Sociale, Direzione Generale della Cooperazione) 1952.

TOSTI, M.: "L'area umbro-sabina", in: S. ZANINELLI: *Mezzo secolo di ricerca storica sulla cooperazione bianca*, Verona (SCA) vol. 2, 1996.

TRAMONTIN, S.: "La prima cassa rurale cattolica", *Bollettino dell' Archivio per la Storia del Movimento Sociale Cattolico in Italia*, 9 (1974).

TREVIGLIO, CASSA RURALE DI: *Verbali dei Consigli d'Amministrazione*, vol.1, 29/3/1899 - 13/11/1907.

UDRY, C.: "Credit Markets in Rural Nigeria: Credit as Insurance in a Rural Economy", *World Bank Economic Review*, 4 (1991).

VARIAN, H. A.: "Monitoring Agents with Other Agents", *Journal of Theoretical and Institutional Economics*, 146 (1990).

VENERUSO, D.: "Le organizzazioni sindacali, sociali ed economiche cattoliche a Genova e in Liguria del 1918 al 1926", in: S. ZANINELLI (Ed.): *Il sindacalismo bianco tra guerra, dopoguerra e fascismo*, Milano (Giuffrè) 1982.

WENNER, M. D.: "Group Credit: A Means to Improve Information Transfer and Loan Repayment Performance", *Journal of Development Studies*, 32 (1995).

ZAMAGNI, V.: *The Economic History of Italy 1860-1990*, Oxford (Clarendon) 1993.

ZANINELLI, S.: *Mezzo secolo di ricerca storica sulla cooperazione bianca*, Verona (SCA) 1996.

Chapter 4

Entrepreneurial Minorities: A Typology

WILLIAM D. RUBINSTEIN

I. Entrepreneurial Minorities: The Historical Problem

It is not easy to offer a clear and cogent definition of 'entrepreneurial minorities'. One might cut the Gordian knot merely by defining them as members of a group, usually religious or ethnic in nature, which has a well-deserved reputation for high ability at business life and entrepreneurship. Clear-cut examples of such groups include Quakers and Unitarians in Britain after c. 1700, Island Greeks (those from Chios, the Ionians, etc.), Overseas Chinese, Germans in eastern Europe from c. 1750-1939, Armenians, Parsees, and Jews throughout all of modern history. Other groups who might well be brought under this heading include overseas Scots, East India Company 'Nabobs', and 'Old China Hands', i.e. Western (chiefly British and American) merchants and traders resident in Chinese trading ports for many years. The most cursory glance at this list reveals the enormously wide variety of groups one might include among 'entrepreneurial minorities.' The term is, moreover, one based largely in repute. Where no repute exists, the entrepreneurial qualities of the group in question are generally ignored, while reputations, especially where ethnic and religious groups are concerned, may easily descend into negative (or overly positive) stereotypes. In Nigeria, the Ibos are known as 'the Jews of Africa,' but this reputation is probably unknown in the West except to the cognoscenti. In Australia, where census data may be used to correlate religion with income, it has been found that Presbyterians consistently enjoy the highest incomes of any religious group. Yet few if any think of Presbyterians as a definable group, let alone an extremely successful one, and they do not enjoy a reputation for entrepreneurial success (apart from the stereotype of the 'canny Scotsman'). Such examples may be repeated many times. Yet everyone also knows that some groups are renowned for their entrepreneurial abilities, and are mentioned time and again by serious scholars as such - Quakers and other Dissenters in the English industrial revolution, for instance. Entrepreneurial minorities are thus important, probably extremely important, in explaining many types of economic development. Despite this, comprehensive studies of such groups appear to be limited. The best-known theory of the behaviour of entrepreneurial minorities remains the celebrated 'Weber Thesis' (1904-05) linking Protestantism with capitalism. Weber's thesis brought religion to the forefront of this subject. Yet a glance at the range of groups well-known as entrepreneurial minorities shows that religious similarities can hardly be a common denominator. This paper is an attempt to find commonalties among all or virtually all entrepreneurial minorities in as straightforward a classificatory schema as possible.

In my opinion, the 'Weber Thesis,' as valuable as it undoubtedly is, is inadequate to encapsulate all of those groups which are both minorities and demonstrate an apparent facility at capitalist entrepreneurship. Most certainly, not all are Protestant. Weber was, in my view, partially correct in identifying the affinity of smaller Protestant sects for successful entrepreneurship, but failed to identify the most accurate and cogent typology of such groups. As noted, he also pointed to religion and religious doctrine as central to Protestant success. This is somewhat misleading, since both non-Protestant religious groups, and groups definable in ethnic and national terms, rather than religious terms, may readily be seen as among the most notable entrepreneurial minorities. For all his brilliance, Weber thus muddied the waters of this question to a certain extent.

II. Entrepreneurial Minorities: A Schema, 'Chosen' Groups

In my view, the most fruitful way of classifying the best-known entrepreneurial minorities in the modern West (and elsewhere) is embodied in the following schema (see diagram).

Entrepreneurial Minorities

Emigration and Return

Examples:

Overseas Scots
"Old China Hands"
Island Greeks
Lebanese

Examples:

Huguenots
Quakers
Unitarians
Parsees?

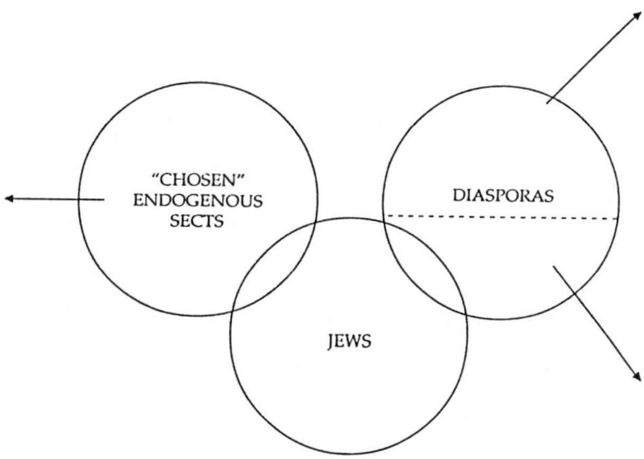

True Diasporas

Examples:
Armenians
Germans?

It will be seen that this schema divides entrepreneurial minorities into two essentially different types: 'Chosen' endogenous sects and Diasporas. Jews as a group contain elements of both and uniquely straddle the two. These two types of entrepreneurial minorities are often conflated and confused, but have essentially different characteristics. 'Chosen' endogenous sects (the term 'Chosen' derives from the Biblical Hebrew notion of 'Chosenness') are typically small Protestant sects, of which the Quakers and Unitarians are probably the best-known. Historically, such sects are commonly endogenous, intermarrying exclusively among themselves and, in the case of the Quakers, long expelling those who 'married out.' They maintained separate educational systems and had an agreed version of their history based centrally on memories of persecution. Although English Protestant groups are the best-known 'Chosen' groups, other non-Protestant sects may perhaps also be classified here, such as the Parsees and, especially, the Jews themselves, the original 'Chosen people' who exhibit most of the qualities of the later smaller Protestant sects.

'Chosen' groups are seemingly always religious in nature, although some 'intellectual aristocracies,' such as the famous Cambridge University 'intellectual aristocracy' from the time of Darwin to Keynes also seemingly exhibit similar qualities (although in this case not manifested in business life.) The 'Weber Thesis' is normally construed as interpreting the success of Protestant sects, and especially of smaller sects of this type, in terms of the religious beliefs of such groups, especially their 'this-worldly ascetism,' the ploughing back of profits, wealth as a sign of God's grace, and the notion of an occupational 'calling' from God. The 'Weber Thesis' cannot readily come to terms with non-Protestant groups which may exhibit similar characteristics. Max Weber maintained, against, in particular, his right-wing contemporary Werner Sombart, who argued that capitalism was 'Jewish,' that modern capitalism was specifically 'Protestant,' especially in its ploughing back of profits and 'deferred gratification,' qualities more closely associated with Protestantism than with the mercantile and financial pursuits long associated with Jews.

While, since Weber, the success of Protestants at entrepreneurship has traditionally been explained by religious factors (those outlined above), non-religious explanations of the success of such groups are also possible and are in many ways more plausible and convincing. In particular, 'Chosen' endogenous groups are often hallmarked by constituting national (or international) networks which, especially before the late nineteenth century, provided information on business conditions in widespread places, gave credit and loans, diminished risks, formed a pool of trustworthy partners and marriageable daughters, ostracised dishonest members, taught basic entrepreneurial and business skills and methods through apprenticeships among the extended network, etc. Together, these gave 'Chosen' groups a tremendous advantage in pre-corporate, pre-modern times. Some Diaspora groups functioned in the same way, and here it is often difficult to distinguish between the two, although 'Chosen' groups often operated within their own homeland rather than outside of it (to name one difference), while Diasporas often lacked a self-conscious religious identity. Non-religious explanations of the success enjoyed by entrepreneurial religious minorities paradoxically probably better explains the success of non-Protestant groups than the 'Weber Thesis' about Protestantism alone.

One other, in my opinion, central characteristic among 'Chosen' endogenous groups, including most emphatically the Jews, is that they almost invariably combined high marginality with high self-esteem. High self-esteem is a component of their 'Chosenness,' while high marginality stems from their status as religious minorities which were frequently persecuted. The combination of these two qualities may in my opinion be one of the key determinants of high achievement in a variety of fields and may fruitfully distinguish high-achieving minorities from other minorities which have no reputation for business (or intellectual) achievement, such as Roman Catholics in Britain or blacks in the so-called 'black Diasporas'. Such groups typically combine high marginality with low self-esteem (although I am perfectly aware that it is very difficult to demonstrate this satisfactorily.) It is also possible to imagine non-religious groups which combine high self-esteem with at least a sense of high marginality, for instance the 'Cambridge intellectual aristocracy' noted above. It would be worth asking here whether high achievement is transmissible among a range of fields apart from entrepreneurial ability. For instance, Jews since c.1850 have produced a grossly disproportionate number of important scientists and seminal thinkers, especially in the social sciences (although they are not so strongly represented in other fields). The 'Cambridge intellectual aristocracy,' if it is in any way comparable to the Jewish case, was entirely non-entrepreneurial, both in the social origins of most of its members (although Darwin and Vaughan Williams were descended from the Wedgwoods) and in its field of achievement. The sense of 'Chosenness' common to such groups is, however, primarily religious in nature and is clearly best engendered by core religious beliefs and values. One wonders whether the notion so central to America's national consciousness of the United States being 'God's own country,' the 'last, best hope of mankind,' a kind of national self-esteem really found nowhere else, has itself acted to facilitate America's amazing entrepreneurial success during the past 150 years.

III. Entrepreneurial Diasporas

This schema distinguishes 'Chosen' endogenous groups from Diasporas. Recent sociologists have divided Diasporas into a number of types, for example Robin Cohen, who distinguishes 'victim diasporas' (Africans and Armenians), 'labour and imperial diasporas' (Indians and British), 'trade diasporas' (Chinese and Lebanese), etc. (Cohen 1997). Although Cohen's divisions are useful on a general level, a different set of emphases is given here, where entrepreneurial Diasporas are further divided into two distinct types, those whose members experience (and intend to experience) emigration and return to their homeland, and true Diasporas, those whose members either have no real homeland or none to which they can return, or wish to return. The Overseas Scots who made a fortune in the Empire, then returned to buy a Highland estate and hopefully found a high status dynasty, are examples of the first type of Diaspora, as were British 'Nabobs' and 'Old China Hands,' while Armenians are a well-known example of the second type. Armenians made their homes wherever they found themselves, and had no independent homeland to return to, although there were heavily Armenian areas of settlement, especially in what is today the Armenian Republic in the Caucasian mountains, in eastern Turkey, and throughout the Ottoman Empire, especially western Turkey, prior to the 1915 genocide. Armenians also formerly lived throughout eastern Europe, comprising a major part of the mercantile class, and indeed throughout the whole of the Levant.

Very similar to the Armenians were the Island Greeks, who since the early nineteenth century have controlled a grossly disproportionate share of the world's cargo shipping trade (and still do). They are also merchants and bankers, and until the early part of this century were dominant in the export trade from southern Russia to all parts of the world (Harlaftis 1996). Island Greeks came from a number of different places in the Greek Mediterranean islands and the coast of Turkey, with an interesting pattern wherein men from one such geographical locale succeeded another group at the same trades at roughly generational intervals. The earliest and best-known shipowning Island Greeks in the modern period came from the island of Chios, and included the well-known Ralli, Schilizzi, Papayanni, and Petrocochino families. By the 1860s the Rallis and others had established their international headquarters in London, where nine members of the Ralli family and five Schilizzis left estates of £500,000 or more between 1868 and 1939. After the 1860s, a second set of Island Greek merchants, originating in the Ionian Islands, gradually replaced them in similar endeavours. A world-wide Greek mercantile Diaspora had been formed by the late nineteenth century. Nevertheless, even in 1990 Greek shipowners apparently owned more than one-third of the world's merchant cargo fleet, vessels either flying the Greek flag or flags of convenience (Harlaftis 1996, pp. 264-267). Aristotle Onassis was, of course, probably the most famous post-war shipowner. It is interesting to note, too, that while Island Greeks were renowned for their business prowess, Greece itself remained a backward, semi-developed country until recently. This pattern is probably a common one among entrepreneurial Diasporas. For instance, the 'Pale of Settlement,' where Jews were confined to live in Czarist Russia down to the First World War, was known for its chronic poverty (caused chiefly by Czarist anti-semitism.)

As indicated in the diagram, Jews were clearly a Diaspora entrepreneurial minority - indeed, once again, the archetypal one, since they literally had no homeland until 1948, apart from shared memories of the Biblical land of Palestine, where virtually no Jews lived and which had not been a Jewish state since Roman times. As is well known, Jews passed the centuries from the Destruction of the Temple in 70 AD until the Enlightenment literally being driven from pillar to post throughout Europe and the Middle East. Only with the rise of the English-speaking democracies and basic changes in definitions of national citizenship to comprise religious and ethnic minorities could Jews securely feel themselves a part of the country they lived in, or were so regarded by the majority.

Unlike 'Chosen' endogenous groups, which are normally religious sects, Diasporas are based in ethnicity/nationality. The success enjoyed by entrepreneurial Diasporas are thus presumably due to the non-religious advantages of internationally-based but interrelated minority communities. Clearly, the 'Weber Thesis' has no relevance to explaining the success of these groups. Indeed, while smaller Protestant sects occasionally acted as internationally-based entrepreneurial Diaspora groups - the transatlantic Quaker 'Cousinhood' of the eighteenth and nineteenth century comes to mind, as do the Protestant German communities of eastern Europe prior to the Second World War - in general Protestants did not as a rule form entrepreneurial Diasporas in the same way as Jews, Greeks, Lebanese, Armenians, and their ilk.

IV. Entrepreneurial Minorities and the Evolution of Capitalism

The success enjoyed by both types of entrepreneurial minorities distinguished in this schema are more typical of the early modern period and of the earlier stages of modern commercial and industrial capitalism (to, say, c. 1870) than of the corporate capitalism of the past 125 years. Corporate capitalism largely renders unnecessary the advantages (trustworthy partners, risk-minimisation, etc.) enjoyed by both groups. It puts in place a professional managerial structure with profit-making goals and criteria, has access to international information networks, institutes rationally-based hiring and promotion criteria, funds research/ development and advertising. Corporations can engage in takeovers and mergers of a kind which kinship-based partnerships find difficult. Theoretically, corporate capitalism should be entirely or very largely free of religious/ethnic modes of organisation. In contemporary America, Britain, and Europe, it is just possible that ethnicity indeed plays almost no role in the hiring and promotion practices of most very large corporations, although in American before c.1960 or so, large corporations were white Anglo-Saxon Protestant (and male) bastions. Professional business school education, and the current popularity of business careers among talented students, suggests that hiring and promotion into the larger corporations will be based largely on talent. Since the mid-1960s, too, virtually every democracy has adopted anti-discrimination legislation which makes overt ethnic discrimination illegal. Democracy, pluralism, secularisation, and the ubiquity of the mass media have done much to remove the shared memories of oppression which bound groups like Protestant Dissenters together until as late as 1914.

Nevertheless, it is clearly the case that some ethnic/nationality groups have remained as strikingly successful entrepreneurial minorities until the present, for instance Jews and Island Greeks. Indeed, new ethnic-based entrepreneurial minorities have become prominent in the contemporary period, for example Overseas Chinese (with a long history of entrepreneurship behind them), the Hindu and Sikh diasporas, and perhaps a Nigerian/West African group. Many shops in impoverished black ghettos in the United States are run by Korean and Indian immigrants. One also wonders whether the past twenty-five years has seen the emergence of a women's business class, centred in certain types of 'tender-minded' shops and services. How conceptually to relate the growing female presence in business life to the impact of previous 'minorities' is an interesting question, but it probably should be linked to the emergence of an affluent, well-educated middle class of consumers, as well as to the removal of discriminatory barriers in entry into business life, the provision of credit, etc., and to non-traditional family and life-style patterns.

Paradoxically, it also seems clear that the heyday of the capitalist 'rugged individual' tycoon was typically found at a later time period than the zenith of the religious or ethnic-based entrepreneurial minorities, which were associated with an earlier phase of capitalism. Very roughly, the 'ideal type' of the (often Methodist) northern factory owner reached his zenith after c.1850, long after, for instance, the Quaker 'Cousinhoods' became prominent. One reason for this is that the advantages enjoyed by the older kinship networks had largely dissipated by that time. For instance, there was, by the later nineteenth century, an independent mercantile and sales network for the products of Britain's manufacturing enterprises (or at least the beginnings of one), local banks which supplied credit, etc. Thus, both 'rugged individual' tycoon capitalism and corporate capitalism may be more typical of the later (post-1850/1870) phases of capitalism than are modes of capitalism exampled by either type of entrepreneurial minority.

V. Entrepreneurial Minorities and Commercial/Financial Capitalism

By and large, both types of entrepreneurial minority were more likely to be found in commercial than in manufacturing capitalism. Indeed, 'middleman' capitalism was often heavily associated with extended kinship and international networks of the types discussed here. In the Middle Ages and early modern period, too, Jews predominated in the role of bankers, money-lenders, and tax-collectors, largely because of the ban on usury among Christians. In the modern era, although the ban on usury no longer exists, Jewish economic activity is certainly still found disproportionately in finance and commerce. However, in contrast, Protestant sects appear to have had a much greater affinity (for reasons which are not obvious) with industrial and manufacturing capitalism as well as with commerce. This may in fact be an important distinction between 'Chosen' groups and diasporas.

Throughout central and eastern Europe and the Levant down to the Second World War, entrepreneurial minorities and Diasporas virtually constituted the business middle classes of many countries which failed to produce a native business class (e.g. Poland, Rumania, much of the Ottoman Empire.) Jews predominated here, but such groups as Armenians, Greeks, Lebanese Christians, and eastern European German Protestants were also very prominent. In general, relations between entrepreneurial minorities were always good, although there were some notable exceptions when rivalries emerged. For instance, some historians have noted the disproportionate involvement of Greeks in the anti-semitic pogroms in southern Russia between 1881 and 1905. This may have been founded in the growing displacement of Greek merchants by Jews in the import-export trade of southern Russia at this time (Klier and Lambrozo 1992; Harlaftis 1996, pp. 70-104).[1]

1 Obviously other factors were at work in the pogroms.

VI. The Unique Position of the Jews

Something should specifically be said about the position of Jews; they uniquely, bridge both 'Chosen' minorities and Diasporas. Sociologists and historians have pointed to a wide range of factors to account for the facility of Jews at business life. In Christian Europe to the Reformation, Jews were the only people who could lend money at interest and were commonly used by kings and royal courts as tax-collectors and money-lenders (e.g. by the Norman kings of England between 1066 and 1290.) As late as the eighteenth century, 'Court Jews' remained as official money-lenders to many central European princes, for instance the Rothschilds to the rulers of Hesse-Cassel. Some Marxist historians have argued that the unique 'wealthy pariah' economic role of Jews was precisely what allowed them to survive so many centuries as the only non-Christian group permitted to exist in most of Europe.

In religious terms, Judaism has no tradition of poverty as a virtue in itself nor of ascetism (although it equally has no tradition of wealth being seen as a sign of God's favour.) Jewish tradition demanded that all Jewish males (and, indeed, females) be literate, while Jewish religious life is obsessively time-conscious (of festivals, sabbaths, etc.) in, perhaps, a modern sense. From a non-religious perspective, Jews were, as a people, a kind of very large extended kinship network all over the Western world and the Levant, with fewer internal class barriers than among most other settled peoples, and a long tradition of wealthy Jews assisting poor and oppressed Jewish communities. Perhaps more importantly than any other factor, practising Jews could not, until the early-mid nineteenth century, enter the nobility or higher status groups of any European country; even if rich, they could not readily buy land, become landed aristocrats, or join the military elite (or, by definition, the clerical elite). Thus Jews could become wealthy only as owners of personalty, not realty; there was no Jewish 'haemorrhage of talent' towards the idle rich among the children and grand-children of successful Jewish businessmen, or at any rate much less of one than among other groups. Furthermore, as successive generations of impoverished Orthodox Jews left the ghettos, especially by heavy emigration to America and other parts of the 'new Diaspora' after 1880, they entered societies which were regularly well-disposed to capitalism and to upward social mobility, with much less rampant anti-semitism than in eastern and central Europe.

The Jewish affinity to capitalism and economic success should, of course, not be exaggerated. By and large, Jews comprised a small, even insignificant portion of the economic elite of the English-speaking world between c.1840 and 1939 (Rubinstein 1998). America's extraordinary economic ascent between 1865 and 1929 was almost entirely judenrein, with northern European Protestants 'taking the place' of Jews, as anti-semites like Werner Sombart pointed out. The contemporary State of Israel is renowned for many things; the quality of its capitalists is not one of them. The persisting economic role of the Jews is an extreme example of a successful entrepreneurial minority, but is obviously on a continuum whose rationale is not very mysterious.

VII. Nationalistic Hostility to Entrepreneurial Minorities

As the Jewish example immediately suggests, entrepreneurial minorities have often been subject to fierce hostility by local nationalists. One of the major underlying factors in modern European anti-semitism has been the often grossly disproportionate overrepresentation of Jews in the local economic elites of central and eastern Europe. Significantly, anti-semitism was always categorically lower in the English-speaking world, where the Jewish percentage of the economic elite was always relatively low. In east Asia, Overseas Chinese have been subject to similar hostility, as have been Hindus and Sikhs throughout east Africa, etc. Armenians were massacred by the Turks during the First World War, while over a million Greeks were expelled by Turkey in the early 1920s. Indeed, it is hardly much of an exaggeration to conclude that much of twentieth-century nationalism, in Europe and beyond, has consisted of eliminating 'alien' entrepreneurial minorities from national economies. In contrast, the English-speaking world has been largely sympathetic to such minorities, particularly in the largest cosmopolitan entrepôts like London and New York. One late nineteenth-century description of the Baltic Exchange in London (which deals primarily in freight chartering on merchant ships) noted that its prominent members included "the wily Greek and the almost wilier Hebrew, the cute Yank and the German with spectacles on both outer and inner eye ... together with some of the shrewdest Britons, metropolitan and provincial" (Harlaftis 1996, p. 59). These ethnic descriptions were ambiguous: half hostile but half admiring. The City of London, in particular, has welcomed entrepreneurial minorities for centuries, while New York was the 'melting pot' itself. The relatively sympathetic attitude of the English-speaking countries presumably stems from the fact that capitalism and democracy were deeply rooted in their local cultures, but also because there was a powerful and successful elite which did not perceive these outsider groups as a threat.

Entrepreneurial minorities were 'elite' groups which should therefore be distinguished from other types of ethnic minorities.[2] Such groups as the Irish in Britain and America and blacks and West Indians in both countries and elsewhere were groups without a reputation for entrepreneurial talent. They were perceived as threats and unwelcome arrivals in very different ways from Jews and Armenians. They were feared for such alleged characteristics as propensity to drunkenness and crime, as well as the dangers they allegedly presented of 'swamping' the demographic balance of a country. (Jews and other groups have also experienced this type of hostility, but not as frequently.) These two types of prejudice and hostility appear to be conceptually separate. It will be interesting to see whether trends to globalization and much higher rates of higher education around the world than in the past produces, in the next century, a world-wide capitalism which is freer from the influence of entrepreneurial minorities than previously, or whether these will persist, either in the same forms as have been known in modern times or in new, perhaps disguised, ways.

---

2 Rather regrettably, the present paper cannot address wider questions of entrepreneurship, such as those highlighted by Joseph Schumpeter in pointing to the inevitable decline of entrepreneurial drive. So long as entrepreneurial minorities remain excluded from the normal status structure of their host society, this regularly acts as a spur to the continuation of entrepreneurial life across the generations. Nor can this paper touch on all minorities, especially those whose relationship to individual entrepreneurships is somewhat complex, for instance the Mormons, whose missionary requirement, mandatory tithing to benefit the Mormon church, and geographical centring specifically in Utah, sets them apart from most other 'Chosen' sects.

References

COHEN, R.: *Global Diasporas: An Introduction,* London (UCL Press) 1997.

HARLAFTIS, G.: *A History of Greek-Owned Shipping: The Making of an International Tramp Fleet, 1830 to the Present Day*, London (Routledge) 1996.

KLIER, J. D., LAMBROSO, S. (Eds.): *Pogroms: Anti-Jewish Violence in Modern Russian History*, Cambridge (Cambridge University Press) 1992.

RUBINSTEIN, W. D.: "Jewish Participation in National Economic Elites and Anti-Semitism: An International Comparison" (unpublished conference paper) 1998.

Chapter 5

Cultural Determinants of Jewish Immigrant Entrepreneurship in the UK and USA and British and American Culture

ANDREW GODLEY

I. Introduction

This paper aims to summarize the main findings of a research programme, which examined the impact of cultural factors on labour market mobility, in particular, the supply of entrepreneurship in the UK and USA between 1880-1914 (Godley 1999). An alleged divergence in the supply of entrepreneurship to the two economies, possibly caused by cultural differences, has been cited as being one of the principal causative factors in the very real divergence in the two economies' performances after 1880 (Wiener 1981). Simply put, this thesis states that upper class antagonism to industry acted as a force against the adoption of cultural values sympathetic to innovation in the UK, whilst the cultural values in the USA were more in favour of self-employment and entrepreneurship. A variation of this theme of culturally induced labour market rigidity in the UK emerges from the writings of David Landes and William Lazonick. This focuses on the dominance of a craft-culture among the working classes which allegedly acted as a drag on innovation and technological diffusion. Finally, the work of A. D. Chandler focuses on the slow adoption of modern corporate structures in UK industry at least partly as a result of a cultural bias to maintaining family control (Landes 1969, Lazonick 1991, Chandler 1990).

Whichever of these, and other, theses is examined the fact remains that late Victorian culture is in some way or some form being used as an explanatory variable in the process of economic retardation before 1914. To those wanting to test this hypothesis and measure the impact of UK culture on UK economic performance a significant problem emerges. This can be seen when considering what would need to be done in order to assess the impact of UK culture on UK economic performance relative to other countries.

For economists brave enough to confront cultural variations in applying neoclassical models, the traditional approach has been to assume that differences are merely manifestations of social and economic backwardness, which, with suitable economic development, will converge to the norm of materialistic individualism. New growth and new institutional economics theories have begun to redress this imbalance with increasing attention being focused on the impact of cultural factors on economic developments, principally through further refinements of the importance of human capital and the theory of the firm and the role of transaction costs in firms and markets. For example, "Economic performance depends on transaction costs, and these mainly reflect the level of trust in the economy. The level of trust depends in turn on culture" (Casson 1991, p. 3). Thus, it follows that if cultures vary then economic actors will respond differently to similar economic stimuli when in different cultures. For historians wanting to use economic analysis as a part of a comparative study of different economies, industries or firms, where different cultural values and practices are evident, this poses something of a dilemma.

Yet it is a dilemma which is similar to that faced in other disciplines when conducting comparative experiments, especially in medical research. For example, the investigation of the aetiology of certain diseases, which are observed to vary with environmental factors, inevitably concentrates on a control population. Thus, it might be variations in heart disease between native Japanese and Japanese migrants in California, or types of diabetes among Asians in the Indian sub-continent and in the UK, or whatever, but medical researchers assume that environmental factors will influence disease and that one way of obtaining scientifically significant measurements of the importance of environment is to concentrate on a genetically identical population (Bodanski et al 1992). For social scientists the problem is slightly different. In order to obtain scientifically significant measurements of the influence of the environment (including cultural factors) on economic decision making isolating a genetically similar population to use as a control is not sufficiently rigorous. The control population has to be one which responds to economic stimuli in the same way. Thus it is not enough to compare migrants of one nation with those who chose to stay at home, as the medical scientists have done, because the difference in levels of geographical mobility may imply different preference sets and so different levels of responsiveness to similar economic stimuli. The answer for the economist has to be to choose as a control population a single ethnic group which has migrated to two locations at the same time, and then to compare the responsiveness of these migrants to the appropriate economic variables in the two destinations. Control groups like this are not exactly thick on the ground. When comparing the UK with the USA the only ethnic group where migration took place to both these countries in sufficient numbers during the years 1880-1914 were the East European Jews.[1] Therefore, it is proposed that, by examining the responsiveness of the East European Jewish immigrants in the UK and USA to the specific economic variables which influenced the supply of entrepreneurship, a uniform elasticity should be observed which would be consistent with a single supply function. If this was not the case then any residual factors can be further examined for any plausible relationship with differences in the cultural values of the two host societies, which may have been absorbed by the assimilating immigrants. The first step then is to consider the levels of entrepreneurship among East European Jewish immigrants in the UK and USA during this period.

1 The Irish also emigrated to both destinations during these years, but they were considered to be less suitable than the East European Jews for the purposes of comparison, because of the close geographical proximity and political unity of Great Britain and Ireland.

ANDREW GODLEY

II. East European Jewish Entrepreneurship in the UK and USA, 1880-1914

The Ashkenazim Jews settled in what were the kingdoms of Poland and Lithuania during the 16th and 17th centuries. As a result of Russian expansion and the partition of Poland by Russia, Prussia and Austria-Hungary the population of East European Jews was almost entirely divided into these three empires by the end of the Napoleonic era, the exception being a group which had migrated over the Carpathian mountains into what became Rumania. The majority were resident in the western portion of the Russian Empire, a section which became known as the Pale of Settlement. During the nineteenth century the East European Jews experienced one of the most rapid population increases in all Europe. Starting at the beginning of the century with approximately 1-1½ million people the East European Jews grew to about 8 million by 1913 (Frankel 1981). This pace of growth was faster than that experienced even in Britain during the period. Not surprisingly such a rapid population growth led to intense pressures on the economic viability of the East European Jewish community, pressures which were exacerbated by the Russian imperial governments' use of discriminative legislation and their toleration, even encouragement at times, of racial hatred (Baron 1964, Dubnow 1918-19). Emigration eventually came to be seen as an option for the East European Jews to escape their poverty and, once started, it took on the proportions of an exodus. Before 1880 the number of East European Jews who had left for either western Europe or the USA totalled a few thousand, by 1914 approximately 2½ million had left (Kuznets 1975, Godley 1999). Most of these went to the USA (2m) but 150,000 settled in Britain. In both destinations the main centres of settlement were the great metropoli, New York and London.

When the levels of Jewish immigrant entrepreneurship are measured in the two nations there are three problems which need to be addressed before any results can be considered. The first two are issues of methodology, the last of data. The first problem is related to the definition of entrepreneurship. Entrepreneurship is conventionally seen as a source of dynamism in economic development, which means it fits in less easily than it might to the normal comparative static approach to economic analysis. In this paper it is most appropriate to adopt Casson's definition of the entrepreneur as "someone who specializes in taking judgmental decisions about the co-ordination of scarce resources" (Casson 1982, p. 23). This allows the proxy of heads of firms to be used as a measurement of entrepreneurs because the heads of firms are going to be the ones most responsible for economic decision making within the firm. It is readily apparent that this is a measure of quantity rather than quality of entrepreneurship, but, in the absence of any acceptable method of differentiating between good and bad entrepreneurship, this is the best indication available to historians.

The second issue to be resolved before considering the results is that of actually how to measure and compare Jewish immigrant entrepreneurship in the two locations, especially bearing in mind the differences in the sizes of the two immigrant communities. It was held that the only reasonable way was to measure entrepreneurship as the share of immigrant entrepreneurs in the immigrant workforce.

Finally the question of data needs to be considered. The published census reports of USA and UK, whilst providing much important information relevant to the study, do not actually differentiate between the entrepreneurs and workers among the Jewish immigrants. When considering the information recorded in the census manuscripts by census officials differences in status are sometimes but not always apparent. Differentiation between masters and workers was clear for the USA, where the work of Thomas Kessner on the Jewish immigrants in New York City provides one data-set (Kessner 1977, Kessner 1983). In the UK the original enumerators' books are less helpful. Workers have been listed under their occupation but without any indication of rank. However, an alternative data-set provided the necessary results to compare with Kessner's New York data. This data-set was the occupational information on the marriage records of London's East End and City synagogues, which is discussed in detail elsewhere (Godley 1999). Combining these two data-sets gave occupational information at the required level of detail enabling the differentiation of employer from employee. The comparison then is of Jewish immigrant entrepreneurship in the two principal centres of settlement on either side of the Atlantic, rather than the nation states in which they were located. All these caveats and considerations aside, the two sets of figures are broadly representative of the Jewish immigrant experience in the two nations.

III. The Results

Table 1 shows the levels of East European Jewish immigrant entrepreneurship in London and New York between 1880 and 1914, expressed as the percentage of entrepreneurs among the workforce.

Table 1: East European Jewish Immigrant Entrepreneurship in London and New York, 1880-1914 (%)[2]

Entrepreneurs in Workforce [N]	1880-89 [91]	1890-99 [264]	1900-06 [315]	1907-14 [291]	Increase 1880s-1914
London	14.2	10.9	13.1	18.0	3.8
	1880 [524]		1905 [963]	1925 [1535]	Increase 1880-1914 est.
New York	18.0		34.3	36.0	17.0

The results in table 1 show how the Jewish immigrant working population in London and New York began the era of mass migration with a broadly similar share of entrepreneurs in the workforce. The 18% in New York would most probably be matched by the London figure if 1880 alone were chosen as the sample year (there were insufficient number of observations in the London sample for that method to be chosen). In London the share of the workforce employed in entrepreneurial occupations fell during the 1880s and 90s. However, the level of entrepreneurship among the Jewish immigrants in London reached its nadir in the early-1890s and then began to increase, reaching a peak of 18% by 1907-14. In New York, by contrast, the share of entrepreneurs in the immigrant workforce almost doubled to over 34% as early as 1905, a level from which it remained

2 Reproduced from GODLEY (1999, table 3.6). Note, the New York estimate for 1914 was 35%, the straight-line interpolation of 1905-25, to the nearest whole figure.

roughly stable. This represents a net increase in the share of entrepreneurship of 17% in New York compared to a net increase in London of 3.8% over the period. The growth of entrepreneurship among Jewish immigrants in New York was over four times greater than in London over the period. How could such a large difference between the two communities have occurred? The next two sections aim to provide, first a conventional economic analysis focusing on the market for entrepreneurship in London and New York, and second a modified model of the market for entrepreneurship which relaxes the assumptions about actors responding to pecuniary signals only.

IV. The Market for Entrepreneurship Among Jewish Immigrants in London and New York

The first attempt at interpreting the fourfold difference in the rate of increase of entrepreneurship in London and New York is by considering the market for entrepreneurship in London and New York. Such differences in the supply of entrepreneurship by Jewish immigrants should indicate similar changes in the demand for entrepreneurship and the price paid to entrepreneurs for supplying entrepreneurship. Before going on to consider the market for entrepreneurship among Jewish immigrants in London and New York in more detail, however, it is important to pay more attention to one vital assumption made about the two immigrant groups, namely that of homogeneity. It has, thus far, been assumed that the East European Jewish immigrants in New York and London were homogeneous. This is clearly not true in one area. The majority chose to settle in New York, the minority in London. Space constraints here do not permit any detailed answer of these important questions other than to report that they have been dealt with elsewhere (Godley 1999). It is sufficient to note here that the most powerful explanatory variable of migrants' choices of destination was the size of pre-existing Jewish immigrant community. It was a migration movement which followed chains. The destination was determined by whom the potential migrant knew and how much they were prepared to subsidise his or her passage. Consequently, the patterns of migration flow to the UK and USA were remarkably similar. The chronology of settlement in the two destinations was almost identical, as figure 1 shows, which makes for a distinct contrast with East European Jewish emigration to any other destination. The similarity between the Jewish migration movements to London and New York is further underlined with the regional background, literacy rates and composition of the migrant population according to age and gender almost identical for both destinations. As far as the propensity to entrepreneurship is concerned there are no grounds upon which to question the homogeneity of the Jewish immigrant population in both New York and London during this period.

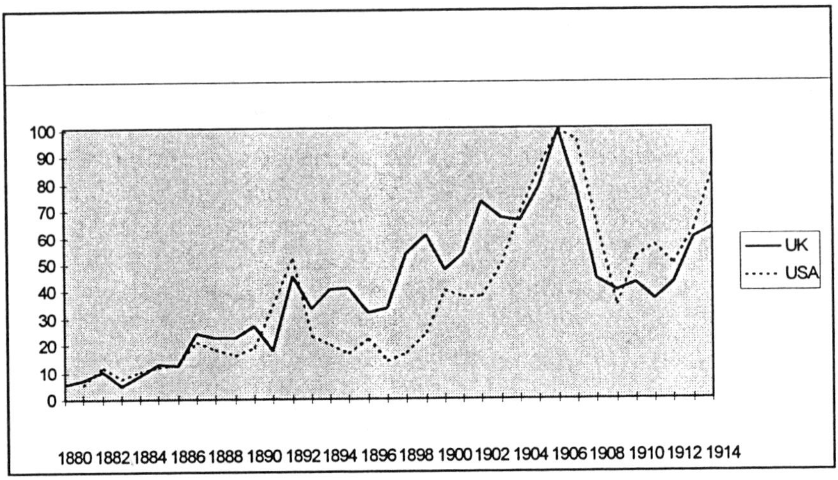

Figure 1: East European Jewish immigration to the UK and USA, 1880-1914 (1906 = 100).

If we return then to the concept of there being two markets for entrepreneurship among Jewish immigrants in London and New York, the next step must be to note the existence of a qualification mark for entry into these particular markets. For entrepreneurship to be exercised the specialist in the making of judgmental decisions must have access to scarce economic resources requiring co-ordination. The entrepreneur therefore must have access to capital in order to gain access to economic resources. The difference between the levels of entrepreneurship between the two Jewish immigrant communities might, therefore, be explained by varying institutional constraints on the supply of capital to would-be immigrant entrepreneurs, with easier access in New York than in London. Again space constraints permit little more than a notification of the results of the research, which show that there was no difference in the availability of venture capital to potential entrants into the market for entrepreneurship. The supply of capital was a function of individual savings and the supply of outside sources of small loans. Business loans were obtainable but from charitable organisations rather than banks, and there was no greater provision of venture capital from charitable sources in New York than in London. Entrepreneurs who invested their savings into businesses were common in both cities. The amount of capital needed to set up a shop in the immigrant trades was notoriously little. However, despite real wages being higher in New York, disposable income was closer to parity with London because of the much higher living costs in Manhattan. Savings for investing in business ventures, as for returning to Russia in the form of remittances or to subsidise passage fares, were essentially similar in the two cities' Jewish immigrant communities (Godley 1996a).

If the conditions of the supply of entrepreneurship were no different in the New York and London Jewish economies then perhaps the demand for entrepreneurship varied, with a much higher and faster growing demand for entrepreneurs among the Jewish economy in New York rather than in London. In the Pale of Settlement the Jewish workforce was dominated by traders, artisans and providers of ethnic services to the Jewish community, such as specialist food retailers and religious and educational instructors. In the West however, the occupational structure of the two principal immigrant communities was dominated by one industry above all others: the clothing industry. Almost two-thirds of the Jewish immigrants in both New York and London were employed in the various branches of the clothing industry, with men's tailors the most important by far (Godley 1997a, Godley 1997b). Aside from the clothing industry the two Jewish economies provided employment for a stable proportion of those providing ethnic goods and services (Jewish butchers, bakers, rabbis, teachers and so on), and a number involved in commerce and other forms of semi-industrialised manufacturing, such as furniture-making.

There were some minor differences between the two local economies. There was a higher share of the Jewish immigrant workforce employed in cabinet-making and boot-making in London compared to New York, and, conversely, a higher share employed in the food processing and property sectors in New York, but the differences were insignificant. Both immigrant economies were dependant on the fortunes of what was a rapidly growing clothing industry. Clothing can be seen as the main source of 'exports' from the Jewish to the Gentile economies of the USA and UK. The dominant source of demand for entrepreneurship in both immigrant economies was firmly located in the two clothing industries. Thus, the main source for any changes in profits which would stimulate further changes in the supply of entrepreneurship must be looked for there.

For the supply of entrepreneurship, to have risen by so much more in New York than in London would imply a fundamental change in the ratio of real profits between the two, in favour of New York. Thus, assuming opportunity costs to have been equal and further assuming the price elasticity of supply of entrepreneurship among the Jewish immigrants to have been uniform, an increase in the share of entrepreneurs in the workforce which was four times greater in New York than in London would have to have been caused by a greater increase in profits in New York than any increase in London. It is therefore surprising, when the available evidence is examined, that the trend was for profits to fall in New York Jewish immigrant community and rise among London Jewish immigrant entrepreneurs. In both cases the opportunity cost for potential entrepreneurs was the prevailing wage level, and among Jewish workers wages were generally sticky throughout the period, neither falling much nor rising a great deal. Among the New York entrepreneurs in the clothing industry the level of profits declined considerably between 1880 and 1905, the two years for which we have figures for the level of entrepreneurship. In London, however, Jewish entrepreneurs were complaining bitterly of falling profits in the 1880s, yet by 1907-1914 the Jewish economy in London was relatively buoyant, the clothing industry was experiencing record output and considerably higher wages and profits than the 1880s (Godley 1995, Godley 1996b, and Godley 1996c).

This provides something of a paradox. The economy where the supply of entrepreneurship increased less was the economy which experienced the increase in profits. The economy where the supply of entrepreneurship increased more experienced a fall in profits, something which should have stimulated a move out of profit-earning occupations and into wage-earning ones. Before going on to suggest a possible interpretation of this paradox it is worth examining the evidence of Jewish immigrant labour market mobility in the two cities during this period in more detail.

Table 2: East European Jewish socio-economic structure in London and New York, 1880-1914[3]

New York (%)		1880		1905	
White-collar	Entre-preneurs:	18.0		34.3	
	Non-Entre-preneurs:	3.0		6.1	
	TOTAL	21.0		40.4	
Blue-collar					
	TOTAL	79.0		59.6	
London (%)		**1880-82**	**1890-99**	**1900-06**	**1907-14**
White collar	Entre-preneurs:	14.2	10.9	13.3	18.0
	Non-entre-preneurs:	3.4	3.0	1.8	1.4
	TOTAL	17.6	13.9	15.1	19.4
Blue-collar	Skilled:	14.6	14.0	23.8	24.0
	Semi/-Unskilled:	67.8	71.3	56.9	30.2
	Journey-men:	-	0.8	4.2	26.3
	TOTAL	82.4	86.1	84.9	80.5

Table 2 gives the picture of the two immigrant labour markets more detail. The story of a rather dramatic increase in the share of the workforce who were in business in New York is confirmed. The smaller increase in

3 GODLEY (1999).

the share of entrepreneurs among the London Jewish immigrants proves to be only one part of a more complicated picture, where the changes in blue collar employment are more important, particularly the gain in relative importance of skilled workers and journeymen. Indeed, the rather dramatic point demonstrated by table 2 is not the predictable increase in skilled workers but the sudden and very rapid rise of a group of Jewish immigrant workers who were calling themselves journeymen. Rising moderately from a position of negligible importance to only just over 4% of the workforce by the early years of this century, the Jewish immigrant journeymen suddenly increased their share of the workforce to more than one-in-four by 1907-1914. This is a curious artefact of the data and needs some explanation.

Journeymen in Britain were craftsmen. Having served their apprenticeships they were highly skilled. Within the British working class to be called a journeyman was a sign of moderately high status, higher than the ordinary worker, but not as high as a master craftsman. Within the industries where the Jewish journeymen proliferated - the clothing and furniture making industries - the term denoted a rank of skill, which in turn demanded high wages. Journeymen tailors in London were concentrated in the West End, with Saville Row the centre of the bespoke trade. Yet very few Jewish immigrants were bespoke tailors, nor were there many working for the established firms in the West End. Indeed, the idea of Jewish immigrant tailors rising to the ranks of journeymen would have been considered with derision by the English tailors. English tailors were craftsmen who shunned the machine, Jewish tailors were little more than profiteers, running up cheap and shoddy garments, using the latest Singer and deskilling a once noble craft, so the allegations rang (Schmiechen 1984, Wechsler 1979). They were clearly not journeymen tailors as the term was generally understood. A journeyman tailor, as far as the Jews were concerned, at least by the 1920s and 30s, had come to mean someone who could make a garment all the way through, from the cutting of the material to the sewing, basting and pressing. Thus, before World War Two it was a term denoting skill and status for the Jews. Yet in the workshop dominated trade before World War One there was no room for highly skilled generalists, only the semi-skilled specialists were in demand. Indeed, the exact nature of who or what the pre-1914 Jewish journeyman was defies exact definition. It was certainly not an import from the Pale of Settlement as there is no Yiddish equivalent for journeyman. But it was an indication of status to those grooms registering their occupations, and one which evidently became very popular.

Econometric evidence shows that the Jewish immigrant journeymen grooms were more likely to be assimilated than the average Jewish immigrant groom. They were more likely to be able to sign their names in English, to take English born brides and to marry in the synagogues of the established UK Jewry. Thus, they were more likely to have been exposed to English cultural values than the average Jewish immigrant, other things equal, and so to have assimilated these values. Their preference for journeyman status indicates that they had absorbed some of the values of the English craft culture, with its extreme considerations of rank and status. What did they do to deserve this status? Not what their Gentile equivalents did. Within the structure of the East End Jewish tailoring industry their was no room for the highly skilled worker who was more familiar with the needle and thread than the Singer and treadle. It is most likely that Jewish journeymen tailors were simply skilled machinists.

If this explanation of the rise in importance of Jewish journeymen is accepted then table 2 can be reinterpreted as follows. If the most dramatic part of the story of the Jewish immigrant labour market in London - the rise of the journeymen - is depicting the acquisition of a culturally determined status by the assimilating immigrants, then perhaps it is worth reconsidering the market for entrepreneurship among Jewish immigrants in London and New York as merely a part of a larger story.

V. Cultural Assimilation and the Market for Status Among Jewish Immigrants in London and New York

Beginning to consider status as a good which can be obtained through occupational rank brings a complication to the conventional labour market model so far used here to interpret the differences in socio-economic mobility in New York's and London's Jewish immigrant communities. That complication is, of course, the one introduced at the beginning of this paper, the extreme assumption of economic rationality as a rationality defined by responsiveness to material rewards only. Thus, the conventional model of a labour market focuses on the role of wages as the only reward structure, ignoring status considerations per se.

As far as our Jewish immigrants are concerned it is possible to postulate that as the two immigrant communities became established and as the two immigrant economies developed, the process of assimilation continued. This process of assimilation involved the adoption by the immigrant community of host cultural values, in particular in relation to work status. Thus, it is now possible to incorporate cultural values, at least in this limited sense, in preference sets and apply this modified model of the labour market to the experience of Jewish immigrants in New York and London.

If it is accepted that the cultural values of America gave self-employment a higher status than in the UK, it is equally the case that in the UK the status accorded to the skilled working class was higher than in the US, a legacy of a highly developed pre-industrial craft culture. If status is to be incorporated into the model of labour market activity, then it is possible to compare how the Jewish immigrants in both cities accumulated occupations with higher status as well as higher income. In New York American cultural values would give high status to all the white-collar occupations, which, as table 2 shows, increased in importance among the Jewish workforce from 21.0% in 1880 to 40.4% in 1905. In London, where English cultural values predominated and where the skilled blue collar workers were recognised as the aristocracy of the working class, the high status occupations would include the white-collar ones, but also the highly skilled blue collar ones. Thus, if we include the journeymen class with the white collar workers table 2 shows that the higher status occupations increased from 17.6% of the workforce in the 1880s to 45.7% of the workforce in 1907-14. This is a rate of increase which is very similar to that of the Jewish immigrants in New York.

VI. Conclusion

The more detailed results of the study of Jewish immigrant labour market behaviour in New York and London between 1880-1914 shows two rather striking phenomenon. Namely the rise in importance of entrepreneurs in New York and the rise in importance of journeymen in London. The most convincing interpretation of these results so far, would appear to be that East European Jewish immigrants were adopting the cultural values of their host nations, which was reflected in how they were describing their occupational status. It is unlikely that the Jewish immigrant tailors classified as entrepreneurs in New York were, in fact, performing much of a different function in the clothing workshop than the Jewish immigrant journeymen tailor in London. There was little or no difference in the disposable income available to the New York Jewish entrepreneurs or the London Jewish journeymen as far as the available evidence shows.

The results of the research suggest that cultural values play an important, and, indeed possibly an increasingly important, role in co-ordinating labour market activity. The control population despite having very similar occupational distributions were, nonetheless, describing themselves in very different fashions by the end of the period, seemingly reflecting different aspirations. These different aspirations could only have come from the two host cultures. It follows then that the two host nations had different cultural values relating to work activities and, particularly, to the co-ordinating function in the labour market. American values would appear to accord with the Horatio Alger ideal of entrepreneurial dynamism and innovation according to the evidence presented here. British values, with a longer history, emphasized the importance of craft skill and traditional methods of production, with a more conservative approach to change.

The evidence also suggests that this particular control population - the East European Jewish immigrants in New York and London - were sensitive to host country cultural values and to a degree which has previously perhaps not been recognised. The emphasis of a very great deal of earlier sociological research has been to assume that Jews were somehow distinct from other ethnic groups and particularly predisposed to pursuing entrepreneurial occupations (Rubinstein, this volume). The evidence here suggests that, while there may be some truth in their propensity to entrepreneurship, the more important factor was the prevailing conditions (including cultural values) of the economies to which the Jews migrated.

If the evidence of labour market activity of this control population in the two nations can be considered representative of wider trends in the two economies, the implications for the understanding of long term economic development of the two nations need at least to be noted. Successive studies have shown that despite the Horatio Alger ideal, the American economy cannot be said to have been blessed with an abundance of rags-to-riches entrepreneurs, indeed the Jewish immigrants appear to have been the only ethnic group to have approached the ideal (Sarachek 1978, Sarachek 1980, Thernstrom 1973).

However, the more important implications lie with the way that these results apply to what is understood of British economic development during this era. Here, the results of the evidence presented in this summary suggest that the existence of a pre-industrial craft culture was an important determinant of labour market co-ordination. Moreover, this would have acted as a constraint on the supply of entrepreneurship from the working classes and could, therefore, have had repercussions on economic development. The evidence presented here, therefore, supports the hypothesis that Britain had a relatively anti-entrepreneurial culture, but not because of aristocratic values, but more because of the continuation of a strong pre-industrial craft culture.

References

BARON, S. W.: *The Russian Jew under Tsars and Soviets*, New York (MacMillan) 1964.

BODANSKI, G., et al: "Evidence for an Environmental Effect in the Aetiology of Insulin Dependent Diabetes in a Transmigratory Population", *British Medical Journal,* 304 (1992).

CASSON, M.: *The Entrepreneur: An Economic Theory*, Oxford (Martin Robertson) 1982.

CASSON, M.: *The Economics of Business Culture: Game Theory, Transaction Costs and Economic Performance*, Oxford (Clarendon) 1991.

CHANDLER, A. D.: *Scale and Scope: The Dynamics of Industrial Capitalism*, Cambridge Mass. (Belknap) 1990.

DUBNOW, S.: *History of the Jews in Russia and Poland*, Philadelphia (Jewish Historical Society of America) 3 volumes, 1918-19.

FRANKEL, J.: "Introduction", in: A. KAHAN: *Essays in Jewish Social and Economic History*, Chicago (Chicago University Press) 1986.

GODLEY, A. C.: "The Development of the UK Clothing Industry, 1850-1950: Output and Productivity Growth", *Business History*, 37 (1995).

GODLEY, A. C. (1996a): "Jewish Soft Loan Societies in New York and London and Immigrant Entrepreneurship, 1880-1914", *Business History,* 38 (1996).

GODLEY, A. C. (1996b): "Immigrant Entrepreneurs and the Emergence of London's East End as an Industrial District", *London Journal*, 21 (1996).

GODLEY, A. C. (1996c): "Singer in Britain: the diffusion of sewing machine technology and its impact on the clothing industry in the United Kingdom, 1860-1905", *Textile History*, 27 (1996).

GODLEY, A. C. (1997a): "The Development of the Clothing Industry: technology and fashion", *Textile History*, 28 (1997).

GODLEY, A. C. (1997b): "Comparative Labour Productivity in the British and American Clothing Industries, 1850-1950", *Textile History*, 28 (1997).

GODLEY, A. C.: *Enterprise and Culture: Jewish Immigrants in London and New York, 1880-1914*, 1999 (forthcoming).

KESSNER, T.: *The Golden Door: Italian and Jewish Immigrant Mobility in New York City 1880-1915*, Oxford and New York (Oxford University Press) 1977.

KESSNER, T.: "The Selective Filter of Ethnicity", in: D. BERGER (Ed.): *The Legacy of Jewish Migration: 1881 and its impact*, New York (Brooklyn College Press) 1983.

KUZNETS, S.: "Immigration of Russian Jews to the United States: background and structure", *Perspectives in American History*, 9 (1975).

LANDES, D.: *The Unbound Prometheus: Technological Change and Industrial Development in Western Europe from 1750 to the Present*, Cambridge (Cambridge University Press) 1969.

LAZONICK, W.: *Business Organization and the Myth of the Market Economy*, Cambridge (Cambridge University Press) 1991.

RUBINSREIN, W. D.: "Entrepreneurial Minorities: A Typology", in this volume.

SARACHEK, B.: "American Entrepreneurs and the Horatio Alger Myth", *Journal of Economic History*, 38 (1978).

SARACHEK, B.: "Jewish American Entrepreneurs", *Journal of Economic History*, 40 (1980).

SCHMIECHEN, J. A.: *Sweated Industries and Sweated Labour: the London Clothing Trades, 1860-1914*, London (Croom Helm) 1984.

THERNSTROM, S.: *The Other Bostonians: Poverty and Progress in the American Metropolis, 1880-1970*, Cambridge, Mass. (Harvard University press) 1973.

WECHSLER, R.: "The Jewish Garment Trade in East London, 1875-1914: A study of conditions and responses" (unpublished Ph.D. thesis, University of Columbia 1979).

WIENER, M.: *English Culture and the Decline of the Industrial Spirit, 1880-1980*, Cambridge (Cambridge University Press) 1981.

Chapter 6

Jurisprudence, Expected Value, and the Culture of Innovation

FRED V. CARSTENSEN

"Nothing is more mischievous than uncertainty in commercial law."

Lord Mansfield, Chief Justice, King's Bench:
Medcalf v Hall, 1782

Perhaps no development offers a greater challenge to economic historians than the remarkable growth in material well-being that characterise Anglo-American history over the four centuries from 1500 to 1900. While there is much disagreement about when English incomes began their sustained growth that separated them from others,[1] no one denies that that differentiation did occur, or that America in the nineteenth century quickly achieved a comparable or higher standard. Joel Mokyr has offered a powerful argument (Mokyr 1990) that this growth flowed fundamentally from technological innovation. David Landes' *The Wealth and Poverty of Nations* digs behind the innovation process to argue the criticality of culture. What follows is a 'stylised' essay that seeks to give a critical role to the unique quality of Anglo-American political economy that common law jurisprudence (and the American constitutional framework) provided. This framework, as developed by judges (and to a lesser extent by parliaments), was responsive to the evolving needs of a dynamic economy, articulating an expanding meaning of property rights (e.g. property rights in goodwill and trademark) through case law, providing relative certainty in the rights of property and contract-thus permitting formation of meaningful 'expected value' for economic initiatives-through the stability of relying on precedent, and mechanisms for continual adjustment, even enlargement, of those rights through new cases that permitted a continuing assessment of the symmetry between legal principle and commercial need.[2]

The essay begins with a broad characterization of a critical element of the intellectual climate. That reflects my belief that Anglo-American jurisprudence came to be deeply imbued with a concern with economic growth, or in J. W. Hurst's (1956) felicitous phrase, 'release of creative energy,' and the capacity of markets to facilitate such growth. Thus it is important to appreciate the emergence of the idea of a 'positive sum' world, and idea which ultimately lies at the heart of Smith's justification of the 'invisible hand.'[3] Such an appreciation of markets stands in contrast to the neo-

---

1 Robert Allen argues that that divergence began in 1500; Gunder Frank argues it didn't begin until much later (ALLEN 1999, FRANK 1998). But no one denies that it was massive by the mid-19th Century, or that the overall process of modern growth is not sustainable in a way fundamentally different from early period of growth.

2 Lord Mansfield would convene panels of merchants to alert him to the broad implications of commercial cases being heard before King's Bench. See J. S. ROGERS (1995), especially pp. 210-222.

3 ADAM SMITH (1937 orig. 1776) offers a rich explanation for trade: it arises from the scale effects of specialization and thus would arise even if there were identical tastes and resources. Such trade enlarges the universe within which economic actors function. More critically, Smithian trade generates growth

classical emphasis on individual utility maximization. The essay then offers an outline of the evolving institutional context, one shaped largely by judges, but one in which the American constitution also plays a central role.[4]

I. The Intellectual Climate: Understanding the Utility of Markets and Discretionary Choice

What is the value of the 'market mechanism.' Mainstream economic analysis emphasises the benefits that flow from achieving Pareto-optimal allocations and exploiting the mutual benefits of Ricardian comparative advantage. But both of these processes, once carried through, while having enhanced welfare (by assumption) give rise to no addition change in economic conduct. Indeed, one might argue that, once achieved, either the process of exchange ceases altogether or it settles into a perpetual equilibrium. Neither one gives rise to a dynamic process that generates change in the capabilities of economic actors or the array of goods and services offered. Thus one could argue that such markets do not provide a socially

through innovation, in what is a potentially endless process. In this, Smith is much closer to Schumpeter than to his declared intellectual descendants, and his insights into the progressive enlargement of the market are underappreciated and underdeveloped.

4 This is an argument quite different from that of D. North, who sees the events surrounding the Glorious Revolution (1688) as being decisive. Rather, this is a long, gradual process, one that begins before 1600, is well-developed before 1688-which helps to explain why the events of that year happened-and which continues right down to the present. A recent salient example of this process has been the creation of new property rights in pollution, specifically in atmospheric emissions. Creation of such a market creates for the first time a framework which will generate, it is reasonable to believe, coherent price information, and hence incentives, for assessing the tradeoffs between the market value of the pollution rights and the cost of buying or creating appropriate pollution reduction technology. See NORTH (1991 and 1993), and NORTH and WEINGAST (1989).

desirable outcome. Thus Pareto optimality and Ricardian comparative advantage seem a thin reed on which to validate reliance on market mechanisms. (As Schumpeter (1934) observed, it may be a matter of 'comparative indifference' whether an economic system generates such outcomes; they are not the stuff of which economic growth is made.)

II. The Intellectual Climate: Appreciating the Value of Change

If it is true that people in general prefer stability (risk-avoiding behaviour), and that changing a system-whether through introducing new processes, new products, new organizational forms, or permitting entry of new participants - typically produces losers as well as winners, then developing an ideological or intellectual framework that justifies protecting, even encouraging, such change would be central to creating an institutional framework that achieves that outcome. To put it in a different way, if a people (society) believe that they live in a 'zero-sum' world, or even in a 'negative-sum' world, they would almost certainly oppose permitting people discretion in the use of their resources. Such discretion could, at best, only re-allocate income and wealth; it could not increase the aggregate material welfare of society. Indeed, in such an environment, it would be highly advantageous for every individual to have an assigned role, economically, socially, politically, because then every individual would have an assured (safe) place within that socio-economic structure. Thus markets - here understood to embrace not simply exchange, but discretionary control over assets and thus their creative use - are broadly inconsistent with a 'negative-sum' or 'zero-sum' world. But if a society broadly accepts the proposition that the world is a 'positive-sum game', one in which change generates socially beneficial outcomes (e.g. economic growth), then the argument turns on the question of what mechanism best facilitates such change. In the Anglo-American experience, the argument came to focus on the market mechanisms that, by permitting discretionary use of assets and comparatively open entry (participation), maximised the number of 'innovators' and thus maximised the social benefits that flowed from successful innovation. Anglo-American jurisprudence specifically came to recognise the inherent link between legal (and political) frameworks, formation of expected values, the level of innovative energy, and economic growth beneficial to society as a whole.

III. The Intellectual Climate: Facilitating Discretionary Conduct and Innovation

The challenge that any individual economic actor must confront is how to develop a reasonable 'expected value' for their current conduct. In a simple case, if someone makes the effort to develop a trade in a given commodity (e.g. playing cards), how can that individual be assured that that trade will not be taken away through the intervention of civil authority (e.g. a granting of a royal monopoly)? In a more complex case, how does one know that one can capture the benefits that flow from making superior quality goods when the producer is anonymous to the purchaser, known only by an identifying 'mark' which others can duplicate? And in a still more complex case, if an individual purchases a 'going concern' - that is both the assets of the firm but also its underlying business activity (today we call it 'goodwill') - what assurance does that purchaser have the seller will not in fact simply re-emerge as a direct competitor? These are all essentially questions of property rights (what rights do you have to conduct your existing trade? can you 'own' a distinctive 'mark'? can you sell your right to compete?). But developing 'expected value' relies not simply on the framework of enforceable property and contractual rights within which economic activity takes place, it also depends upon measurements of value, i.e. money. If money, in its intertemporal role as a store of value, does not provide a stable measure and vehicle for value over time, it diminishes the ability of actors to develop a coherent sense of 'expected value.' Insofar as rights of property, enforceability of contract, and the validity and stability of the measure of value - i.e. money - are creatures of civil authority, jurisprudence comes to occupy a central place in the articulation by individual actors of 'expected value' and thus in their willingness to seek opportunity through innovation. In stylised form, socially productive market activity thus depends upon money and contract, that is, on the two instruments which stores value over time on the one hand and which permits co-ordination of the flow of factors of production, again over time, on the other. And it is through appropriately constructed and constrained civil authority that those two instrumentalities of market activity find articulation and protection.

IV. The Intellectual Climate: Critical Actors

The articulation of these ideas about living in a 'positive-sum' world, the critical importance of providing a stable rules environment ('certainty') within which people could utilise their property, including protections not only against the actions of other individuals but also against interventions by the state (what becomes embodied in the notion of limited government), providing a stable monetary system, and, at the same time, accommodating change, begins in the late Elizabethan period and continues through (and beyond) development of the political economy embedded in the American constitutional system. From Coke through Hobbes, Locke, Mansfield, Smith, the Federalists, and Hamilton, these ideas develop and evolve, ultimately generating a political economy which see markets as giving rise to a socially beneficial dynamic, most clearly captured in Smith's self-reenforcing cycle of market expansion leading to increased specialisation leading to innovation generating enhanced productivity and thus to expanded markets.

V. The Institutional Context: Developing Modern Property

The intellectual history had a parallel institutional history. In a series of critical cases in the early Stuart period, King's Bench reconfigured common law to create new forms of property. Thus the court established property rights in trademark and goodwill. Parliament extended this process by recognising a limited property right in individual creativity with the first patent law. Thus, between 1603 and 1625, one can see the emergence of forms of property which are explicitly the product of dynamic market activity, and which served to enhance the 'expected value' of innovative uses of assets or creativity. In the 1730s, then new printing technology permitted reproduction of artistic work, the widespread unauthorised duplication of Hogarth's Marriage a la Mode lead to enactment of the first copyright law-defining the property right that resides in artistic or literary creativity. In that same period, the courts facilitated market transactions by separating the validity of underlying transactions from the enforceability of inland bills, thus vastly expanding liquidity. Critically, all of these new forms of property and limitation on liability (attached to use inland bills) were ones to which anyone could lay claim through participation in market exchange; they were not distributed by a central (capricious) political authority. And because of the 'open entry', they encouraged expansion of markets, hence of specialisation, and thus of innovation-the Smith/Schumpeter formula for growth.

VI. The Institutional Context: Constraining the State

What the initial period of judge-created law did not restrain was the capacity of the state (king) to intervene in transactions or to take property in arbitrary and capricious ways (hence uncertainty). Despite the abolition of the prerogative law courts (Star Chamber) and other attempts to rein in royal autonomy, James II reduced the courts to subservience and threatened to de-stabilise all property rights. After he was forced from the throne, England adopted an 'institutional settlement' which went a significant way to securing the instrumentalities of the market. Creation of the Bank of England, stripping the King of authority over the value of money, and establishing an independent judiciary provided what at the time was surely the most favourable environment for individual discretionary use of resources and for innovation.[5]

5 This is the 'macro' transition on which North focuses; but in fact it only protected 'micro' changes long embedded in common and statutory law, and made possible a continuing adjustment. Thus there is no reason to believe ex ante that these events should have generate a measurably large change in economic performance-which is indeed what critics of North have confirmed.

VII. The Institutional Context: The American Solution

The American constitutional framework in conjunction with the creation of the First Bank of the United States (1791) built on the English framework. But unlike the English who did not develop a written constitution and viewed an independent judiciary as a restraint only on royal authority, the American institutional settlement, a written social contract, both created a far more (potentially) powerful Supreme Court, which could constrain both executive and legislative, and a structure of representative government intended, through the artfully constructed framework of checks and balances, to make policy with a maximum of public scrutiny, a minimum of speed, and relatively safe from the capriciousness of an ephemeral majority. Like case law, the legislative framework of American government was to add policies incrementally; and when larger change loomed, the legislative framework assured multiple points of 'entry' for affected parties, including even the opportunity to challenge new policies in the courts on constitutional grounds. The objective here was to create a framework which provided a stable rules environment (hence certainty) even as it provided mechanisms for change. But that change would occur through a process and at a pace that would permit adjustment in 'expected values.' Thus the American system of political economy, predicated on a presumption of a 'positive-sum' world, sought to provide that distinctive blend of stability and flexibility necessary to sustaining a culture of innovation.

VIII. Concluding Comment

Discussions of the relationship between the state and markets is often framed as one in which the range of individual discretion and the realm of civil authority each occupy some fixed space, the two arenas being inherently dichotomous, their intersection at best a zero-sum game. Such a view finds confirmation in the comparative statics that lies at the core of neoclassical economic analysis, and easily reduces government 'intervention' to rent-seeking behaviour which has, and can have, no productive impact. Such a conceptualisation is easily grasped, offers a seductively appealing calculus, and finds quick confirmation in myriad instances where public power has been used to benefit clearly private ends; it is also profoundly misleading.

The perspective offered here sees the purpose of civil authority, animated by a 'positive sum' conception, is to create a stable framework for the security of tangible and intangible property and of contract, within which individuals can develop reasonable expectations about the future and thus make rational calculations about the likely outcomes of various paths of economic conduct. The vitality of market activity lies precisely in such calculability. Thus the issue is not cast in terms of a rivalry between public power and private initiative, but in terms of how civil authority, properly formulated and applied, creates and expands the arena for private initiative.

Historically, the defining characteristic of Anglo-American economic history has been neither equilibrium nor stasis, but sustained, long-term growth. This essay sees civil authority playing a critical role in creating, shaping, and sustaining the competitive frameworks that gave rise to intense competition and, through expanding markets, specialisation - the twin sources of those Schumpeterian innovations that generate economic growth. Specifically, the essay thus argues that, proceeding from an acceptance of a 'positive sum' view of the world, Anglo-American jurisprudence embraced to a significant degree a presumption that individual innovative activity was socially beneficial (generating economic growth). Thus law (and, in America, political structure) should facilitate, through encouraging formulation of appropriate expected values, innovation. That leads, logically, to a profoundly anti-majoritarian conception embedded in the sanctity of private property and enforceability of contract. Such a view is deeply antagonistic to 'culture' in the broad sense of fully defining and constraining behaviour of all members of a society, but it generates an alternative, highly individualistic 'culture' that (largely) ignores attributes other than those that are 'functional' - primarily the ability to innovate. The Anglo-American - and especially the American - record of economic growth can then be interpreted within a framework of ideas and institutions that put the release of creative energy at its centre.

References

ALLEN, R.: "Wages and Prices in Europe, 1375-1913", *Journal of Economic History*, 59 (1999), forthcoming.

FRANK, A. G.: *ReOrient: Global Economy in the Asian Age*, Berkeley (University of California Press) 1998.

HURST, J. W.: *Law and the Conditions of Freedom in the Nineteenth Century United States*, Madison, WI (University of Wisconsin Press) 1956.

LANDES, D. S.: *The Wealth and Poverty of Nations* New York (Norton) 1998.

MOKYR, J.: *Lever of Riches: Technological Creativity and Economic Progress*, New York and Oxford (Oxford University Press) 1990.

NORTH, D. C.: "Institutions", *Journal of Economic Perspectives*, 5 (1991).

NORTH, D. C.: *Institutions, Institutional Change and Economic Performance*, New York (Cambridge University Press) 1993.

NORTH, D. C., WEINGAST, B. R.: "Constitutions and Commitment: The Evolution of Institutional Governing Public Choice in Seventeenth-Century England", *Journal of Economic History*, 49 (1989).

ROGERS, J. S.: *The Early History of the Law of Bills and Notes: A Study of the Origins of Anglo-American Commercial Law*, Cambridge (Cambridge University Press) 1995.

SCHUMPETER, J. A.: *The Theory of Economic Development*, Cambridge MA (Harvard University Press) 1934.

SMITH, A.: *Wealth of Nations*, New York (Random House/Modern Library Edition) 1937 (originally published 1776).

Chapter 7

Constitutions, Liberties, and Growth in Pre-Modern Europe

STEPHAN R. EPSTEIN

I. Economic History and Culture

Economic historians are generally diffident towards cultural explanations of economic phenomena. This attitude stems partly from the lack of any obvious progress in linking symbolic, cultural meanings to economic practice since Aristotle condemned the social consequences of market exchange (exchange for profit) in the 4th century B.C.E.,[1] and partly from methodological concerns. Two questions in particular arise with respect to cultural

1 Aristotle's condemnation of all forms of exchange that did not aim to meet the household's self-sufficiency as causing the dissolution of the basic social set the terms of subsequent discussion. Both medieval theories of usury and of the just price, which were premised on the normative and positive view that personal and collective moral precepts ('culture') applied to economic practice and gave rise to specific forms of economic behaviour, and the 20th century contributions of Durkheim, Weber, Mauss and Polanyi appeal to Aristotelian ideas: as Marx put it, with the spread of market relations 'all that is solid melts into air'.

explanations of economic behaviour. The first is connected with the fact that beliefs can only be apprehended at second hand; the second has to do with the difficulty in identifying the causal links between cultural and economic practices in ways that are not tautological.

The fact that historians can only apprehend symbolic meanings indirectly from the observed outcome of economic activities is an oft-voiced criticism of cultural models. The issue revolves in essence around the methodological question that engaged the anthropological debate between the 'substantivists' (who argued that exchange in non-Western, non-modernized societies was regulated by `traditional' values which could not be submitted to modern economic theory) and the 'formalists' (who claimed the opposite). The choice between the two claims cannot be a matter of subjective and ideological preference, however, for they rest on very different epistemological grounds. Whereas economic explanations yield predictions that can in principle be tested, statements about unobserved values (traditional or otherwise) lack any external verification: they are simply a subjective and untestable construct by the historian. By taking observed economic consequences as evidence of their cultural causes, cultural models are also inevitably circular and raise questions such as how can historians have access to thoughts that were differently thought? On what authority do they stake their claim to knowledge? How, if past modes of thinking were so alien and at the same time all-encompassing, did these modes of thought ever change?

The second major source of concern with cultural explanations comes from recent anthropological research that casts doubt on the existence of direct causal links between systems of belief and individual economic practice. Despite huge cross-cultural variation in the way in which economic activities are conveyed symbolically, different human societies appear to share two critical features. On the one hand, most societies combine quite relaxed views about individual short-term acquisitiveness and competition associated with production and trade, with normative controls over consumption that aim at maintaining a longer term social and cosmic order. In other words, non-Western or non-'modernised' societies display a similar combination of individual acquisitiveness, and concern with its destructive collective consequences, which has been a feature of European societies since Aristotle's day. These structural similarities raise the question whether differences in cultural form produce any systematic and predictable difference in economic performance.

On the other hand, anthropologists also question how far one can infer actual economic practice from culturally charged statements about that practice. The link between economic function and symbolic meaning is uncertain, in the first place because people do not do what they say; and secondly, because the cultural meaning of an economic practice is not fixed. An economic practice can mean different things to different people or to the same person in different circumstances within the same culture; acquisitiveness and competition can be conceived at the same time as subversive of social relations and as a means to their reproduction.[2]

The de-coupling of cultural from economic practice has important methodological implications for economic history. Firstly, if what someone does doesn't allow us to predict what she believes she is doing, and what she believes does not straightforwardly determine what she does, the premise for cultural explanations of economic behaviour collapses. Second, the volatility of cultural meaning and its dependence upon context suggest that interactions between belief and practice are better analysed at the level of individuals than of whole societies. This is not something economic historians who apply the law of averages are very good at doing. Although in strictly pragmatic terms their approach seems to provide a suitably parsimonious explanation of observed individual behaviour,[3] economic historians are ill-equipped to discuss linkages between cultural and economic practices that are only visible at the individual level and over short periods of time.

In recent years neo-institutionalist economic historians, spearheaded by Douglass North, have tried to circumvent these difficulties by reducing culture, defined as an informal system of rules embodying mainly non-pecuniary (moral) sanctions, to institutions defined as formal systems of

2 "The meanings with which money is invested are quite as much a product of the cultural matrix into which it is incorporated as of the economic functions it performs" (PARRY and BLOCH 1989, p. 21).

3 Even though the economists' rational choice model of 'culture' is based on a very primitive theory of cognition, in the long run - which is the time scale most economic historians work in - it appears to 'work'. One reason for this could be that societies `select' economic institutions that maximize returns relative to certain goals; in this case, institutions provide the cognitive 'scaffolding' for individual choices which are, in effect, little more than interchangeable bearers of efficient practices. See CLARK 1997, pp. 272-73.

rules that embody mainly pecuniary or quasi-pecuniary sanctions.[4] By transforming arguments couched in terms of cultural preferences into statements that appeal to individual economic self-interest, neo-institutionalists have turned the classic culturalist arguments on their head.[5] In this model, societies do not create specific institutions in order to uphold and further their beliefs, but instead they develop specific behavioural patterns (and therefore, beliefs) as a consequence of the institutions they are endowed with. Therefore, societies whose institutions foster behaviour or cultural preferences that bring private returns closer to social returns will experience more rapid economic development. Institutions that promote greater individual choice, individualism and stronger relations of trust will promote faster growth than institutions that foster individual insecurity, mistrust, and 'familistic' behaviour.

The Whig belief that constitutional freedoms breed economic success is a central feature of recent explanations of the English industrial revolution and the 'European miracle' (Jones 1981, Gellner 1988, and pursued by Carstensen in chapter 6 of this volume). They argue that the institutional prerequisite for the breakthrough to capitalist industrialism in late eighteenth-century England was England's and part of Europe's unique array of political freedoms in comparison with the rest of the world. These consisted most notably of the natural liberties and common law entrenched by the English civil wars, in particular by the Glorious Revolution of 1688, but also of the freedoms enjoyed by Republican city-states in early modern Italy, Switzerland and South German and in the Dutch United Provinces (North and Thomas 1973, Hall 1985, Mann 1989, Olson 1982, Cameron 1989). By contrast, the autocratic or absolutist Continental monarchies[6]

---

4 See the recent collection of essays in North's honour (NYE and DROBACK 1997).

5 David Hume was an early exponent of this strategy. His explanation of the investment strategies pursued under absolutism is couched in terms both of cultural preferences (commerce and industry are spurned because they are seen as less honourable than `birth, titles, and place') and of institutional incentives [the distortions are caused by the tax system, which is not excessive in absolute terms but is oppressive at the margin (HUME 1993 (1777)]. For a similar argument see HOFFMAN and ROSENTHAL 1997.

6 OLSON's (1991) equation of absolutism with autocracy is disputed by HOFFMAN and ROSENTHAL (1997, p. 50), who however maintain a sharp distinction between absolutist and parliamentary regimes that I do not follow.

stifled their economies through oppressive taxation, other punitive forms of redistribution, and the absence of the rule of law.

The reduction of culture to institutions or 'rules of the game', as North has called them, does not however resolve the methodological and measurement problems previously described. To see why this is so, we must distinguish between the two quite different claims being made by neo-institutionalists. The first claim is that governance systems influence the pursuit of material wealth: thus openness to trade, savings policies, commercial and financial regulation and educational policies will all affect a country's rate of economic growth. The second, more contentious claim is that different forms of governance sanction different norms and forms of behaviour, which in turn are more or less conducive to economic growth (Fogel 1997, p. 22; Scully 1992).

The historiography of English and European exceptionalism relies crucially on the second argument. It asserts that economic growth was the effect of systems of political governance which sanctioned greater individual liberty: it is because the post-1688 parliamentary regime in England was a freer, more equitable system of governance that the country first experienced the industrial revolution. In this chapter I discuss the basis for this claim.[7] I provide evidence to suggest that the economic consequences of English and Republican freedoms were less positive than assumed. I show that, paradoxically, the main effect of the Glorious Revolution was to allow England to catch up economically and institutionally with the Continent, rather than to gain a decisive advantage. The result contradicts the view that the allegedly more authoritarian Continental regimes were at a permanent institutional disadvantage (Section III). In the case of Republican states, on the contrary, I find that political power was inversely correlated with economic success. This result runs counter to the claim, most recently restated by Mancur Olson (1991), that economic growth promotes political freedom (Section IV). Both cases raise serious doubts about the possibility of inferring patterns of behaviour (individualism, trust, security) and economic

7 Here development is narrowly defined as increase in per capita income. On a broader view that incorporates general measures of well-being such as basic civic and political freedoms, a democracy (however qualified) would nearly by definition be more conducive to development than a non-democratic regime. Since such modern democratic freedoms are not immediately apparent in any pre-industrial society, however, the issue can be safely ignored.

performance from constitutional arrangements, thus confirming the methodological concerns spelled out in the opening to this chapter. Finally, I raise the question whether systems of governance made any difference to economic performance (Section V). I conclude that constitutional structures did matter, but for reasons that had little to do with liberal concepts of freedom or individualism.

II. Negative and Positive Economic Freedom

The point of departure of arguments that draw a direct link between forms of institutionalised freedom and economic growth is the view that growth before the Industrial Revolution was mainly Smithian; that is, it was based on an increasing spatial and organisational division of labour (e.g. Persson 1988, Jones 1988). Since the extent of specialization is essentially a function of the technical and institutional limits to trade,[8] neo-Smithian economic historians have paid particular attention to institutional barriers to the efficient allocation of resources and to the free flow of goods. In so far as market imperfections cause unequal access to economic resources, this approach brings the issue of freedom firmly onto centre stage. Social norms and rules (property rights and rights of entitlement) that are defined and are thus potentially contestable in the political, rather than the purely economic realm sanction and reproduce the access to income streams. It follows that the politically sanctioned distribution of freedom - and hence of power - within societies will strongly influence economic growth.

It thus seems that the exercise of economic freedom is inextricably linked to the exercise of power. Yet, within the negative definition of freedom most often subscribed to by economic historians (that is, freedom from constraint), power and freedom stand opposed.[9] On the common definition

8 Market size is a function also of demand within a given territory, which however in pre-industrial societies tends to change more slowly.

9 This purely negative definition of freedom is a consequence of economists' suspicion of normative ideas like power to explain the economic institutions of the past. The suspicion arose following the analytical distinction established during the late nineteenth century between the allocative and the redistributive functions of markets, i.e. between efficiency and equity - neo-classical

of economic power as a person's ability to further her interests by imposing (or credibly threatening to impose) sanctions on another person where the converse is not true,[10] freedom in the economic historian's sense becomes the absence of such sanctions. In this sense, the relationship between power and freedom emerges as a zero-sum game: one can gain only as much freedom as someone else must lose power, and vice versa.

In fact the relation between freedom and power is far more ambiguous. On the one hand, freedom as the ability to achieve a desired goal implies an active exercise of control. On the other hand, freedom can be defined only in relation to unfreedom; to be free there must be a condition one wishes to escape from. Freedom has scarcity value: if everyone has it, it is of no worth (what value the rights of citizenship, if all foreigners had them also?). In both cases, freedom is based on an institutional asymmetry: freedom was born as a privilege and has remained so ever since (Bauman 1988, p. 9). Rather than following naturally from someone else's lack of power, a condition of freedom always implies the agent's exercise of power.[11] In other words, the negative definition of freedom as what we are at liberty to do implies a positive meaning of freedom as what we are able to do. This ambivalence, which lay at the heart of pre-modern concepts of legal and economic 'freedom', is important for understanding how political institutions shaped pre-modern growth.

---

economics being concerned only with the former (DE MARCHI and MORGAN 1994, Introduction). The belief that lack of political coercion is a precondition for economic growth, which appeals to Adam Smith's attack on ancien regime and mercantilist restrictions, is based on a projection of nineteenth- and twentieth-century definitions of political freedom as universal suffrage and participatory democracy onto Smith's quite different political categories (see WINCH 1978, pp. 83- 6).

10 A related voluntarist definition focuses on an agent's ability to affect the incentives facing another agent so that it is rational for the latter to do something she would not otherwise have chosen to do.

11 This claim does not contradict the more common statement that an agent's freedom involves exerting control over what happens to her.

III. 1688 and All That: England's Fiscal and Economic Revolution?

In a recent paper, North and Weingast (1989) have made a powerful economic case for the argument that the changes in political representation caused by the Glorious Revolution of 1688-89 set the English economy on a unique growth path leading directly to the industrial revolution. The story is a familiar one. In the early seventeenth century the Stuart kings could no longer fund their increasing requirements with traditional sources of revenue. Sale of these lands did not make up the shortfall, and the Stuarts were forced to find new sources of income. This set them against Parliament, which had the right to grant new taxes, typically for extraordinary purposes such as war but also by increasing excise on trade. Faced with parliamentary resistance, James I and especially Charles I imposed new taxes without the Commons' consent. They also resorted increasingly to forced loans (which they repaid, if at all, with considerable delay), to the sale of monopoly rights and of patents of nobility, to purveyance (the requisitioning of goods below market prices), and to other less overt forms of involuntary redistribution. The more the landed and commercial interests represented in Parliament traded their financial support in exchange for limitations to the Crown's authority, the more the Crown was led to avoid insolvency through underhand expropriation.

The Stuart monarchy could act in this way because it combined executive, legislative and judicial powers and possessed a comparative advantage in coercion. Because Parliament's capacity to check royal power was restricted, the Crown could renege on prior agreements and modify the existing structure of property rights. The situation set in motion a coalition of subjects who sought to preserve personal liberties, rights, and wealth, and led to the Civil War. However, only the Declaration of Rights of 1689, which enshrined parliamentary sovereignty, created truly secure property rights. Parliament re-established authority over the right to tax, gained the right to audit government accounts, curtailed royal prerogative powers, and established the independence of the law. These political rights laid the foundations on which economic rights were built.

North and Weingast measure the gains in economic freedom through changes in government finances and in capital markets. Although government expenditure and indebtedness mushroomed (by 1720 public debt stood at over 50 times the level of 1688), official rates of interest fell and the government avoided the trap of inflationary finance. Government financial reforms also sustained the expansion of private capital markets and benefited the wider economy. Thus, the Glorious Revolution enforced economic freedom in the shape of secure property rights and promoted financial efficiency. By making it impossible for the Crown to change the rules of economic activity ad libitum, Parliament made government behaviour more predictable and lenders were consequently forthcoming.[12]

This interpretation implies three further conclusions which the authors do not however pursue. First, because English property rights before 1688-89 were insecure, the required rate of return on capital and restricted private investment must have been higher than after the revolution; second, Continental, absolutist European states must have faced higher credit risks and greater instability than eighteenth-century England; third, the latter's military success is evidence of the wider economic benefits created by the new regime.

We can test the first two arguments against comparative data on interest rates. Since changes in the security of property rights should be reflected in the expected rates of return on capital, the theory predicts that the Glorious Revolution would be followed by a sharp decline in rates of return. In fact, analysis of rates of return to the main capital input, land, shows no significant link with political or constitutional events throughout the period between 1540 and 1837. Although rates of return did decline after 1688, the decline was part of a secular trend that had begun in the first half of the seventeenth century and which ended in the middle of the eighteenth. Therefore, the evidence from domestic imputed rates of interest suggests that "secure private property rights existed in England at least as early as 1600, and probably much earlier. As far as most private investors were concerned, nothing special happened in 1688, or, for that matter, in any period between 1600 and 1688. The information from capital markets implies that the move to representative democracy (sic) was not necessary for the establishment of secure private property rights" (Clark 1996, p. 565).

---

12 Strictly speaking, therefore, North and Weingast address the economic effects of secure property rights and of a government's pre-commitment to binding rules, not those of freedom. Secure property rights are not a critical measure of freedom, not even in the sense of equality before the law (MUNZER 1990, ch. 7; RYAN 1987, ch.7; and see below).

This result does not, however, address the claim that England enjoyed institutional and economic advantages over its more oppressive Continental neighbours; the chronological origins of the country's cultural or institutional advantage (such as the existence of the common law) might simply go back further in time.[13] We can verify this proposition by comparing interest rates paid by different European governments, on the basis of the hypothesis that autocratic regimes paid significantly higher rates than republican governments and than England after 1688 because the reneged more frequently on their debts. The astonishing decline in English prime rates from 8-10 per cent just before the Glorious Revolution to 3 per cent by 1750 lends prima facie support to this claim.

Table 1 lists the prime interest rates current in several European states between the early sixteenth and the mid-eighteenth century. It tests whether different constitutional arrangements were reflected in significantly different premiums by distinguishing between Continental monarchies, England, and urban-based republics. With the significant exception of England before 1688, which lacked a long-term funded debt and therefore resorted to short-term loans, quoted rates of interest refer in the main to long-term loans, which measure the borrower's credibility more accurately than money market rates.[14]

The data do not support the neo-institutional arguments. Although most urban republics enjoyed an interest rate premium over monarchies for much of the period under review, the explanation does not seem to lie in their constitutional differences. The rule applied neither to Geneva nor, more significantly, to the Dutch United Provinces before the mid-seventeenth century; moreover, the lowest rates of interest were present in Genoa, which was formally an independent state but was in practice under Spanish tutelage and acted as the empire's main financial clearing house. These examples suggest that the lower interest rates found in some city-states may have been due to their greater supply of capital and financial specialization, rather than to a general security premium enjoyed by republics over monarchies.

---

13 See e.g. MACFARLANE (1978), HAYEK (1973), SCULLY (1992).

14 Long-term interest rates reflect both the state's fiscal fungibility (whether the present value of expected income equals the present value of expected outlays) and the public's perception of the security of claims to future income streams.

Table 1: European Prime Interest Rates, c.1500-1750[15]

A. REPUBLICS

		Rate	*Source*
Alsace, S. Germany, Switzerland	early 16th c.	10	14:520
Geneva	1538	5	2: 119
	1557	6.67-7	A
	1572	8.33	A
	1613	8	A
	1648	6.67	A
	1668	5-6.67	A
	1681	5	A
Switzerland	18th c.	3-4	14:536
Genoa	1522-24	3-4.25	12:118
	1550	4.375	"
	1575	4.25	"
	1600	2.875	"
	1620	1.25	12:132
Holland (Habsburg)	c.1500	8-12	12:118
	1550s	6.25-8.33	12:118; 21:117
	1550-60	8.33	12:118
(United Provinces)	1572	8.33	"
	1600-40	6.17-8.33	12:131
	1640-72	3.75-5	"
	1672-1700	3-3.75	A
	1709-13	4-4.5	10:474
	1724-5	3-4	A
	1740	3.5-4	A

15 Sources: (1) ASHTON (1960), (2) BERGER (1962), (3) BONNEY (1981), (4) CALABRIA (1991), (5) CARBONI (1995), (6) COLLINS (1988), (7) COVA (1991); (8) DENT (1973), (10) DICKSON (1967), (11) GOUBERT (1970), (12) HOMER and SYLLA (1991), (13) KELLENBENZ (1986), (14) KÖRNER (1995), (15) MUELLER (1997), (16) PEZZOLO (1994), (17) PEZZOLO (1990), (18) PIOLA CASELLI (1991), (19) RUIZ MARTIN (1975), (20) STUMPO (1988), (21) TRACY (1990), (22) VAN DER WEE (1977).

	1750-2	2.5-4.5	A
Nuremberg	1540-50	5	12:117
	1561	6	"
	1565	5	"
Venice	1500	9.6	12:118
	1502	6.76	"
	1509	5	15:474-75
	1521-99	2.5-5	16:738
	1593	3	17:178
	c.1600	4	13:334
	1616-17	5	16:740
	late 17th c.	4-5	14:532
B. MONARCHIES			
Denmark	18th c.	4-5	14:536
France	1522-43	8.33	12:117
	1594-1601	8.33	3:19
	1601-34	6.25	A
	1600-10	3.5-4.3	6:73
	1630s	4-5	6:86
	1656-61	14.5	3:318
	1661-9	5.5-7	6:47; 18:376
	1679	5-5.875	12:131
	1698-9	5	11:227
	1717-18	4	22:379
	1719	3	"
	1735	5	12:170
	1749	5	"
Habsburg Austria	late 17th c.	5-6	14:532
	1700-40	5-6	14:536
	1760-80	3-4	A
Piedmont	1680s	5	20:662
Papal States: Bologna	1555-95	7.01	5:131
	1575	7.01	"
	1595	7.03	"
	1625	7.04	5:132

	1655	6.18	"
Papal States: Rome	late 16th c.	6-8	18:467
	early 17th c.	6	16:740
	1686	3	18:466
Spanish Empire: Castile	1504	10	19:14
	1526	9	"
	1540	7.5	"
	1545-50	6.25	"
	1584-98	5.8	"
Spanish Empire: Milan	1598	7	7:344
	1602-14	5.25	7:73
	1637	5	8: 330
	1655-58	7	7:73-76
	1659-61	2-4.5	7:81-86
	1706-30	4	7:108
Spanish Empire: Naples	1520-29	8.3-10	4:143-45
	1530-38	9.7-11.7	A
	1540-46	8.7-10.5	A
	1550-59	8-9.4	A
	1560-75	8.8-9.3	A
	1580-98	6.8-8	A
Tuscany	early 18th c.	4-6	14:536
	post 1726	3.5-4	"
England	1546-58	13-14	13:113
	1603-24	10	1:155
	1624-40	8	A
	1693	14	12:126
	1694	8	22:385
	1710	8.3	12:156
	1717	5	22:388
	1727	3.57	12:161
	1736	2.86	"
	1750	3	"

We can verify the two hypotheses by examining the interest rate differentials more closely. If the difference was the effect of a permanent risk premium, it would remain constant over time, whereas if it was mainly due to technological factors, one would expect the differentials to narrow over time as monarchies caught up in financial sophistication. The data, which show a strong tendency for prime interest rates to decline and converge over time, strongly support the second hypothesis. Rates of 8-12 per cent towards 1500 had dropped to 8 per cent half a century later; by the early seventeenth century they had slipped to 6 per cent, declined further to about 4 per cent by 1700, and inched a few points lower in the following decades.

The one significant exception to European convergence was England before the Glorious Revolution. Still during the 1690s the English crown was forced to offer rates of 10 per cent, compared with rates of 3-3.75 per cent in the Dutch Republic, of 4-5 per cent in Venice, of 5 per cent in France, and of 5-6 per cent in Habsburg Austria. The comparison with conditions on the Continent turns the Whig interpretation of the Glorious Revolution on its head. The sharp decline in English interest rates after 1700 reflected a process of convergence to the European, Republican and absolutist norm, rather than a bifurcation in England's favour. England was catching up with its neighbours, not initiating a revolution in government security.

Why was pre-1688 England so backward, and why were interest rates there so high? High interest rates imply that the early Stuarts were significantly less reliable and more prone to default on their fiscal commitments than their European counterparts.[16] The explanation for this appears to be the early modern English monarchy's political and military isolation. England's effective insulation from Continental warfare between the mid-fifteenth and the late eighteenth centuries was an effect of its inefficient fiscal system, which was incapable of raising the inflated sums needed to wage early modern warfare, and of the excessive costs of invasion that protected it from foreign attentions (Brewer 1990: 12-13). Whereas on the Continent the constant threat of foreign-backed insurrection, civil war and invasion acted as an effective deterrent against unchecked expropriation,[17]

16 By the 1630s the Stuarts' reputation had so deteriorated that they were no longer able to raise funds on international financial markets (NORTH and WEINGAST, p. 820, n. 36).

17 The fact that the French and Spanish monarchies never entirely lost their credit, and that they were able to transform short term into long term government debt indicates that financial crises and 'bankruptcies' were essentially moratoria on interest payments (VAN DER WEE 1977, p. 391; KÖRNER 1995, p. 520).

in England those competitive constraints were far weaker. Moreover, precisely because the English Crown faced fewer external threats, it remained wedded to an archaic system of expensive short-term finance based on a floating debt far longer than any of its larger Continental competitors. While England established a consolidated debt only after the foundation of the Bank of England in 1694, the pressures of war made France, Spain and lesser Continental monarchies move towards the systems of debt management pioneered by the late medieval Italian city-states already during the sixteenth century. Somewhat ironically, the cost of England's absence between the mid-fifteenth and the late seventeenth centuries from the major European zones of military engagement may have been an autocratic government that kept average rates of interest 50 percent above those prevailing on the Continent. Although the system of constitutional checks and balances that emerged in 1688-89 and the financial pressure caused by war with France (1689-97)[18] did help secure more effective property rights in England, its principal economic effect was an unusually rapid convergence to the European fiscal and political norm.[19]

The English case proves that constitutional differences in systems of governance are not accurate predictors of economic performance. It is just as misleading to take eighteenth-century England's military successes as

18 "Nearly all that was 'revolutionary' about the years following 1688 was the product of war, not of some novel ideology (...) All the distinctive themes of constitutional evolution (...) were, in large measure, developments enforced (...) by the most expensive conflicts that England had yet fought". However, one should not exaggerate the impact of 1688 on administrative practice. Many of the techniques extended to government finance after 1688 had been developed by the Treasury in the period 1665-79 with the "ambition to revolutionize the basis of government borrowing" (ROSEVEARE 1983, p. 708).

19 England managed to turn its relative backwardness into a latecomer's advantage, as it adopted and perfected the best available financial institutions happily at hand in the allied United Provinces. Thus eighteenth-century England was the only country to offer perpetual loans. The more specific benefits of late seventeenth-century fiscal reform and of England's convergence to the European norm are more difficult to identify. Any benefits accruing from sharply lower interest rates on the national debt were probably balanced by the sharp rise in the levels of debt and taxation after 1700, although the claim that private investment was crowded out by state debt is disputed (ROSEVEARE 1983, p. 703-7).

evidence of superior economic performance (North and Weingast 1989). As early modern Sweden and Brandenburg-Prussia proved to great effect, a state's military standing depended more on the efficiency with which it extracted taxes than on the disposable wealth of its subjects. Eighteenth-century England confirmed this point. In England, the share of national income appropriated as taxes rose from approximately 3.5 per cent in the 1670s to between 11 and 12 per cent during the American War (Mathias and O'Brien 1976). The fact that these levels were unmatched elsewhere in Europe proves that the most significant effects of the Glorious Revolution of 1688- 89 were at the level of the fiscal administration. Those reforms underpinned the change in England's international status, from a marginal player under the Tudors and Stuarts to a competitor for European leadership after 1700. A period noted for its praise of liberty actually witnessed the creation of the fiscal-military state (Brewer 1990: xi, xvii).

Several features of the English tax system set it apart from the Continental monarchies. Firstly, tax collection was more centralized and was based on larger numbers of centrally appointed and professionally trained government officials. Second, England's lack of internal jurisdictional and revenue boundaries made it easier to police and repress tax evasion compared to most Continental countries, where jurisdictional fragmentation and administrative heterogeneity made revenue policing an administrative nightmare (Bonney 1995). Third, the English tax system applied uniformly throughout the country, again in striking contrast with rivals such as France and the Dutch Republic, where innumerable regional, group and individual privileges and immunities compounded the lack of fiscal compliance. Lastly, the openness of the English revenue system to public scrutiny created a greater degree of public confidence than in more secretive countries, and conversely made it harder to voice opposition to taxes once Parliament had granted its consent. The English fiscal system was thus more efficient and less subject to evasion or resistance than under nominally more powerful absolutist Continental regimes. The critical advantage of the English system of governance over its neighbours was its superior ability to solve problems of co-ordination and conflict between rival claimants (Brewer 1990).

This conclusion corresponds to recent re-evaluations of the character of ancien régime Europe, in particular of French absolutism. The current view among historians of the French monarchy contrasts strongly with the portrait of a despotic regime (North and Thomas 1973, chs.8, 10; North and

Weingast 1989; Macfarlane 1987; Olson 1991). If one had to sum up the regime's failings in a word, it would be: ineffectiveness. I have already mentioned the main constraint on royal authority: the towering pyramid of inherited and newly established powers and jurisdictions, which gave local and regional societies substantial margins of political manoeuvre and at times de facto independence in their dealings with the Crown (Beik 1985). In a society in which legal propriety was sacrosanct, the ruler could not by law (of which there were different and competing kinds) encroach upon the privileges and rights - the liberties, as they were known - of the provincial elites, the town councils, and the myriad other corporate bodies that made up the pre-modern body politic. Both in theory and in everyday practice, the ruler was supreme political mediator rather than autocrat (Mettam 1990).

This condition defined absolutism's - and indeed all pre-modern governments' - basic predicament. The vast number of sectional interests endowed with legally sanctioned liberties made it necessary to insulate the French royal councils from outside pressure by surrounding them with a high degree of secrecy. This fact in turn transformed lawmaking and especially economic regulation into a discretionary prerogative of the bureaucracy (Root 1991). Although political secrecy and bureaucratic discretion, which made it easier to lobby for privileges outside the glare of public scrutiny, are the hallmarks of authoritarianism, the state's ability to enforce its decisions and to mediate between conflicting claims faced frequently insurmountable barriers. Local and regional representative institutions (parliaments, estates, urban councils and suchlike) could challenge the legitimacy of royal jurisdiction; the country's administrative complexity resisted attempts at uniform enforcement; and even the laws' application was frequently in local hands, which had every opportunity to stall, delay or boycott any centrally legislated decision.

In brief, despite their ostensibly greater authority, French and indeed other absolute monarchs were less able to put their will to good effect than their English counterparts. However, absolutist inefficiency - its failure to co-ordinate and cut through competing economic claims - was not the result of unbridled tyranny and a lack of individual freedom, but of the surfeit of sanctioned liberties and of the absence of a coherent, unified system of law. Moreover, legislative confusion was not the outcome of deliberate state action.[20] It was the inescapable consequence of the way Continental states

20 As argued by HOFFMAN and ROSENTHAL (1997).

were formed, through organic growth and piecemeal accumulation that left pre-existing institutions by and large untouched, rather than by right of conquest which could be used to wipe the political and institutional slate clean. By contrast, the English settlement of 1688-89 was effective because it relied on a highly centralized state that faced little local and provincial opposition. Although the relative openness and size of the English assembly made it harder to reach agreement than in more secretive systems such as the French one, laws passed by the English Parliament had greater legitimacy and could be implemented more consistently than in most Continental states (Levi 1988, ch. 6).

IV. Urban Capital, Republican Coercion

The belief that the emergence of political and civil liberties was inextricably linked to economic freedom also sustains the old view that western Europe's break with feudalism and economic stagnation owes much to the existence of independent cities (Smith 1976, III, iii-iv). The proposition comes under two distinct but connected forms. In the first place, the economic and social changes linked to European modernisation, that is, to the transition from a traditionalist, corporatist, religiously-minded society, to the increasingly secularised, individualistic and mobile world of capitalism, originated and developed in towns (Langton and Höppe 1983, Hicks 1969). The growing material wealth, new codes of law, religious beliefs and aesthetics, nation states and, ultimately, world expansion associated with western European modernisation can all be traced back to the peculiar dynamism of its urban society, and to the social tensions and innovations it brought about. Second, European sovereigns were forced to meet their fiscal requirements by allying with the towns against the feudal aristocracy in exchange for financial support; bargaining over taxes promoted forms of parliamentary representation and thus led, over time, to modern parliamentary democracy.

In the first view, western European cities derived their unique historical role from being both the main and often the only fora of exchange, and the main and often the only centres of cultural, economic and institutional innovation. The view that the medieval Western city is the source of modern legal and political freedoms is often credited to Max Weber (Weber 1978, vol. 2, 1212-372; Käsler 1988: 42-8, 200; Berman 1983, ch.12). However, as Weber pointed out, the origin of those freedoms lay in an act of usurpation of legitimate (feudal) power by groups of burgers who acted collectively to establish their free status - that is, subject to a special and autonomous law (Weber 1978, vol.2, 1254). Therefore, the emergence of free citizen status also defined non-citizens as unfree; urban freedom was the outcome of a legally sanctioned privilege that distinguished the town from the feudal or subject countryside. It thus comes as no surprise that during the medieval and the early modern periods, `freedom' was used in the sense of `privilege' (Bridbury 1986).

During the past two decades this stark contrast between urban modernity and freedom and rural conservatism has been challenged by a large body of research, which has shown that rural or proto-industry contributed as much as urban manufacture to pre-modern economic growth. However, because towns tended where they could to ban all rural activities that threatened their own industries, a critical institutional pre-condition for proto-industrial success appears to have been protection from, or absence of, urban competition. The latter were generally strongest in republican city-states, which were politically independent and could therefore extend their jurisdiction unchallenged over the rural hinterland; as a consequence, rural industries under those regimes were generally weaker. In this way urban privileges, which had originally established the towns' autonomy from feudal authority and had provided the legal basis for their economic expansion, turned later into fetters on rural freedom and growth. Conversely, successful rural manufacture required the same kind of positive freedoms backed by legal privileges and immunities on which 'usurping' towns had originally built their economic fortunes. Rural `freedoms' gave nascent proto-industries the equivalent of infant industry protection against urban encroachment; perhaps paradoxically, such freedoms were more likely to arise in monarchical states in which the sovereign could override the privileges of towns (Pollard 1997, Epstein 1999).

Similar criticisms apply to the second model that links urban economic and political freedom. While also owing something to Weberian analyses, this approach emphasises the capacity that pre-industrial European cities had to avoid the embrace of the tax-hungry state, and it postulates a dichotomy between urban 'capital' and state 'coercion' (Tilly 1990). Pressure to increase political coercion came from rising military competition between states. The early modern `military revolution' had to be paid for by greatly increased rates of taxation; since towns were both wealthier and more easily assessed than the countryside, they bore the brunt of the states' financial needs. However, this was in danger of killing the goose with golden eggs, for military expenditure and bureaucratic controls were antithetical to early commercial capitalism. Therefore, where fiscal pressure could not be restrained, the commercial and financial metropolises were stifled; conversely, where cities were independent of the larger monarchies, they became the core of the rising merchant capitalist economy. The inherent fiscal hostility between feudal and royal authority and the cities meant that monarchs strove for total territorial control, whereas cities pursued commercial profits and preferred open routes of travel and communication along coasts and rivers to politically enforced borders (Blockmans 1989, pp. 733,735). In general terms, economic growth could only occur in towns or regions where state control was weak or non-existent (Blockmans 1989, p. 752; see also Tilly 1990, pp. 52- 3).

These conclusions are however contradicted by evidence about the political status and activities of cities. In politics, cities were strong allies of the monarchs in the latter's attempts to extend full sovereignty over the feudal aristocracy. In exchange for the towns' support expressed through parliamentary institutions, rulers in France, the Crown of Aragon, the southern Netherlands and Piedmont vested cities with political and economic privileges that transformed the urban elites into rentiers (Blockmans 1989, p. 752). Instead, where towns were politically independent, representative institutions were simply ignored. Either one metropolis established control over its region, as did Florence, Milan or Venice in central and northern Italy, or a loose federation of towns like the North Sea Hanse emerged in its place. In the first case, the dominant city's elites employed their new-found powers to exploit the subject territories (Epstein 1999); in the second case, the federated cities suffered from a lack of organization and in due course fell under the sway of more powerful territorial rulers.

Thus just as the economic freedom of the Hansa cities was incapable of sustaining their political independence, political freedom (in the form of parliamentary representation or of an independent republic) was incapable of sustaining subject cities' economic freedom. Urban political and economic freedoms conflicted for two reasons. First, the parcellization of sovereignty characteristic of pre-modern Europe meant that for most cities, jurisdictional powers over trade were a fundamental source of profit. Urban elites therefore had a strong vested interest in preserving their political privileges. Second, monopolistic competition between cities created a Prisoner's Dilemma that placed city-dominated states at an economic disadvantage compared with larger monarchies. In sum, the political power of cities stood in inverse relation to their economic efficiency.

The early modern Netherlands provide a good example of this. The history of the Dutch Republic - governed by a federation of 58 independent cities with equal voting rights and having the most developed and urbanised European economy of its time - seems to confirm that urban political freedom led to economic success. In fact, the country's constitutional structure was among the causes of the country's relative decline from the 1680s ('t Hart 1989). When the Dutch constitutional settlement emerged in the late 1570s, no single city was yet hegemonic, and it was therefore decided that all 58 cities had to vote unanimously on issues of national concern such as war, peace and taxation. However, the compromise entrenched a permanently weak national leadership, which subjected decision-making to constantly shifting coalitions and debilitating bargaining between rival towns. Up to the Peace of Westphalia (1648), the all-out war of independence against the Spanish Empire gave the cities a shared external focus that papered over their main differences. Thereafter, however, the dispersal of political authority among competing commercial and industrial centres restricted the Dutch state's capacity to make timely decisions, particularly in matters concerning the country's commercial and political interests in the international arena over which urban interests differed. The need for unanimity made it harder to respond quickly to evolving international conditions, and became a cause of Dutch decline in the late seventeenth and eighteenth century when England and France challenged the country's hold over international trade (`t Hart 1989, 681). Although economic success achieved the country's political freedom by enabling the Dutch to finance an 80-year war of independence against the world's most powerful empire, the opposite did not apply: in the longer run, political freedom was preserved at the cost of relative economic decline. As we saw with rural manufacture, the political preconditions of urban economic success had turned over time into institutional fetters to further growth.

V. Did Governance Matter? The State as Institutional Co-ordinator

Having begun with the hypothesis that political freedom was essential for economic success, we are being led to conclude that the two may be incompatible. The answer to our initial question, whether there was a direct relation between systems of governance and economic performance in pre-modern Europe, is at first sight negative. We appear generally to have confirmed the initial criticism, that culture - defined as sanctioned behaviour or the 'rules of the game' - cannot be deduced from a given constitutional arrangement. However, this is not an entirely surprising conclusion. Although it is in principle true that an autocratic government (that is, one not subject to constitutional checks and constraints) will be unable to provide the necessary commitment to existing property rights, and will therefore stifle opportunities for growth, it is well known that the converse does not follow. Free (in the sense of liberal democratic)[21] institutions do not necessarily lead to a superior degree of commitment.

A priori, there is little reason to believe that democratic freedoms will be associated either with secure property rights or with a credible pre-commitment to constitutional rules. The modern argument that democratic freedoms may actually threaten economic growth is based on two claims (Przeworski and Limongi 1993). First, democracies fall prey to pressure groups, whose elected representatives pursue the particularist goals of their constituencies rather than collective or national interests, thus favouring policies aimed at economic redistribution rather than generalised growth (Olson 1982, Becker 1983). Secondly, democracies can overturn past laws and decisions, if a qualified majority so decides and if there are no constitutional constraints on such change (Elster and Slagstad 1988). This causes uncertainty and inhibits strategic planning and investment. The tyranny of particularism and the lack of pre-commitment therefore make it essential to insulate the state's decision-making processes from competing interests.

21 I follow this middle-of-the-road liberal definition of democracy to avoid the complications that arise if one argues with Hayek that a democracy may be illiberal and a dictator liberal, where liberalism is defined as a system of individual freedom under the rule of law with wide scope for free-market activity (ARNESON 1993, pp. 145- 6).

Democratic inefficiencies mean that authoritarian rule is necessary to ensure long-term growth.

These arguments suggest that the main economic limit of democracy is one that I have imputed also to absolutism: the excessive and debilitating hold of particular interests. Although we should not push the analogy too far (whereas liberal democracy is based on universal equality before the law, ancien régime liberties were premised on legal inequality), it indicates why differences in constitutional rights across pre-modern Europe were not critical for relative economic performance. In this respect, the Whig and neo-institutional contrast between English and Continental forms of governance is based on two misunderstandings. The first, which underlies the assumption that absolutist monarchies faced higher interest rates than constitutional ones, confuses the normative and political issue of freedom from autocratic or absolutist government with the positive (economic) issue of pre-commitment to rules, and on both points we can do no better than cite David Hume:

> Private property seems to me almost as secure in a civilised European monarchy as in a republic; nor is danger much apprehended, in such a government, from the violence of the sovereign, more than we commonly dread harm from thunder, or earthquakes, or any accident the most unusual and extraordinary. Avarice, the spur of industry, is so obstinate a passion, and works its way through so many dangers and difficulties, that it is not likely to be scared by an imaginary danger, which is so small, that it scarcely admits of calculation. It may now be affirmed of civilized monarchies, what was formerly said in praise of republics alone, that they are a government of Laws, not of Men. The source of degeneracy which may be remarked in free governments, consists in the practice of contracting debt, and mortgaging the public revenues, by which taxes may, in time, become altogether intolerable, and all the property of the state be brought into the hands of the public. Absolute princes have also contracted debt; but as an absolute prince may make a bankruptcy when he pleases, his people can never be oppressed by his debts [Hume 1993 (1777), pp. 53-55].[22]

22 Hume seems to be saying that public debt under a constitutional or mixed government is subject to moral hazard and can therefore get out of hand, whereas an absolutist ruler will not be trusted with excess sums and will therefore keep debt under check. There are obvious similarities between this

The second misunderstanding relates to the character of pre-modern states. The source of institutional inefficiency in pre-modern states was less a lack of concern in enforcing contracts, a despotic lack of predictability, or parliamentary weakness, than the absence of full sovereignty over the public sphere. The reason why pre-modern societies conceived no clear distinction between the public and the private spheres was, precisely, because the state did not monopolise jurisdiction within its borders. Feudal lords, cities and other 'public' corporate bodies within the state's boundaries received private income streams from jurisdictional rights that were sanctioned by law. Monarchs confirmed these rights, but they did not control them. This explains the clear contemporary distinction drawn between absolutism - defined as a constitutional arrangement in which legally chartered 'freedoms' were respected and upheld - and despotism - defined as a system in which they were not (Kelley 1981, pp. 314-22; Black 1984, ch.11).

If one takes the view that the main thrust of pre-modern state formation was a process of ever-expanding sovereignty (Rosenberg 1994), rather than the instantiation of individual political liberty, the links between institutional and economic change become much clearer. Because the most important institutional source of pre-modern economic inefficiency was the near-universal parcellization of sovereignty, which followed from the way states (except England) expanded leaving most existing laws, rights, and privileges in place, the main way pre-modern states could contribute to economic growth was by overcoming that parcellization.

Jurisdictional fragmentation was the source of two fundamental institutional constraints on exchange, specialization and growth. The first, frequently remarked source of economic inefficiency was the panoply of tariff barriers that raised the direct and indirect costs of trade; the second, even more pervasive bottleneck arose from the multiple Prisoner's Dilemmas and market failures caused by competing, politically sanctioned monopolies. One previously remarked instance of market failure was the need to gain some kind of jurisdictional privilege to establish rural industry against urban competition successfully. Another major market failure occurred in systems of food distribution, in which monopolistic competition between towns and states increased both the level and volatility of consumer prices (Epstein 1999).

---

argument and my preceding explanation for the different levels of interest rates in Continental Europe and pre-1688 England.

Pre-modern states could extend their sovereignty and thus limit sources of market failure in two ways. Firstly, and most dangerously, they could usurp feudal or corporate rights - in wartime, under cover of fiscal necessity, by right of territorial conquest, or by reverting feudal rights to the state upon the death of an incumbent. Alternatively, rulers could bypass existing jurisdictional claims by granting new charters of economic 'freedom', new privileges that restrained and weakened the effects of the old.[23] These solutions were both dangerous and circuitous. The first was politically and legally fraught and encountered strong resistance, including accusations of autocratic oppression; it was the negative aspect of that beneficial constraint by subjects on their rulers' actions that I discussed in the context of public debt. The second solution created additional sources of rent-seeking and co-ordination failure which took additional time and effort to solve.[24] In such a world, state 'efficiency' was a relative concept, which consisted in gaining sovereignty over collective income streams earlier and at lesser cost than in competing states. In other words, an 'efficient' pre-modern state was necessarily also a strong and centralized (albeit not autocratic) state. The only European polity that came anywhere close to this benchmark before the late eighteenth century was England, in virtue not of its unique individual liberties but of its precocious political unification (Koenigsberger 1978, Brewer 1990, chs. 1, 4).[25]

23 "In a society organized on a corporative basis personal initiative could only flourish under the protection given by exemption and privileges" (DEYON and GUIGNET 1980, p. 626).

24 One might speculate that weak sovereignty could shape collective expectations (culture), insofar as a society of 'liberties' tended to allocate entitlements along corporate lines and rewarded redistribution over aggregate expansion. It is however difficult to see how such a claim could substantiated.

25 It is for this reason that England achieved national market integration a century before the rest of Europe (REED 1973, KUSSMAUL 1990, CHARTRES 1995).

References

ARNESON, R. J.: "Socialism as the Extension of Democracy", in: E. F. PAUL, F. D. MILLER Jr. and J. PAUL (Eds.): *Liberalism and the Economic Order*, Cambridge/New York (Cambridge University Press) 1993, pp. 145-71.

ASHTON, R.: *The Crown and the Money Market, 1603-1640*, Oxford (Oxford University Press) 1960.

Banchi pubblici, banchi privati e monti di pietà nell'Europa preindustriale. Amministrazione, tecniche operative e ruoli economici, Genoa (Società Ligure di Storia Patria) 1991.

BAUMAN, Z.: *Freedom*, Milton Keynes (Open University Press) 1988.

BECKER, G. S.: "A Theory of Competition among Pressure Groups for Political Influence", *Quarterly Journal of Economics*, 98 (1983), pp. 371-400.

BEIK, W.: *Absolutism and Society in Seventeenth-Century France,* Cambridge (Cambridge University Press) 1985.

BERGER, J.: "Taux de l'intérêt et crédit à court terme à Genève dans la seconde moitié du XVIe siècle", in: *Studi in onore di Amintore Fanfani*, Milan 1962, 4, pp. 89-119.

BERMAN, H. J.: *Law and Revolution. The Formation of the Western Legal Tradition*, Cambridge MA/London (Harvard University Press) 1983.

BLACK, A.: *Guilds and Civil Society in European Political Thought from the Twelfth Century to the Present*, London (Methuen) 1984.

BLOCKMANS, W.: "Voracious States and Obstructing Cities. An Aspect of State Formation in Pre-Industrial Europe", *Theory and Society*, 18 (1989), pp. 733-55.

BONNEY, R.: *The King's Debts: Finance and Politics in France, 1589-1661*, Oxford (Oxford University Press) 1981.

BONNEY, R.: "Revenues", in: R. BONNEY (Ed.): *Economic Systems and State Finance*, Oxford (Clarendon Press) 1995, pp. 423-506.

BREWER, J.: *The Sinews of Power. War, Money and the English State, 1688-1783,* Cambridge MA/London (Harvard University Press) 1990.

BRIDBURY, A.: "Markets and Freedom in the Middle Ages", in: B. L. ANDERSON and A. J. H. LATHAM (Eds.): *The Market in History*, London (Croom Helm) 1986, pp. 79-119.

CALABRIA, A.: *The Cost of Empire: The Finances of the Kingdom of Naples in the Time of Spanish Rule*, Cambridge (Cambridge University Press) 1991.

CAMERON, R.: *A Concise Economic History of the World*, Oxford (Oxford University Press) 1989.

CARBONI, M.: *Il debito della città. Mercato del credito fisco e società a Bologna fra Cinque e Seicento*, Bologna (Mulino) 1995.

CHARTRES, J. A.: "Market Integration and Agricultural Output in Seventeenth-, Eighteenth-, and Early Nineteenth-Century England", *Agricultural History Review*, 43 (1995), pp. 117-38.

CLARK, A.: "Economic Reason: The Interplay of Individual Learning and External Structure", in: J. N. DROBAK, J. V. C. NYE, (Eds.): *The Frontiers of the New Institutional Economics,* 1997, pp. 269-90.

CLARK, G.: "The Political Foundations of Modern Economic Growth: England, 1540-1800", *Journal of Interdisciplinary History*, 26 (1996), 4, pp. 563-88.

COLLINS, J. B.: *Fiscal Limits of Absolutism. Direct Taxation in Early Seventeenth-Century France*, Berkeley-Los Angeles (U. of California Press) 1988.

COVA, A.: Il Banco di S.Ambrogio nell'economia milanese dei secoli XVII e XVIII, Milan 1972.

COVA, A.: "Banchi e monti pubblici a Milano nei secoli XVI e XVII", in Banchi pubblici cit., pp. 327-39.

DE MARCHI, N., MORGAN, M. (Eds.): *Higgling: Transactors and their Markets in the History of Economics*, Durham (Duke University Press) 1994.

DENT, J.: Crisis in Finance. Crown, Financiers and Society in Seventeenth Century France, Newton Abbot (David and Charles) 1973.

DEYTON P., GUIGNET, PH.: "The Royal Manufactures and Economic and Technological Progress in France Before the Industrial Revolution", *Journal of European Economic History*, 9 (1980), pp. 611-32.

DICKSON, P. G. M.: *The Financial Revolution in England. A Study in the Development of Public Credit, 1688-1756*, London 1967.

DROBAK, J. N., NYE, J. V. C. (Eds.): *The Frontiers of the New Institutional Economics*, San Diego/London (Academic Press) 1997.

ELSTER, J., SLAGSTAD, R. (Eds.): *Constitutionalism and Democracy*, Cambridge (Cambridge University Press) 1988.

EPSTEIN, S. R.: *Freedom and Growth. The Political Economy of Markets in Renaissance Europe*, London (Routledge) 1999.

FOGEL, R. W.: "Douglass C. North and Economic Theory", in: J. N. DROBAK, J. V. C. NYE (Eds.): *Frontiers of the New Institutional Economics*, 1997, pp. 13-30.

GELLNER, E.: "Introduction", in: J. BAECHLER, J. A. HALL, M. A. MANN (Eds.): *Europe and the Rise of Capitalism*, Oxford (Basil Blackwell) 1988, pp. 1-6.

GOUBERT, P.: *Louis XIV and Twenty Million Frenchmen*, transl. A.Carter, London 1970.

GUARDUCCI, A. (Ed.): *Prodotto lordo e finanza pubblica. Secoli XIII-XIX*, Florence (Le Monnier) 1988.

HALL, J. A.: *Powers and Liberties. The Causes and Consequences of the Rise of the West*, Oxford (Basil Blackwell) 1985.

HAYEK, F. A.: *Law, Legislation and Liberty, 1. Rules and Order*, Chicago (University of Chicago Press) 1973.

HICKS, J. R.: *A Theory of Economic History*, Oxford (Oxford University Press) 1969.

HOFFMAN, P. T., ROSENTHAL, J.-T.: "The Political Economy of Warfare and Taxation in Early Modern Europe: Historical Lessons for Economic Development", in: DROBAK, J. N., NYE, J. V. C. (Eds.): *The Frontiers of the New Institutional Economics*, San Diego/London (Academic Press) 1997, pp. 31-56.

HOMER, S., SYLLA, R.: *A History of Interest Rates*, New Brunswick - London 3rd ed. 1991.

HUME, D.: "Of Civil Liberty", in: D. HUME: *Selected Essays*, ed. by S. Copley and A. Edgar, Oxford (Oxford University Press) 1993 [1777], pp. 49-56.

JONES, E. L.: *The European Miracle*, Cambridge (Cambridge University Press) 1981.

JONES, E. L.: *Growth Recurring.Economic Change in World History*, Oxford (Oxford University Press) 1988.

KÄSLER, D.: *Max Weber. An Introduction to His Life and Work*, Oxford (Polity Press) 1988.

KELLENBENZ, H.: "Wirtschaft und Gesellschaft Europas 1350-1650", in: W. FISCHER et al. (Eds.): *Handbuch der Europäischen Wirtschafts- und Sozialgeschichte*, 3, Stuttgart (Klett-Cotta) 1986, pp. 1-386.

KELLEY, D. R.: *The Beginning of Ideology. Consciousness and Society in the French Reformation*, Cambridge (Cambridge University Press) 1981.

KOENIGSBERGER, H. G.: "Monarchies and Parliaments in Early Modern Europe. Dominium Regale or Dominium Politicum et Regale", *Theory and Society*, 5 (1978), pp. 191-217.

KÖRNER, M.: "Public Credit", in: R. BONNEY (Ed.): *Economic Systems and State Finance*, Oxford (Clarendon Press) 1995, pp. 507-38.

KUSSMAUL, A.: *A General View of the Rural Economy of England, 1538-1840*, Cambridge (Cambridge University Press) 1990.

LANGTON, J., HÖPPE, G.: *Town and Country in the Development of Early Modern Western Europe*, Norwich (Institute of British Geographers) 1983.

LEVI, M.: *Of Rule and Revenue*, Berkeley/Los Angeles (California University Press) 1988.

MACFARLANE, A: *The Culture of Capitalism*, Oxford (Basil Blackwell) 1987.

MANN, M.: "European Development: Approaching a Historical Explanation", in: J. BAECHLER, J. A. HALL and M. A. MANN (Eds.): *Europe and the Rise of Capitalism*, Oxford (Basil Blackwell) 1989, pp. 6-19.

MATHIAS, P., O'BRIEN, P.: "Taxation in Britain and France, 1715-1810: A Comparison of the Social and Economic Incidence of Taxes Collected for the Central Government", *The Journal of European Economic History*, 5 (1976), pp. 601-50.

METTAM, R.: "France", in: J. MILLER (Ed.): *Absolutism in Seventeenth Century Europe*, Houndmills (Macmillan) 1990, pp. 43-67.

MUELLER, R.: *The Venetian Money Market*, Baltimore (Johns Hopkins) 1997.

MUNZER, S. R.: *A Theory of Property*, Cambridge (Cambridge University Press) 1990.

NORTH, D. C., THOMAS, R. P.: *The Rise of the Western World*, Cambridge (Cambridge University Press) 1973.

NORTH, D. C., WEINGAST, B.: "Constitutions and Commitment: Evolution of Institutions Governing Public Choice in Seventeenth-Century England", *Journal of Economic History*, 49 (1989), pp. 803-32.

OLSON, M.: *The Rise and Decline of Nations. Economic Growth, Stagflation, and Social Rigidities*, New Haven/London (Yale University Press) 1982.

OLSON, M.: "Autocracy, Democracy and Prosperity", in: R. J. ZECKHAUSED (Ed.): *Strategy and Choice*, Cambridge MA (MIT Press) 1991, pp. 131-57.

PARRY, J., BLOCH, M.: "Introduction: Money and the Morality of Exchange", in: J. PARRY, M. BLOCH (Eds.): *Money and the Morality of Exchange*, Cambridge (Cambridge University Press) 1989, pp. 1-32.

PERSSON, K. G.: *Pre-Industrial Economic Growth. Social Organization and Technological Progress in Europe*, Oxford (Basil Blackwell) 1988.

PEZZOLO, L.: "La finanza pubblica", in: A. TENENTI, U. TUCCI (Eds.): *Storia di Venezia, VI. Dal Rinascimento al Barocco*, Rome (Istituto Enciclopedia Italiana) 1994, pp. 713-73.

PEZZOLO, L.: *L'oro dello Stato. Società, finanza e fisco nella Repubblica veneta del secondo '500*, Treviso (Fondazione Benetton) 1990.

PIOLA CASELLI, F.: "Banchi privati e debito pubblico pontificio a Roma tra Cinquecento e Seicento", in: *Banchi pubblici* cit., pp. 461-95.

POLLARD, S.: *Marginal Europe. The Contribution of the Marginal Lands Since the Middle Ages*, Oxford (Clarendon Press) 1997.

PRZEWORSKI, A., LIMONGI, F.: "Political Regimes and Economic Growth", *Journal of Economic Perspectives*, 7 (1993), pp. 51-69.

REED, C. G.: "Transactions Costs and Differential Growth in Seventeenth Century Western Europe", *Journal of Economic History*, 33 (1973), pp. 177-90.

ROSENBERG, J.: *The Empire of Civil Society. A Critique of the Realist Theory of International Relations*, London (Verso) 1994.

ROSEVEARE, H.: "Government Financial Policy and the Money Market in Late Seventeenth Century England", in: A. GUARDUCCI (Ed.): *Prodotto lordo*, pp. 703-35.

RUIZ MARTIN, F.: "Crédito y banca, comercio y transportes en la época del capitalismo mercantil", in: *Actas de las I jornadas de metodologia aplicada a las ciencias históricas. III. Historia moderna*, Santiago de Compostela 1975, pp. 723-49.

RYAN, A.: *Property*, Milton Keynes (Open University) 1987.

SCULLY, G. W.: *Constitutional Environments and Economic Growth*, Princeton, NJ, Princeton University Press) 1992.

SMITH, A.: *An Inquiry into the Nature and Causes of the Wealth of Nations*, ed. by E. Cannan, Chicago (Chicago University Press) 1976 [1776].

STUMPO, E.: "Reddito nazionale e debito pubblico. La finanza pubblica in Piemonte nella seconda metà del secolo XVII", in: A. GUARDUCCI (Ed.): *Prodotto lordo*, pp. 653-702.

'T HART, M.: "Cities and Statemaking in the Dutch Republic, 1580-1680", *Theory and Society*, 18 (1989), pp. 663-87.

TILLY, C.: *Coercion, Capital, and European States, AD 990-1990*, Oxford (Basil Blackwell) 1990.

TRACY, J. D.: *Holland under Habsburg Rule 1506-1566*,Berkeley - Los Angeles (U. of California Press) 1990.

WEBER, M.: *Economy and Society*, ed. by G. Roth and C. Wittich, 2 vols., Berkeley/Los Angeles/London (University of California Press) 1978.

WEE, H., VAN DER: "Monetary, Credit and Banking Systems", in: E. E. RICH, C. H. WILSON (Eds.): *The Cambridge Economic History of Europe, V. The Economic Organization of Early Modern Europe*, Cambridge (Cambridge University Press) 1977, pp. 290-393.

WEINGAST, B.: "The Political Foundations of Limited Government: Parliament and Sovereign Debt in 17th- and 18th-Century England", in: J. N. DROBAK, J. V. C. NYE (Eds.): *Frontiers of the New Institutional Economics*, pp. 213-46.

WINCH, D.: *Adam Smith's Politics. An Essay in Historiographic Revision*, Cambridge (Cambridge University Press) 1978.

Chapter 8

Culture and the Myth of Economic Determinism in Global History and World Politics

KEN DARK

I. Introduction

This paper offers a critique of 'economic determinism' in global history and world politics. In particular, this will be achieved by highlighting the relationship between culture and economic change. The explanation of large-scale changes in global history and world politics are used as a case-study, although the points made here are of far wider relevance than simply to those subjects. These areas offer especially clear-cut examples with which to consider this, as in recent years the economic determinist paradigm has been deployed in these subjects in an overt and explicit form.

In these fields 'economic determinist' approaches have been employed to explain a very wide range of phenomena. This range extends from the rise and fall of states, empires, and international political and economic systems, through an array of 'developmental' issues, to the growth of political integration and globalization[1]. It encompasses changes which took place in the 'distant' past, such as the origins of the earliest states and empires, to those affecting contemporary global trends and even the possibility of forecasting future global political development. Obviously, change on these scales relates not only to politics and economics but to the growth and decline of cultures and civilizations[2].

Many of these issues relate closely to key concerns of Economists and Economic Historians and the points made here affect, too, how one envisages the relationship between economics, history and politics as a whole. So, this debate strikes at the core of the relationship between history and economics, economics and culture, and particularly to that between economic growth and large-scale political and cultural transformations. The argument proposed here will be that this relationship has been so severely distorted in much contemporary analysis as to undermine both the basis of more effectively integrating aspects of these subjects and our ability to produce more satisfactory explanations for large-scale political and economic change as a whole.

II. What Is 'Economic Determinism'?

The term 'economic determinism' needs to be clarified at the outset. This expression is used in many academic disciplines to refer to the theoretical paradigm that 'economic factors' - usually simply defined as the production and control of material resources in such analyses - dictate the history of all non-economic aspects of human activity. The economic determinist paradigm in this sense is the basis of most materialist concepts of human history, including Classical Marxism. This paradigm assumes that 'economic change', understood in this somewhat limited way, is the basis of all other change in human societies. Economic determinists argue that culture, politics and the like are mere secondary features of underlying 'eco-

1 For an overview, see DARK (1998, chs. 1 and 2).

2 For the context within Economics and Economic History, see CASSON and GODLEY (this volume, ch.1).

nomic realities'. To its supporters, therefore, economic determinism is believed to exist as a 'real world' process, not simply be an analytical procedure.

Thus, economic determinism and economics are not at all the same thing. Economic determinism is not the analysis of social or political life using the methods and theories of the academic field of Economics. It is not only the assumption that economic factors play some role in these other aspects of human existence.

So, an Economist who simply applies neoclassical political economic theory to the study of politics is not an economic determinist.

To give a well-known example, Mancur Olsen's work on the 'rise and decline of nations' is not economic determinism, because it does not locate causal primacy in production and the control of material resources (Olsen 1982). To take an economic determinist approach, the analyst must adopt the view that such factors so entirely shape all human decision-making as to make rationality and optimisation no more than self-delusions on the part of individual actors operating under specific material circumstances. In this way, economic determinism is opposed to the very core of conventional economic theory.

III. Global History, World Politics and Economics

Although in this paper I shall illustrate the problems of economic determinism with reference to global history and world politics the points made here are, therefore, equally valid in any other sphere of human activity. However, first it is necessary to define what is meant by 'global history'. By this term I mean the entire human past worldwide. This may be preferred to the alternative 'world history' as the latter has come to designate a specific approach to the study of history. Likewise, the term 'world politics' requires a definition. This is used here to refer to political units, institutions, relationships and interactions examined on a worldwide scale. World politics is the subject of the academic field which is, perhaps confusingly, known as 'International Relations'.

At the outset it is also worth stressing that it is not my intention to present an argument about 'why economics does not matter in the study of global history or world politics'. Nor do I intend to argue that approaches developed within the academic fields of Economics and Economic History cannot be applied to the study of global history or world politics. Far from it, this contribution is based on an assumption that economic considerations are of importance to both the study of global history and world politics. But this is one of the reasons why the economic determinist approach is so pernicious.

Any theoretical premise which distorts our understanding of the relationship between economics and either global history or world politics must be countered if a fruitful dialogue is to be developed between those studying these subjects.[3] Moreover, this paradigm denies the very basis of most Economic analysis. 'Economic determinism' does not merely lead to 'bad History' but to 'bad Economics' too.

The latter observation also serves to introduce the purpose of this contribution. It is not the rejection of economic determinism that reduces the relevance of economics to these two fields of study. Rather, it is a belief in economic determinism itself which - more than any other factor - hinders our ability to analyze the role of economics in these areas in theoretically sophisticated - and historically more credible - ways.

These clarifications are necessary because there is a widespread, but erroneous, scholarly view that historical or political interpretations based on economic determinism are more solidly-founded than those emphasising other factors. Of course, such studies have the advantage of offering apparently clear causal links and an illusion of the easy quantifiability of causal factors in historical or political change. They can be expressed in a format which sometimes resembles that of Economic analysis more closely than is usual in studies of large-scale historical or political change. Moreover, in that such interpretations put economic activity 'centre-stage' it might be supposed that economic determinism enhances the significance of Economics to other disciplines, but this not the case.

Far from furthering our understanding of the importance of economic factors in global history and world politics, economic determinism obscures all the critical issues in understanding this significance. Not least it creates confusion as to the central issues of why, when, where, how, and to what extent, are these factors important? If causal relevance is simply assumed, it is no longer incumbent on the analyst to demonstrate it! This paradigm also,

3 For my own view, see DARK (1998).

as we have already seen, encourages a sort of 'pseudo-Economic' analysis. In this the basic premises and principles of mainstream Economics are rejected when analyzing economic factors in favour of simplistic correlations and an explicit denial of agency. Using an economic determinist paradigm one would need to set aside most of the theoretical basis of neoclassical economics, and opt instead for a 'hard' materialism in which issues of rational calculation would be seen as self-deception.

Many Economists may argue that a paradigm which interprets material outcomes as the determinants of human behaviour, rather than vice versa, is so intrinsically flawed that it is clearly obsolete. Conversely, therefore, it may be felt by some scholars working outside the study of either global history or world politics, that economic determinist theories are already redundant. That is, they may assume that this contribution takes issue with an already obsolete theoretical position.

At this stage it is, therefore, perhaps helpful to give a brief impression of some of the recent approaches to these subjects employing an economic determinist perspective. This will serve to demonstrate the current resurgence of this framework of analysis in the study of global history and world politics and the need for such a critique. Ironically, far from being outdated, economic determinism has recently become quite fashionable!

IV. Economic Determinism in the Contemporary Study of Global History and World Politics

Economic determinism has a very long intellectual history. Perhaps its most celebrated exposition was in the writings of Marx himself and those of the later Marxian writers of the later nineteenth and early-mid twentieth centuries. Their work has made this theory into both a formidable theoretical school and a political ideology, in the last century or so.

Thus, it is especially ironical that the rapid decline of Marxism in the Soviet Union and eastern Europe in the late 1980s and early 1990s was broadly contemporary with a resurgence of this paradigm among Western scholars seeking to explain large-scale political changes such as the collapse of the U.S.S.R.[4]. As a result of this there is the curious spectacle of the 1990s 'transition' in eastern and central Europe being discussed in 'historical materialist', or even explicitly 'Marxist', terms. That is, as Marxism collapsed as a political force, International Relations specialists and historians rediscovered historical materialism as an analytical perspective with which to study this collapse.

Moreover, economic determinism forms the basis for several analytical frameworks, notably 'world systems theory', which seek to become overall paradigms for International Relations and history alike. While explaining of the inadequacies of historical materialism in historical materialist terms might seem strange - even bizarre - to the layperson, in the last decade it has become part of the implicit orthodoxy of most analysis of large-scale change in a wide range of academic fields.

It is perhaps worth outlining in a little more detail some of the questions such scholars are trying to address using this approach.[5] In addition to the collapse of the Soviet Union and its aftermath (mentioned above) key issues discussed using this paradigm have included: the emergence of pre-eminent ('hegemonic') states, the rise and fall of states and empires in general, the origins of the modern international political system, regional political integration, globalization, and the occurrence and timing of wars and revolutions. This is but a selection of what might be a far longer and more diverse list. These are not issues of relevance only to scholars of politics, culture or society, but which have profound implications for Economics. A particularly curious application of the economic determinist paradigm is, in fact, its use to explain economic change on a similar scale, such as the Industrial Revolution or origins of capitalism. Here, one economic change is supposed to have caused another in a direct and immediate manner. This, of course, begs the question of to what extent such explanation would be successively repeatable, from one economic change to another through time. Where does this stop!

At this point, it may be useful to illustrate this scholarly trend toward economic determinism with two examples, one each from global history and world politics. As a historical example, we may cite the well-known work of Paul Kennedy (Kennedy 1989). Kennedy has charted the 'rise and fall of the great powers' in exactly this way, seeing a close link between excep-

4 This work has been reviewed by SMITH (1994).

5 The following is based on examples given in DARK (1998, chs. 1 and 2).

tional 'national' economic growth and the growth of 'great power' status. Kennedy has been very keen to emphasise that he is a historian and, if so, his work must surely be classifiable as 'global history'.

Likewise, Robert Gilpin - one of America's most renowned scholars of International Relations - has employed a very similar approach to studying the emergence and decline of leading states.[6] Writing explicitly as a scholar of world politics, Gilpin sees patterns in the accumulation and depletion of 'national wealth' as lying behind the growth and decline of leading state-actors in international politics.

So, here we have examples of major scholars in both fields using what are clearly economic determinist approaches. Moreover, both Kennedy and Gilpin are alike in that they assume that there is a direct causal correlation between the growth and decline of 'national' economies and the growth and decline of specific states as 'great powers'. In their view, economic factors do not merely play a part in, but actually determine, which states will become politically and militarily dominant at any time.

So, it is argued, by tracing current patterns of economic growth it is possible to forecast the world politics of the twenty-first century (For example: Kennedy 1993). Alternatively, global political history for millennia can be seen as no more than the outcome of long-term economic changes.

Kennedy and Gilpin are, of course, far from alone in this belief. Here, their work is cited merely as highly-visible examples of the use of this paradigm in the last decade. In particular, other scholars adopting a state-centric perspective on world political change (so-called 'Realism') have employed a similar approach.

Among the leading contemporary Realist scholars of international politics, George Modelski has recently proposed an evolutionary approach to the whole of global political history along exactly these lines (Modelski 1996). In his view, states and their economies 'co-evolve' to produce long cycles of international political hegemony. In these, the economically dominant state will also be the 'hegemon', capable of recasting the whole international system (Modelski and Thompson 1995). Whereas until recently Modelski favoured political strategies as the key factor in such long-cycles of growth and decline, his recent work proposes that it is economic factors which drive these political changes.[7]

---

6 For examples, see GILPIN (1996, 1981).

7 For his earlier views, see MODELSKI (1987).

All these scholars are united by their state-centric view of world politics and global history. However, many commentators on recent theoretical developments within the academic field of International Relations have observed that such state-centric views have been themselves in sharp decline.[8] Especially relevant here is that this decline has generally been ascribed to the explanatory inadequacy of state-centric perspectives. In particular, 'Realism' of this sort has been seen as wholly incapable of explaining the end of the Cold War and the collapse of the Soviet Union (Collins and Waller 1992, Harris 1996).

It might, therefore, be asked whether this 'Realist' interest in economic determinism is merely a reflection of the outmoded approaches encompassed within that school. This raises the question of whether similar concentration on economic factors is found elsewhere in the study of global history or world politics. Is this more than the last grasp at explanation by a troubled theoretical school seeking self-justification by the addition of a new (and seemingly more credible) addition to its repertoire of explanatory tools? Or is economic determinism of this sort - in which political changes can effectively be 'read off' from 'underlying' economic change- a more widespread analytical trend?

Far from finding a contrast between state-centric analysts and other scholars of world politics, a similar focus on economic explanation is found in most other contemporary schools of International Relations theory (Dark 1998, ch. 1). For example, many scholars belonging to the 'Neo-liberal' school - usually supposed to be the principal competitor (in theoretical terms) to the state-centric approach - also favour a determining role for economics.

Neo-liberalism is a much more diverse, and some Realists might say diffuse, school of thought than Realism.[9] But one can take as examples two well-known mainstays of this approach: 'interdependence theory' and 'integration theory'. These assert that economic integration and economic interdependence will, necessarily, bring about an increasingly peaceful and more co-operative world.

Once again, then, these theorists assume that economic changes not only closely coincide with, but directly cause, political changes. Moreover, spe-

8 For example: KRATOCHWIL (1993).

9 By far the best survey of contemporary Neo-liberalism is: ZACHER and MATTHEW (1995).

cific types of economic change are meant to cause specific types of political change - pure economic determinism. It has even been suggested that sufficiently intensive economic interdependence will bring an end to war altogether and so economic factors will automatically lead to world peace.

There can, therefore, be no doubt that Neo-liberalism too often encompasses a far from 'half-hearted' form of economic determinism. This is not to say that all Neo-liberals are economic determinists, but neither are all Realists. However, this paradigm is widespread in both schools. Thus, as in state-centric approaches, we see here that economic changes are supposed to automatically produce political changes according to Neo-liberals too.

Probably the third most widely used theory of world politics (after Realism and Neo-liberalism) is 'world systems theory' (classically expounded by Wallerstein 1974-88). Like both Realist and Neo-liberal approaches, the world systems perspective is shared both by some International Relations analysts and some historians. In the former discipline, it has been rapidly growing in the previous decade.

World systems theory is more explicitly based on an economic determinist understanding of global history and world politics than either Realism or Neo-liberalism.[10] World systems perspectives encompass a wide range of theoretical variation, from explicitly Marxist perspectives, to those somewhat closer to 'World History' in McNeill's sense (Sanderson 1995)

Despite their other differences, all world systems analysts see world politics as an inevitable product of economic relations. They all assign economic factors causal primacy in bringing about change. Moreover, they suppose that particular patterns of economic relationships (such as 'exploitation of the periphery by the core') are directly causally related to specific political relationships such hegemony and imperialism. So, world systems theory is even more 'economic determinist' than these other schools.

This is, of course, to leave aside those historians and, albeit far fewer, scholars of world politics who still explicitly employ a Classical Marxist, or less modified neo-Marxist, theoretical framework (for examples: Halliday 1994, Cox 1987, Cox and Sinclair 1997). These, too, are founded on a determinist understanding of the supposedly causal relationship between economic 'substructure' and political and cultural 'superstructure'.

Of course, by no means all historians or scholars of world politics adopt any of these approaches. By no means all employ economic determinism as

10 A recent survey of the field is provided by CHASE-DUNN and HALL (1997).

their framework for analyzing global history or world politics. However, the economic determinist approach is now widespread in the three most numerous theoretical schools in the latter field, and very prevalent in the study of global history.

Among the scholars that abjure this approach there is great theoretical diversity. In History these include, for example, structural historians or historical particularists who do not favour an economic determinist view. Likewise, in International Relations there are also whole schools of analysis which do not depend upon economic determinism (Dark 1998, chs. 1 and 2).

Nonetheless, economic determinism - rather than waning as one might expect - has been growing dramatically in popularity in recent years in both fields. This growth has been part of a wider interdisciplinary trend, and similar approaches are widespread in other disciplines within the Humanities and Social Sciences. In Geography, Archaeology and Anthropology, economic determinism has also been making something of a 'comeback' since the end of the 1980s.

For instance, Peter J. Taylor (Taylor 1989), arguably the leading living Political Geographer of 1990s, has explicitly adopted world systems theory as the framework for his work. In Anthropology the work of Marvin Harris has popularised a strongly determinist materialist perspective (Harris 1979). In Archaeology, the long-dormant Marxist school revitalised itself in the early 1980s to become one of the major theoretical traditions of the discipline.[11]

In several of these disciplines a curious development has been the alignment of scholars adopting an explicitly economic determinist viewpoint with post-modernism (For example: Friedman 1994). Although one might suppose that materialist determinism and anti-foundationalist/anti-essentialist relativism were incompatible, such a synthesis of perspectives has taken place in several disciplines. These include International Relations, History, Sociology, Geography, Anthropology and Archaeology. In the latter it has become, perhaps, the dominant theoretical paradigm of the 1990s, in the form of 'Post-Processualism'. In this theory, economic determinism, a particularly extreme form of post-modernist relativism and radical feminism combine to form a distinctive perspective.[12]

---

11 For discussion of this, see DARK (1995, pp. 27-9).

12 For a review of this see DARK (1995).

Thus, from post-Cold War world politics to the study of long-extinct human societies, economic determinism has become one of the most widespread analytical frameworks in use in the 1990s. There seems no indication at present that this theoretical growth in slowing down.

However, there seems to have been remarkably little theoretical or analytical discussion of the basis of such an approach in recent scholarship (an exception is Dark 1998, ch .3). In the remainder of this contribution, I shall try to look again at the theoretical basis for economic determinism in global history and world politics. The main purpose of this investigation will be to ask whether there are any logical grounds whatsoever for a belief that economic determinism actually 'works' as a theory at all?

In order to approach this question, it will be useful to examine a specific historical theme. Here, therefore, discussion will centre on the extent to which economic determinism offers a convincing explanation for large-scale political change in global history. As we shall see, it is also a topic which exposes some of the serious flaws found in the economic determinist approach.

V. Two Types of Economic Determinism

When examining large-scale global political change, economic determinism can usefully be subdivided into 'crude' and 'subtle' forms. These two types of determinism may be only approximate and general categories, but we shall see in due course that they prove useful in discussing the shortcomings of this approach.

In 'crude' economic determinism, large-scale economic changes are chronologically compared to large-scale political changes. When a major change in the economic system occurs, a major change in the political system will be expected to follow it. In this way, the chronology of economic changes forms the basis for the chronology of political changes. So, economic growth is seen as the principal driving force in global history. If there is especially rapid economic growth affecting a specific state, for example, a new political system based on that state can be anticipated, only to decline in a subsequent economic slump (Arrighi 1994).

As simple, some might say naive, as this approach sounds, it has surprisingly often been the basis for discussions of world politics (Dark 1998 ch. 1). For example, almost all of the current heated discussion over whether or not the USA is in decline as a 'superpower' has been in these terms (Dark with Harris 1996, esp. ch. 1). Likewise, one often hears the assertion - made on exactly these grounds - that 'the globalization of the world economy will transform world politics'.[13]

That is, in both cases it is assumed that preceding large-scale economic transformation will automatically lead to large-scale political transformation. To give a more 'theoretical' example, much world systems theory proceeds in very much this way. According to many world systems analysts economic long-cycles bring into existence repetitive patterns of exploitative and unequal economic core: periphery relations. These, in turn, lead to the emergence of identical patterns of political and military relations.

The second, or 'subtle', form of economic determinism does not make such straightforward correlations. It points to the way in which specific trajectories of economic change produce specific outcomes in given societies. Thus, identical economic changes in different societies might produce quite different outcomes in political terms, but each of these outcomes would be determined by those specific economic trajectories.

Usually, scholars working within this approach draw attention to the reflexive and intricate relationships which exist between natural and economic resources, modes of production and exchange, technologies and social relations. They highlight the non-teleological or contingent dimensions of these relations. They assert that their own analyses are, therefore, 'not deterministic', while making highly-deterministic assumptions about the relationship between economic and political change.

This type of argumentation characterises Marxist analyses of world politics. The specifics of economic history can be interpreted in this manner according to Marxian analytical concepts (for example: Chase-Dunn 1990). Of course, there are yet other studies both by historians and International Relations analysts in which economic and political change is interpreted in this way, but in a more implicit manner (For example: Weiss and Hobson 1995).

Using these two broad categories we may now look at the credibility of economic determinist explanations of large-scale political change. This will

13 For a recent survey of academic discussions of globalization, see JONES (1995).

demonstrate first the problems with 'crude determinism'. Then analysis will focus on the more deep-seated theoretical difficulties which undermine not only the basis of both 'subtle' economic determinism but of the whole paradigm.

VI. Crude Economic Determinism

A clear and simple test of crude economic determinism can be formulated by comparing large-scale economic and political changes in western Europe (this section is based on, and expands, ch. 3 of Dark 1998). If large-scale economic change automatically causes large-scale political change, then fundamental economic transformations should be seen to have some political effects on a concomitant scale. If not, then crude economic determinism cannot be said to be credible.

So, all that is required is a simple historical comparison of the chronology of large-scale economic and political changes. Here, let us look at ten fairly uncontroversial and widespread - if not Europe-wide - large-scale economic changes, from the origins of agriculture to the Industrial Revolution.[14]

1. The origins and spread of agriculture, in the Neolithic period. This enabled the first widespread sedentary economies to come into existence, after millennia of hunter-gatherer economies.
2. The first extensive evidence of crafts specialization in the early Bronze Age.
3. The establishment of the first Europe-wide network of trade, which probably dates to the later Bronze age.
4. The establishment of the Roman imperial economy outside Italy, which in western European terms occurred in the first century AD.
5. The collapse of the Roman economy, probably in the seventh century AD.
6. The re-emergence of urban-based trading networks on a European scale in the later seventh century.

14 For the historical framework, see PARKER (1993), DARK (1998 chs. 5-7).

7. The Viking Age trading system, established following Viking settlement in the ninth century onward.

8. The feudal economy, perhaps first discernable in the tenth century.

9. The origins of mercantile capitalism in the fifteenth and early sixteenth centuries.

10. The late eighteenth century Industrial Revolution.

In order to compare these ten profound economic changes with political transformations of a comparable scale, let us take ten political changes which are usually seen in historical and political studies as of approximately the same magnitude. That is, periods in which the whole basis of political organization was transformed across much of western Europe.

Of course, as with the economic changes selected, any choice of which changes to include is open to debate, but few scholars would probably dispute the inclusion of at least the majority of the following changes.

1. The origin of the earliest chiefdoms found in western Europe. This probably occurred in the late Neolithic or early Bronze Age. Such polities were probably the first to form inter-polity networks.

2. The formation of the earliest western European states. The earliest of these was probably the Etruscan polity in Italy.

3. The establishment of the Roman empire, which in western European terms principally belongs to the first centuries BC and AD.

4. The fall of the Roman empire. This occurred in western Europe in the fifth century AD.

5. The formation of barbarian kingdoms in the fifth-seventh centuries. In most of western Europe, outside Italy, these were the first non-Roman states.

6. The rise of the Carolingian empire, culminating in the coronation of Charlemagne in AD 800. This was the first empire centred in north west Europe.

7. The Viking Age. Beginning c. AD 800, this was a period of Europe-wide political change contemporary with the Viking incursions and settlement.

8. The emergence of medieval feudal kingdoms in the tenth and eleventh centuries. This established the kingdoms which dominated western European politics throughout the middle ages.

9. The transformation of feudal political organization in the Renaissance period, to form early modern states.

10. The formation of the Westphalian international political system, in the early seventeenth century. This is usually accredited with forming the contemporary international system.

It will be immediately apparent from these two lists that there is only a very partial parallel in the dates of the two sets of transformations. The chiefdom appears long after the 'agricultural revolution', but before the earliest evidence of widespread crafts specialization. In fact, it is usually suggested that the emergence of chiefly patronage enabled crafts specialization to take place.[15]

The Etruscan state postdates the establishment of Europe-wide trading systems (in which it participated) and of course predates the Roman imperial economy (Spivey and Stoddart 1994). Roman economic institutions, in turn, were established in western Europe only after the Roman conquest.[16]

More remarkable, perhaps, is that the collapse of the Roman economy postdated Roman political collapse by some two centuries, while the new urban-based trading network which succeeded it formed within already-existing barbarian kingdoms (Hodges and Whitehouse 1983, Herrin 1987). The Carolingian empire, while it benefitted from the existence of these trading contacts, was not itself associated with Europe-wide economic innovations, despite its profound political, military, cultural and religious affects (Pounds 1994, esp. pp. 47-61, 74-77).

In the following Viking Age, Scandinavian settlers and raiders alike moved within the existing trading network at first.[17] It was probably only after they formed their own kingdoms in western Europe that they established a 'successor' economic system.

One exception to this general lack of correlation seems to be the simultaneous emergence of feudal society and economy, although recent work has problematised our understanding of feudalism overall. However, a conventional historical understanding of the emergence of feudalism might be to correlate the rise of feudal society and economy very closely. So, here

---

15 For recent discussions, see EARLE (1997, 1991), CLARK and PARRY (1990). See also RENFREW and SHENNAN (1982).

16 For an interesting regional study of this, see MILLETT (1990).

17 For a recent survey of the period, see ROESDAHL (1991).

we might accept one point of direct correlation between large-scale political and economic change.

However, no such correlation can be found between the emergence of the Westphalian international system - which most International Relations scholars consider still exists today - and the Industrial Revolution. The Westphalian System is universally considered to have come into existence in 1648, more than two centuries before the Industrial Revolution.

Thus, although in the specific case of medieval European feudalism it is possible to argue that large-scale political and economic change may have closely coincided, there is no other correlation between these two sets of changes. The most interesting relationship is, conversely, the very way in which large-scale political changes have usually preceded large-scale economic changes. Of course, it might be argued that the economic transformations affected other aspects of politics, but this still does not explain why these political changes occurred. Nor does it explain why these economic changes apparently had so little affect on the forms of political organization established by these major political transformations.

That is, from this comparison alone it would be more plausible to argue that large-scale economic change had been the outcome of large-scale political change, rather than visa versa! Of course, this latter possibility is not intrinsically unlikely on *a priori* grounds. However, it is not necessitated by this comparison.

It is easy to imagine how changed political circumstances could, in each case, have facilitated new possibilities for technological innovation, for experimentation with untried or risky economic forms, or for the redistribution of wealth and patronage.[18] They might have provided new opportunities for entrepreneurs, businesspeople and merchants. If so, this is hardly economic determinism!

The principal problem with this view is that the timing of these changes still seems too far distant to draw a link between them. Can political changes centuries before really have triggered later economic change? So, by far the safest interpretation is to forge no link between these two sets of changes at all. Of course, it might be said that this 'test' is to make too broad and simplistic a correlation between economic change and political

18 For a cognate argument, see KRATOCHWIL (1989).

change. Or, it could be claimed, this might be to conceive of the relationship between these too narrowly.[19]

This line of argument brings us to consider what was termed earlier 'subtle' economic determinism. But before doing so, it is worth noting that what has been discussed so far is exactly the sort of correlation which has recently been especially favoured by many scholars of global history and world politics.

VII. Subtle Economic Determinism

If large-scale economic change does not automatically trigger large-scale political change, what of more 'subtle' causal relationships. It might be argued that these are a more promising area of academic exploration in seeking a firm scholarly basis for economic determinism. However, there are serious theoretical problems with this approach too.

Obviously, if the causes of large-scale political change lie in the precise details of individual economic trajectories, then the sort of broad analyses so far presented might not constitute a very convincing critique of them. It might be claimed that, if we could trace the individual economic histories of each region, each town, each state or each institution, then we would be able to see the true economic causes of political change. This is, of course, a somewhat different concept of what is meant by economic determinism, but it is economic determinism all the same.

Claims such as this are naturally very hard to verify. Too often, therefore, they remain based on mere assumption. No matter how much empirical work has been done which fails to find a convincing economic cause for non-economic change, it can always be claimed that further study would reveal this. That is, on empirical grounds one can always assert that these relationships exist, but are simply so subtle, or so elusive, as to evade scholarly reconstruction or discovery.

Perhaps for that reason, subtle economic determinism might be supposed to be almost irrefutable as well as unprovable. Once it is established as a

---

19 For an example of an attempt to develop a more sophisticated understanding of such relationships, see Cox (1983, 1987).

preconception, then economic factors are simply assumed to have a determinant character in the subsequent analysis.

It is somewhat surprising, then, to discover that even subtle economic determinism may be easier to refute than has often been supposed. Empirically, as we have seen, it may be almost impossible to refute subtle determinism of this sort. Theoretically, however, subtle economic determinism has some very serious weaknesses which do not seem to have been previously exposed in published work.[20]

The role played by culture is absolutely central to this argument. For it is cultural analysis which sounds the final death knell both for this type of determinism and for economic determinism overall.

VIII. Culture and Economic Determinism

Like crude economic determinism, subtle economic determinism rests on the assumption that economic factors are the 'bottom level' of human activity. That is, these factors underlie all other aspects of human life.

Given that economic practices are bound up with the provision of food, drink, and other requirements of human life, this at first sounds a common-sense proposition. But theoretical problems arise from the need to disengage economic practices from society as whole. This sort of argument requires the separation of economic activity from all other aspects of human life, so that this activity can become their basis.

It may be obvious to note that the firms, companies, guilds, or whatever, involved in economic activity are always comprised of human individuals. However, the implications of this seem seldom to have been realised in studies of the relationship between economics and global history or world politics.[21]

The simple recognition that all of these organizations are groups of individuals has deep-running implications for how they must be analyzed. For one very well-attested universal of human societies is that humans always

20 In addition to those discussed here, note GIDDENS (1981).

21 For a more extensive discussion of this point, see DARK (1998, ch. 4).

have cultures (this is so widely accepted by anthropologists that it has even to be incorporated into sociobiological analysis: Boyd and Richerson 1992).

There seems no doubt among scholars that all individuals exist within a cultural context (for example: Gaenslen 1986). That is, their everyday actions are bound up in a cultural matrix comprised of customs, values, beliefs, perceptions, attitudes and habitual or repeated practices.[22] This lies implicit in their every act and in every aspect of their understanding of the world around them.

Thus, human action is always 'encultured': within and existing as part of a culture. Although individuals in some societies may be presented with a range of cultural options, even the option of rejecting aspects of their own culture and taking on new cultural attributes, this and their attitude to such options are both parts of their culture. The adoption of culture, in this sense, begins in infancy and continues throughout the individual's life. Culture is both consciously learned, and passively acquired. Even if we try to change our culture in a conscious way, we do so within the pre-existing culture.

So, cultures are not entirely consciously chosen, nor are they always explicitly expressed. They permeate every aspect of every human community, and at all times. Although cultures also change, except under exceptional circumstances, they do so through the practices and understandings of those already entwined by them.[23]

Work by anthropologists, sociologists, organizational analysts and other scholars also leaves no doubt that culture permeates all aspects of human life (for example: Goldstone 1987). Cultural values affect every aspect of political, social and economic organization. They shape the attitudes and perceptions of every individual in every society.

Not merely firms and economic institutions are culturally-situated, but every other aspect of every human society. Empirical studies have also made it clear that this is one important reason why societies which share similar social and economic forms of organization are so dissimilar in the specific forms which these take (for example: Thomas 1991).

---

22 For discussions, see for example HOFSTEDE (1994), ARCHER (1988).

23 The extent to which culture is transformable by agency has been the subject of an ongoing debate between Giddens and Archer, see for example, GIDDENS (1984), ARCHER (1995).

Like other human activities, economic practices are not merely always permeated by culture but always enacted within a cultural context (Narotzsky 1997). Value, perceptions of resources, needs and wealth, and of the meaning and utility of work are all culturally-dependent. That is, they differ from one culture to another both across the globe today and over time. A clear example is the relationship between the history of slavery and attitudes to the human individual, to work and to value.

The history and anthropology of money is another excellent example of this (Williams 1997). Not only has the physical form of money changed dramatically - literally from cowrie shells to cashcards - from one society to another, but the units and values of money are even more variable (Cribb 1986). That is, even such an apparently 'solid' form of wealth as a coin, is no more than a cultural product. To put it another way, money has no absolute value: it is simply 'culture'.

Likewise, it is impossible for money to function without shared relationships of trust, as well as implicit understanding. If a banknote says 'I promise to pay the bearer...', then this may not be taken literally - but the note will be useless as a form of currency without acceptance of its (culturally) ascribed value by both those involved in the transaction.

If even such a basic part of economic exchange in the contemporary world as money cannot be disentangled from its cultural matrix, it is clear that we must see economics as part of culture, not as a separate sphere of human activity. Economic systems, such as 'capitalism', or concepts such as 'profit', are highly culturally variable (Hampden-Turner and Trompenaars 1993).

That is, while economic trajectories are specific and historically-situated, the fact that they are constituted within - and as part of - a broader cultural matrix is an intrinsic part of that historical specificity. This is implicit in the understanding of the 'periods of human history' used by every economist, historian, archaeologist or anthropologist. Thus, if we wish to define - for instance - the medieval period in Europe, this is conventionally done partly by reference to its cultural specifics.

This realisation, backed up by decades of historical, anthropological and other studies, of course undermines the assertion that economic factors underlie all other forms of human activity. If economic activity always takes place within - and is permeated by - culture, then this implies that these cultural contexts not only permeate but also precede it. If they did not, then the economic forms concerned - such as the banknote in my earlier example - would hold no meaning for the actors involved.

Thus, all economic interactions imply prior cultural understanding. Such cultural categories can themselves be the topic of negotiation, or debate. These categories may encompass what one or another actor involved would characterise as misunderstandings or even deceptions, but that is perhaps the nature of inter-cultural contacts in general.

To return to the example of money for one last time, money-based exchanges could not function without a prior understanding of cultural categories. These include such basic issues as what are 'money', 'value' and 'exchange'. Without these, economic activity is impossible. But if all economic activity implies the pre-existence of its own cultural contexts, how can economic factors be said to bring these cultural contexts into existence? This would require the argument that subsequent changes were brought about by the preceding cultural contexts required for their own existence, which is clearly illogical.

Consequently, economic activity cannot be claimed as a 'base' upon which other aspects of social and political activity are constructed. Rather, economic factors must be seen as a part of a broader set of reflexively-related aspects of communities, including culture.

Of course, this does not mean that all the material commodities of trade (for example) are 'cultural products' in their entirety (cf. Appadurai 1986, Gudemann 1986). Nor does it mean that economic factors are not 'real' in the ways that they affect actors. But it does imply that understanding of the material world, along with forms of economic practice, always takes place 'within' a culture.

As prices, values, economic attitudes, specific modes and means of exchange (such as forms of money) and the physical settings of economic practice are all 'encultured' in this way, 'economic factors' cannot be in any sense a base-line for human societies. Thus, for example, capitalism is a 'really existing' economic system, but it is also an aspect of culture, and so specific to particular times and places.[24]

A further consideration reinforces this view. If one wished to counter the argument that economic factors are so entirely encultured as to deny their primacy, then one would need to demonstrate that some forms of eco-

24 For a clear example of how, to some extent, similar economic changes have been articulated differently: KEMP (1985, 1993).

nomic activity were separate from culture. That is, it would be necessary to assert that actors involved were responding to some sort of essential and universal human need in a universal human manner (Burton 1990, Doyal and Gough 1991).

In this way, it might be claimed, economic activity might cater for needs that precede culture. However, although such pre-cultural precedence might be demonstrable in terms of some biological functions, it is hard to see what specifically economic practices would be encompassed within such a group of activities with no cultural component whatsoever.

A recognition of the encultured character of economic activity also excludes, of course, the argument that culture itself is an outcome of economic factors. If so, at what point in the past were economic factors giving rise to culture not 'encultured' themselves?

It could be claimed that 'if one looked far enough back in history' one would see that economics determined culture. This is not what the empirical evidence for the origins of human cultures shows. In archaeological terms the earliest evidence of cultural production (which is associated with the earliest known hominids) precedes exchange (Toth 1987). Exchange, when it begins to occur, originates within the (culturally-constructed) kinship network (Renfrew and Bahn 1996, ch. 9). Again, cultural precedence is implied in economic activity.

Consequently, the relationship between culture and economics refutes the possibility of subtle economic determinism. Obviously, this consolidates the arguments already made in relation to crude determinism as well. If economic activity takes place within, and is shaped by, cultural contexts, then it is more logical to seek the causes of economic change in cultural change than the opposite.

IX. Conclusion

We can see, therefore, that there are no grounds whatsoever for believing that material production and resource allocation determine the course of global history or world politics. No convincingly consistent correlations between large-scale economic change (in this sense) and large-scale political change have been demonstrated. Nor do such correlations seem at all likely in view of the encultured character of economic activity.

A recognition of the importance of cultural context to economics undermines any prospect of employing even subtle economic determinism to explain global history or world politics. All forms of economic determinism should, therefore, be rejected as invalid in the study of both subjects. Economic factors have undoubtedly played an important part in global history. Likewise economics plays a major role in world politics. But economic activity does not exist outside of culture.

In order to appreciate this role more fully and accurately, it is essential to begin by rejecting notions of economic determinism. We should instead look at the complex interplay of culture and economic activity and study the relationship between these, for instance through the role of language[25] and communication overall (Dark 1998, ch. 7). Current debates in Economics and cognate disciplines regarding the interplay of economic and non-economic factors have an important part to play here. Nor should it be supposed that those fields have nothing to gain - in either theoretical or purely methodological terms - from such a debate with historians and political scientists.[26]

The role of historical analysis in understanding the relationship between economic activity and culture is also highlighted by this discussion. Cultural contexts are important for the understanding of economics, but it is also necessary to remember that these contexts themselves are liable to change. Different aspects of culture may have dissimilar, even conflicting, effects. Cultures may be multi-faceted, with variants belonging to differing groups in society. So, factors such as gender, age, class, and geography may be associated with different forms of a single culture, or with different 'sub-cultures'. When cultural values are implicit they may have different effects from when they are formalised in institutions and law.[27] Obviously, this introduces a great complexity into the cultural analysis of economic forms and activities. This highlights, too, the context-specific character of culture. Both Economic History - and History more generally - may have an impor-

---

25 For one view, see JONES, in this volume.

26 For instance, Economists might find use for 'Regime Theory' developed in International Relations: HANSENCLEVER, MAYER and RITTBERGER (1996).

27 For example, CARSTENSEN and EPSTEIN in chapters 6 and 7 above in this volume).

tant role in elucidating such specifics in relation to issues of economic growth. Moreover, if we understand the relationship between economic change - including economic growth - and cultural change as interlinked, then we must recall that a similar relationship exists between socio-political and cultural change, and between socio-political and economic change. This highlights the need for a view of all these areas of human life which is neither 'static' nor exclusive. This, in turn, may suggest that the increasingly long-term timescales being used to understand socio-political and cultural change - and the theories developed to cope with this type of analysis- may have more general relevance to the study of economics (Dark 1998). Interestingly, these theories include perspectives (notably 'Macrodynamics') which highlight relationships between information, culture, structure and agency.

New and sophisticated theories to analyse these issues may enable us to explore the causes of large-scale change in a multi-scalar fashion, producing explanations on a number of levels which acknowledge the complexity of the phenomena which they investigate. They may permit us to integrate perspectives from many disciplines, recognising that other fields of study may have found means of breaking free of the unidisciplinary problems which hinder current studies. By encompassing theories which envisage active individuals, and encompass both their contexts and the networks of relations between individuals and organizations, we may move closer to comprehending the reflexive links between cultural, political and economic transformation.

These possibilities and this convergence of interest both suggest that further and intensified exchanges between disciplines and perspectives may be fruitful. Only through such multidisciplinary exchanges - and the formation of such interdisciplinary theoretical frameworks - will it, perhaps, be possible to gain a deeper and more satisfactory understanding of the relationship between culture, economic growth and either global history or world politics. Recent work in this area must encourage hope that progress is imminent. We may indeed be on the brink of unlocking what John Lewis Gaddis has called 'the tectonics' of large-scale change. These he sees as processes which lie beyond the normal reach of our perception, but which - reflexively with agency and historical chance - shape the large-scale trajectories of human history (Gaddis 1992, p. 155). Understanding these processes, if they exist, may be no mean goal. Nor is it merely of academic significance. The understanding of such processes may be the first step to the effective management of large-scale change, whether in relation to world politics or the international economy.

References

APPADURAI, A. (Ed.): *The Social Life of Things: Commodities in Cultural Perspective*, Cambridge (Cambridge University Press) 1986.

ARCHER, M.: *Culture and Agency*, Cambridge (Cambridge University Press) 1988.

ARCHER, M.: *Realist Social Theory: the Morphogenetic Approach*, Cambridge (Cambridge University Press) 1995.

ARRIGHI, G.: *The Long Twentieth Century*, London/New York (Verso) 1994.

BOYD, R., RICHERSON, P. J.: *Culture and Evolutionary Process,* Chicago (Univeristy of Chicago Press) 1992.

BURTON, J. W.: *Conflict: Human Needs Theory*, Basingstoke (Macmillan) 1990.

CHASE-DUNN, C.: *Global Formation, Structures of the World Economy*, Cambridge, Mass. (Basil Blackwell) 1990.

CHASE-DUNN, C., HALL, T. D.: *Rise and Demise*, Boulder, Col. (Westview Press) 1997.

CLARK, J. E., PARRY, W. J.: "Crafts specialization and cultural complexity", *Research in Economic Anthropology*, 12 (1990), pp. 289-346.

COLLINS, R., WALLER, D.: "What theories predicted the state breakdowns and the revolutions of the Soviet bloc", *Research in Social Movements, Conflicts and Change*, 14 (1992), pp. 31-47.

COX, R.: "Gramsci, hegemony and International Relations: an essay in method", *Millenniun*, 12.2 (1983), pp. 165-75.

COX, R.: *Production, Power and World Order*, New York (Columbia University Press) 1987.

COX, R. W., SINCLAIR, T. J. (Eds.): *Approaches to World Order*, Cambridge (Cambridge University Press) 1997.

CRIBB, J.: *Money. From Cowrie Shells to Credit Cards*, London (British Museum Press) 1986.

DARK, K. R.: *Theoretical Archaeology*, London (Duckworth) 1995.

DARK, K. R.: *The Waves of Time. Long-Term Change and International Relations*, London (Pinter/Cassell) 1998.

DARK, K. R. (with HARRIS, A. L.): *The New World and the New World Order*, Basingstoke/New York (Macmillan) 1996.

DOYAL, L., GOUGH, I.: *A Theory of Human Need*, Basingstoke (Macmillan) 1991.

EARLE, T. (Ed.): *Chiefdoms: Power, Economy and Ideology*, Cambridge (Cambridge University Press) 1991.

EARLE, T.: *How Chiefs Come to Power. The Political Economy in Prehistory*, Stanford, Cal. (Stanford University Press) 1997.

FRIEDMAN, J.: *Cultural Identity and Global Process*, London (Sage) 1994.

GADDIS, J. L.: *The United States and the End of the Cold War*, Oxford (Oxford University Press) 1992.

GAENSLEN, F.: "Culture and decision making in China, Japan, Russia, and the United States", *World Politics*, 39.1 (1986), pp. 78-103 .

GIDDENS, A.: *Contemporary Critique of Historical Materialism*, Cambridge (Cambridge University Press) 2nd ed. 1981.

GIDDENS, A.: *The Constitution of Society*, Cambridge (Cambridge University Press) 1984.

GILPIN, R.: *War and Change in World Politics*, Cambridge (Cambridge University Press) 1981.

GILPIN, R.: "Economic evolution of national systems", *International Studies Quarterly*, 40 (1996), pp. 411-31.

GOLDSTONE, J. A.: "Cultural orthodoxy, risk and innovation: the divergence between east and west in the early modern world", *Sociological Theory*, 5 (1987), pp. 119-35.

GUDEMANN, S.: *Economics as Culture: Models and Metaphors of Livelihood*, London (Routledge and Kegan Paul) 1986.

HALLIDAY, F.: *Rethinking International Relations*, London (Pinter) 1994.

HAMPDEN-TURNER, C., TROMPENAARS, F.: *The Seven Cultures of Capitalism*, New York (Doubleday) 1993.

HANSENCLEVER, A., MAYER, P., RITTBERGER, V.: "Interests, power, knowledge: the study of international regimes", *Mershon International Studies Review*, 40.2 (1996), pp. 177-228.

HARRIS, A. L.: "Long term perspectives on International Relations theory, the United States and the end of the Cold War", *Contemporary Political Studies*, (1996), pp. 13-20.

HARRIS, M.: *Cultural Materialism*, New York (Random House) 1979.

HERRIN, J.: *The Formation of Christendom*, Oxford (Basil Blackwell) 1987.

HODGES, R., WHITEHOUSE, D.: *Mohammed, Charlemagne and the Origins of Europe*, London (Duckworth) 1983.

HOFSTEDE, G.: *Cultures and Organizations: the Software of the Mind*, New York (McGraw Hill) 1994.

JONES, R. J. B.: *Globalization and Interdependence in the International Political Economy*, London (Pinter) 1995.

KEMP, T.: *Indistrialization in Nineteenth-Century Europe*, London, (Longman) 2nd ed. 1985.

KEMP, T.: *Historical Patterns of Industrialization*, London (Longman) 2nd ed. 1993.

KENNEDY, P.: *The Rise and Fall of the Great Powers*, London (Unwin Hyman) 1989.

KENNEDY, P.: *Preparing for the Twenty First Century*, New York (Fontana) 1993.

KRATOCHWIL, F.: *Rules, Norms and Decisions*, Cambridge (Cambridge University Press) 1989.

KRATOCHWIL, F.: "The embarrassment of changes: neo-Realism as a science of realpolitik without politics", *Review of International Studies*, 19.1 (1993), pp. 65-86.

MILLETT, M.: *The Romanization of Britain*, Cambridge (Cambridge University Press) 1990.

MODELSKI, G.: *Long Cycles in World Politics*, London/Seattle (University of Washington Press) 1987.

MODELSKI, G.: "Evolutionary paradigm for global politics", *International Studies Quarterly* 40 (1996), pp. 321-42 .

MODELSKI, G., THOMPSON, W. R.: *Leading Sectors and World Powers*, Columbia, Cal. (University of South Carolina Press) 1995.

NAROTZSKY, S.: *New Directions in Economic Anthropology*, London (Pluto Press) 1997.

OLSEN, M.: *The Rise and Decline of Nations*, New Haven (Yale University Press) 1982.

PARKER, G. (Ed.): *The Times Atlas of World History*, London (Times) 4th ed. 1993.

POUNDS, N. J. G.: *An Economic History of Medieval Europe*, London (Longman) 2nd ed. 1994.

RENFREW, C., SHENNAN, S. (Eds.): *Ranking, Resource and Exchange*, Cambridge (Cambridge University Press) 1982.

RENFREW, C., BAHN, P.: *Archaeology. Theories, Methods and Practice*, London (Thames and Hudson) 2nd ed. 1996.

ROESDAHL, E.: *The Vikings*, Harmondsworth (Penguin) 1991.

SANDERSON, S. K. (Ed.): *Civilizations and World Systems: Two Approaches to the Study of World-Historical Change*, Walnut-Creek, Cal. (Altamira Press) 1995.

SMITH, H.: "Marxism and International Relations Theory", in: A. J. GROOM, M. LIGHT (Eds.): *Contemporary International Relations: A Guide to Theory*, London (Pinter) 1994, pp. 142-55.

SPIVEY, N., STODDART, S.: *Etruscan Italy*, London (Batsford) 1994.

TAYLOR, P. J.: *Political Geography*, London (Longman) 2nd ed. 1989.

THOMAS, N.: *Entangled Objects: Exchange, Material Culture and Colonialism in the Pacific*, Cambridge, Mass. (Harvard University Press) 1991.

TOTH, N.: "The first technology", *Scientific American*, 256.4 (1987), pp. 104-13.
WALLERSTEIN, I.: *The Modern World System*, New York (Academic Press) 3 vols. 1974-88.
WEISS, L., HOBSON, J.: *States and Economic Development: a Comparative Historical Approach*, Cambridge (Polity) 1995.
WILLIAMS, J. (Ed.): *Money: a History*, London (British Museum Press) 1997.
ZACHER, M. W., MATTHEW, R. A.: "Liberal international theory: common threads, divergent strands", in: C. KEGLEY (Ed.): *Controversies in International Relations Theory*, Basingstoke (Macmillan) 1995, pp. 107-19.

Chapter 9

The Case for a Shared World Language

ERIC L. JONES

I. Introduction

Whereas the biologist, J. B. S. Haldane, could say that the mind of the Creator showed 'an inordinate fondness for beetles', a social scientist might say that it showed an inordinate fondness for languages.[1] There may have been 10,000-15,000 languages in prehistoric times, although today there are commonly said to be 6,000 or 6,500 and the number is decreasing fast.

---

1 This essay was conceived at the Institute for Advanced Study, Berlin. I have benefited, there and elsewhere, from listening to Kate Burridge, Beth Crompton, David Crystal, Hans Magnus Enzensberger, Marc Fumaroli, John Gatt-Rutter, David Henderson, Aneurin Hughes, Sylvia Jones, Reinhart Meyer-Kalkus and Ekkehart Schlicht, although much more than the usual disclaimer applies.

Linguists' interest in language for its own sake leads them to deplore this decline and recommend preserving the most minor remaining languages. Moreover some governments support national languages, at times by discriminating explicitly against others. It will be urged here that these Protectionist efforts are undesirable. The likely benefits of the world adopting a *lingua franca* outweigh the likely costs.

This chapter thus argues that it is reasonable to expose the costs of language diversity and question the opinion that all languages are worth retaining. It urges the advantages of a global *lingua franca*, in particular English; criticises interventions designed to preserve other languages, notably French; discusses costs of preservation and diversity; and points out the contingent nature of language, supporting this by describing the long-run history of language consolidation. The paradoxical role of trade in encouraging simultaneously a proliferation of states and the spread of a shared language is also discussed.

Although any language might in principle fulfil the role of *lingua franca*, the market is selecting English, which is becoming the vehicle of a common world culture. English is an 'open' language, carries the single largest stock of knowledge and creates network effects because of the scale on which it is already spoken. Exclusion from learning English would marginalise people when perhaps one-quarter of the world's population is coming together to speak it. The Black South African writer Es'kia Mphahlele poignantly notes that, because it widens his constituency, "English is therefore tied up with the Black man's efforts to liberate himself" (quoted in Honey 1997, p. 257).

English is the first major language with more second- and third-language speakers than native speakers. Far from being driven by 'linguistic imperialism', English is no longer wholly in the charge of its native speakers. Nor does it depend directly on political power, except perhaps by default, as in the countries of the Former Soviet Union, where the collapse of communism has led to a dramatic increase in the teaching of English, followed by German, with French as a distant third (Singer 1998). What counts most in the choice of English as *lingua franca* is the involvement of the English-speaking countries in international economic integration. Wide diffusion means that canons of grammar, the lexicon and especially pronunciation will deviate from the forms associated with English in Britain and the United States. Nevertheless, modern communications and the desire for mutual intelligibility seem likely to prevent the language devolving into local languages the way Latin once did.

Instances will be assembled here to create a mosaic of the 'cultural wars' over linguistic issues; the full picture would require a book.[2] The case against officially encouraging language diversity will then be indicated. A shared language enlarges trade by reducing transaction costs. Its extension should help to curb rent-seeking by linguistic specialists and ethnolinguistic groups. Although extra languages are not costless and encourage a tribal frame of mind, we should immediately confirm that no suggestion will be entertained here of banning any language: it would be inconsistent to protest at discrimination against one language only to propose this on behalf of another. Let the market decide, which is merely to say, let us allow individuals the freedom to choose which language or languages they wish to speak. As the history of pidgins demonstrates, people are adept at making themselves understood. We can be confident that the advantages of spontaneous co-ordination will be widely recognised.

To avoid misunderstandings, the point should be reiterated that the forcible replacement of any language by any other is not what is being canvassed. If alternatives to a shared language prove valuable for particular purposes, they will remain in use. If important ideas are locked up in a given language and cannot be translated, the language will presumably survive - though if the ideas defy translation they can scarcely be of value to a wider community. Diversity, then, is not something to be eliminated but neither is it to be fostered where doing so would create negative externalities, such as by making it harder for some people to enter the community of shared language. This is precisely what is done by those native English speakers who impose bilingual education on migrant children, despite the wishes of many parents. Put another way, language consolidation should not be hindered, and no-one should be coerced nor scarce resources be actively expended to promote substitutes for the language (currently English) which offers the best opportunity for human interaction and greatest access to the stock of human knowledge.

Although the ramifications of this topic are so wide that any strict cost:benefit analysis would be forlorn, the economic and cultural benefits of a shared tongue are clear. Working towards a common standard has however become unfashionable. Even in English-speaking countries like Australia, Canada and the United States a political preference for cultural diversity runs counter to it. Why is the spread of a shared language, in practice

2 Some additional examples are given in JONES (1995b).

English, so much opposed in some quarters and some countries, although (it proves instructive to note) by no means in all? Those who support language diversity pride themselves on their realism. But theirs is an unhistorical view: language, like culture, is highly contingent. The long-term trend has been towards consolidation and many existing languages, perhaps especially those used by large populations, are comparatively recent and syncretic artefacts.

II. The Economics of Language

The economics of language is a new subfield. Grin estimates there are scarcely more than one hundred papers on the economics of language proper (Grin 1996b, p. 18). Over half are studies of linguistic aspects of the socio-economic status of immigrants. A high proportion is inspired by Canadian or Quebecois issues. Almost none touches on global matters, which may explain why assertions in favour of multiple languages have attracted little scrutiny from economists. We are therefore obliged to consider the less technical pronouncements of specialists in linguistics, bureaucrats, politicians, journalists and so forth; these are the people whose views matter because they form language policy and are responsible for expending resources on it. The rise of cultural protectionism, of which language protectionism is taken to be a part, may however attract more economists to the topic in future.

Linguists themselves seem not to mention transaction costs and the very, very few language economists who touch on them rather surprisingly defend the omission. Arcand, for example, asserts that an information-theoretic approach is superior to the transaction-cost approach associated with neo-institutional economics (Arcand 1996). He draws on claims by Stiglitz about the greater specificity of the information paradigm. Stiglitz takes institutions as endogenous, altering to reflect changing information costs. It is not clear that institutions are thus determined, with only a lag (of unspecified duration) before they adjust to changes in the relative price of information. Transaction cost is a more general concept which requires no such heroic assumption. The present paper takes it for granted that costs should be minimised whenever possible, consistent with maintaining individual linguistic freedom. The natural analogy is with Free Trade and Protection, where the case for openness needs constantly to be reaffirmed.

Linguists, then, take almost no account of costs. On the other hand, Grin, who has written the most comprehensive reviews of language economics, chides economists for being concerned with little else (Grin 1992, Grin 1994, Grin 1996a). He correctly observes that they neglect the non-economic functions of language. He refers to 'language rights' and is among the majority who regard the survival of minority languages as *ipso facto* valuable. In essence he accepts the existing (actually the surviving) pattern of language diversity. His work is therefore 'realistic' in taking account of the loyalties of speakers of particular languages and going on to deal with the decision-making (language planning) required to accommodate competing claims. The underlying question remains, are the non-economic functions of language worth the risks of sundering peoples that they carry with them? A common language is neither a necessary nor a sufficient condition for peace - consider the Serbs and Croats - but language differences make communication harder and breaches harder to heal.

Grin is conscious of the conflicts that arise and does recommend, instead of compulsion, incentives to persuade individuals to adopt languages they would not otherwise choose, e.g. Irish in Ireland. Yet his approach eschews a monolingual solution or the priority of teaching the most widely-spoken language. Here, on the other hand, while loyalties to existing languages are of course recognised, diversity is seen primarily as a burden, a barrier to the free market in ideas, and additional fuel for cultural and ethnic conflagrations. In short, the observed pattern of languages is not seen as necessarily desirable. The economic and cultural benefits of mutual intelligibility amongst the largest number of people come first.

III. Arguments for Language Diversity

The tendency among those who seek to block language consolidation is to assume that the cultures which with particular languages are associated are immutable and desirable. The characteristics of cultures at any one time, and the differences among them, always impress observers of this type. Their view, which I have termed 'cultural fixity', is misleading (Jones

1995a). It is chronocentric because it treats the period in which the observer lives as the culmination of history. Examined historically, cultures can be seen instead to have changed and be changing endlessly. Ironically, the cultural fixity school is the first to lament that history has speeded up, as shown by the accelerating rate of the language extinctions which it deplores.

The fallacy of the cultural fixity position lies in assuming that culture is logically prior to the market and unaffected by it. Cross-sectional observation serves to conceal the process of change, including economically-driven change, and the feedback effect of the market on culture. In the circumstances, thinking of any language as fixed, irreplaceable (a false analogy with biological species is common) and worth preserving at considerable cost in public money, not to mention by curtailing other people's freedom to choose a more mainstream language, is at best somewhat whimsical.

The alternative position, that cultural convergence is occurring and is desirable, does not mean mistaking habits like wearing blue jeans, listening to rap or drinking Coca Cola for evidence that deeper features must be converging, especially political and legal ones. Off duty, so to speak, members of the IRA and the Protestant militias consume similar brands without becoming matey. Despite that, and despite the apparent exceptions, a common style blurs the stigmata of tribalism. There have always been bitter wars between brothers but there have also been successful reunions, for instance in England and the United States after their respective civil wars. A shared language keeps alight hopes of communicating and eventually merging again, Ulster intransigence and the like notwithstanding. Bear in mind the degree of Preference Falsification to be expected in such places, where it is dangerous to announce any genuine cultural preference (Kuran 1995).

Among linguists received opinion is that languages are equal for all purposes or in a slightly weaker version of the hypothesis are instantly (and by implication costlessly) adaptable to every social need. Cultural relativism leads linguists to resist the idea that the intellectual function of Western languages has special merit, since to admit this would 'privilege' them and be 'culturocentric' (Honey 1997, p. 97). Yet, as Honey has demonstrated, standard languages are 'open' to new influences and ideas, whereas minor languages tend, like dialects, to be 'closed'. Scientific terms are hard to incorporate in either minor languages or dialects. Vocabularies of only a few thousand words are simply swamped when faced with incorporating the huge vocabulary of modernity and when the effort is successful the current generation of speakers is still likely to be disadvantaged. Even countries where an appropriate vocabulary has been created, for instance Germany and Japan, find it easier to keep pace with the advance of knowledge by adopting English-language textbooks for graduate courses, a practice extended in Scandinavian countries to Honours and even undergraduate levels.

Honey asks how rational is it for developing countries to devote scarce resources to the enormous effort of creating the terms needed to translate, say, secondary textbooks in chemistry and physics into every local tongue, as language diversifiers have been known to demand (Honey 1997, p. 255). We may merely reaffirm that English is on the receptive side of the language divide and is freely chosen by scientists and others from all countries eager to share in and contribute to the common stock of knowledge. Honey exhorts us not to cling to each and every dialect: "we should be ready to move away from the old, arbitrarily allocated, forms of local community, built on the enforced sociability of common poverty or common dangers... and into kinds of association based on freedom of choice" (Honey 1997, p. 240). Where minority languages have likewise depended on involuntary segregation, perhaps brought about in the past by high transport costs or the actions of nationalist politicians, continued intervention to retain them is similarly unwarranted.

Political supporters of national (as opposed to global) and local (as opposed to national or global) languages nevertheless resist the incursion of more widespread languages as adamantly, sometimes as violently, as speakers of regional dialects resist standard English. Whether the aim of diversifiers is to limit the spread of a *lingua franca* in general, or of English in particular, or to discriminate against any widely-known language in favour of some minor one or even a dead language, they tend to make similar points. They 'privilege' the existing pattern of diversity in categorical but mystical terms.

Consider what was said by Eammon de Valera, President of Ireland: "without a language, without a country" (*The Times* 9.11.1996). The rejoinder of R. C. McCormick, who was obliged to learn Irish at school, is, "what romantic and dangerous nonsense". Boutros Boutros-Ghali, formerly secretary-general of the U.N. and now of the Francophone Agency, has extolled the movement to entrench the use of French world-wide in the words, "it should become a way of defending cultural diversity. If everybody... speaks the same language... we risk having a global fascist-type regime" and "cultural diversity and multi-lingualism... constitute the true quality of the human heritage" (*International Herald Tribune* 14.11.1997).

And the influential linguist David Crystal has claimed that "if everybody speaks English we all have a great time understanding each other but our identities go down (sic) the melting pot," and "suffice to say we should all learn a language that isn't English out of a sense of principle," without explaining what the principle is nor how learning a new language can bolster one's sense of identity (*The Australlian* 12.7.1997).

The French example, detailed below, is paramount among efforts to frustrate choice, but comparable tendencies are evident elsewhere. For example, when the President of the Bundesrepublik recommended that German education should use more English in order to attract a greater share of foreign students he encountered stiff opposition (*Der Tagespiel* 6.11.1997; *Frankfurter Allgemeine Zeitung* 6.11.1997). The riposte was that Europe's cultures need defending against America's, of which they can otherwise be only second-rate copies. Permission is required in some German universities to write dissertations in English on the grounds that works in German and networks of German scholars will not otherwise be cited. This places the national language above educational values: it conjures up no generous vision of scholars moving freely about the world, giving their allegiance more to scholarship than to country. Yet in practice an international 'floating elite' is emerging and its inter-connectedness - not to mention its reliance on English - has been much boosted by the Internet. Russians have switched to the Roman alphabet because the Internet does not employ Cyrillic. English language Internet sites outnumber by 20:1 those in all other languages combined.

IV. Policies to Enforce Language Diversity

Now that telecommunications have reduced the cost of international transmissions and eroded the natural protection of distance, language issues are coming to the fore. Demands for cultural protection are increasing, spurred by NGOs (non-governmental organisations) and some politicians in France, Canada and Australia. An emotive appeal is made to undefined and - given the syncretic nature of all cultures - historically dubious 'cultural identities,' as well as to the rankest nationalism. The effect of exempting cultural products from international trade agreements, imposing local content laws, and so forth, is to reduce consumer choice in favour of otherwise uncompetitive local producers. Requiring the use of local languages has the force of reintroducing the otherwise obsolescent barrier of distance.

Non-market interventions via language planning have sparked a dispute between Grin and Breton (Grin 1994, p. 28-9). Breton allegedly regards language planning as a form of nationalism, that is as investment in ethnicity or nationality secured by confiscating the assets of others. (The effect is to reduce the value of languages previously spoken). Grin's counter is that had the initial distribution of languages reflected only unhampered market forces, it might indeed have represented an optimal allocation. But, he says, more than the market has been involved and he accuses Breton of self-contradiction by relying on market forces to explain certain patterns of language use while citing non-market behaviours, such as military intervention, to account for others. If even part of the distribution was produced by non-market forces, says Grin, Breton should not object to the use of other non-market procedures (i.e. language planning) to correct it. This seems a weak defence of intervention, open to the objection that two wrongs do not make a right.

Interventions are widely approved in Europe. A survey of people between 15 and 35 in five European countries found that 76% agreed with maintaining a diversity of languages.[3] The European Union (EU) intends to spend $US19 million to preserve Europe's multilingualism, apparently because anything else would be 'unfair' to non-English speakers. This is government, or supra-government, spending: multinational companies accept no such liability when they do business and ironically much of the work of the European Commission itself is carried on in English or French. The EU's commitment to language equality is in any case unlikely to survive the incorporation of several new states and is at variance with arguments for European Monetary Union - i.e. that this will reduce transaction costs. As Dennis Mueller observes, "instead of developing a new language that all Europeans would use, existing languages are defended by forcing their use

3 Seventy per cent of respondents outside Britain nevertheless claimed to be fluent in English, *The European* 30.1.1997.

on individuals, and prohibiting the use of competing languages" (Mueller 1996, p. 37).[4]

Attempts to abolish choice are still being made in country after country. The tiniest sample of episodes in 1996 and 1997 follows: two companies and an American university were taken to court in France for having web-sites solely in English (*The Australian* 12.3.1996 and 21.1.97; *Financial Times* 1.3.1997). The Mayor of Moscow, having campaigned to persuade Muscovites to switch back from Coca Cola and hamburgers to kvas and blinis, decreed the banning of foreign (especially English) terms in shops because they displace 'authentic' Russian culture. Vietnam removed foreign company names from buildings and billboards to control 'social evils' and preserve the Vietnamese language. The Algerian government, seeking to distance itself from the French-speaking governing class, decreed Arabic as the official language (which upset not only French speakers but speakers of Berber as well).

Efforts are likewise being made to counter the shrinkage of minor languages, as well as to resurrect dead ones (an option which gives the lie to 'Green Linguistics' analogies between languages and species). UNESCO and the UN support a 'Language Rights' Movement. There is a UNESCO Clearing House for Endangered Languages in Tokyo and the EU has an Office of Lesser-used Languages in Dublin. Cornish, the last speaker of which died in 1777, has been revived as an Advanced Level examination subject in England. In Australia, Peter Muhlhausler, who teaches linguistics in Adelaide, is seeking to revive as an undergraduate course, Kaurna, the last speaker of which died in the 1920s. The South Australian Department of Education wishes this language to be taught by aboriginal teachers (who would first have to learn it) in kindergartens, primary schools and secondary schools.

Muhlhausler claims that the loss of a language means the loss of identity, disorienting people and "often" leading to higher mortality rates and more suicides (*The Australian* 6.8.1997). It is not clear how reviving a language dead for seventy years would remedy this. Whereas studying extinct languages is of scholarly interest, teaching them to schoolchildren appears to serve little educational purpose, especially where there is no

---

4 Mueller does not explain why a new language is desirable; perhaps his position is that only a new Esperanto could overcome the ancient grudges between existing language communities.

literature (Cornish has a small literature, though mostly mystery plays, some of which turn out to be literal translations from English). The opportunity cost should surely be considered. As McCormick commented on the obligatory teaching of Irish, "like most attempts to create a culture by imposing a language, it was a complete waste of time and money... English is the world language and most foreigners rightly spend a lot of time and money learning it, not learning a dead language such as Irish" (*The Times* 9.11.1996).

V. Cultural Protection: The Case of French

Efforts to block English in favour of French most clearly exemplify cultural protectionism (*The Independent* 11/11/97; *International Herald Tribune* 14/11/97 and 16/12/97; *The Economist* 22/11/97; and *Guardian Weekly*, 23/11/97).[5] The efforts include defending the 'purity' of French by legislating against loan-words, which generates absurdity and fails to take into account what Crystal points out: that the chances of its wider adoption were restricted when French opted to be a "closed" language rather than a "vacuum-cleaner" like English (Crystal 1997).[6] France spends almost US$1 billion p.a. to spread French civilisation and language around the world: of this, some $88 million is spent on the Francophone Agency and $100 million on Alliance Francaise centres. Political jockeying is involved: for in-

5 The unhappy background to French attitudes is described by DOMINIQUE MOISI (1998). In Germany language protectionism may again be on the rise, together with nationalism; a 'Club for the Preservation of the German Language' has been founded by a Professor at Dortmund University (*The Age*, 6/2/98). A graphic illustration of the true status of French and German appears in *The Economist Atlas* (1989, p. 116). The minority status of French is further apparent from the observation that there are more speakers of Portuguese in Brazil than French-speakers in the world. Two-thirds of people learning German are localised in Eastern Europe and the Former Soviet Union, while English proves to be the first or second language taught in sixteen countries examined by the Goethe Institute. SINGER (1998, p. 22).

6 Linguistic purism has been shown to endanger the revitalisation of languages DORIAN (1994, pp. 479-494).

stance Jacques Chirac vetoed the appointment of a former Danish foreign minister as secretary-general of NATO on the sole grounds that his French was not good enough to preserve it as one of NATO's official languages. The pro-French campaign was marked in 1997 by the Seventh Francophone Summit conference which took place in Vietnam (where fewer than 0.5% of the population speak French), at a cost of $17 million. Forty-six countries were represented, including some where the language is not French.

The true aim of attempts to extend the use of French is to capture rents which increasingly accrue to users of English. Despite government subsidies to local-language film producers, and in spite of the 'anti-capitalist' hostility of many intellectuals to any cultural work that turns a profit, there is in continental Europe a sizeable market for Hollywood films and English-language books. This is part of what is contested. Little credit seems to be given to the positive reasons for the success of novels and films in English. Where no single alternative to English is acceptable to all, not even French, the reserve protectionist position is to support any and every local language against the consumer's free choice of English. Presumably the calculation is that half a loaf is better than a crust.

VI. Costs of Protection

A straightforward illustration of the costs associated with using more than one language is the expense of translation in the EU. 1,700 of the EU's staff are translators, a formidable trade union that produces over one million pages p.a. (Hughes 1997; *The European* 30.1.97). Its labours are not always successful: a legal suit affecting billions of pounds in customs duty which came before the European Court of Justice hinged on the meaning of the word 'them' in French and English (*The Spectator* 1.3.97). Lawyers' fees for shepherding this case inconclusively through the British courts came to one million pounds. Translation costs could be minimised if member states of the EU made a concerted effort to teach all citizens a common language. But, as Keynes wrote in *The Economic Consequences of the Peace*, "men have devised ways to impoverish themselves and one another; and prefer collective animosities to individual happiness".

As an example of the deadweight costs imposed by attempts to enforce bilingualism, consider the expenditure on public signs in English-speaking parts of Wales, with TACSI next to TAXI and BEICS next to cycles. (Yet, as Kingsley Amis wryly notes, "the words that matter, like DANGER and STOP and NO RIGHT TURN, are in English only" (Amis 1992, p. 132). The matter becomes more invidious when Welsh is insisted on as a condition of employment in the English-speaking parts of Wales. This allows some people privileged access to jobs, whether or not their technical qualifications are the best. It closes out others altogether. Costs rise still further where there is great language diversity but no functioning *lingua franca*. A sad example comes from New York, where translation services in the medical system are being overwhelmed by the growing number of patients who speak little or no English (*International Herald and Tribune* 24.11.97). In Greater New York hundreds of languages are spoken; 14% of the population speaks a language other than English at home. Medical care and disease control are suffering.

Maintaining the use of Icelandic, which is spoken by only 0.005% of humanity, for Iceland's population of under 270,000 has been calculated to absorb 3-3.5% of GDP (*The Economist* 3.1.98). The cost of Quebec's language policies has been estimated at (under) 0.5% of GDP (Grin 1996a, p. 11). Since even 0.1% of GDP would buy a number of schools and hospitals, such proportions are not as insignificant as they look. There is also a loss of personal freedom from the enforcement of the use of French by Quebec's Commission to Protect the French Language (*Guardian Weekly* 11.8.96). Half-a-million Quebecois have emigrated during the past thirty years and between 1976 and 1981 one hundred head offices of Anglophone companies were relocated from Montreal. Effects like these are hard to allow for in calculating the costs of language policies.

An econometric study of African countries since 1945 by Easterly and Levine is an apt example of the costs of using multiple languages (Easterly and Levine 1997). The authors employed an ethnolinguistic index and found that diversity has been the central factor impeding the choice of satisfactory development policies. They found language diversity to be positively correlated with the black market premium, electrical system losses and the percentage of roads unpaved, and negatively correlated with school attainment, financial depth and the number of telephones per worker. According to the model used, these factors have growth or income effects. Yet such an elaborate study may not have been strictly necessary: as Honey remarks, anyone who thinks language diversity is not disunifying should consider Belgium or Canada (Honey 1997, p. 241).

VII. The Contingent Character of Language

The contingent nature of cultures and languages is illustrated in the historical section that follows. Consider the claim by Plamenatz that, "men... are not mere competitors, however benevolent, in a market for the supply of personal wants; they are members of society, and their hopes and feelings, both for themselves and others, would not be what they are apart from their group loyalties" (quoted in Basu, Jones and Schlicht 1987, p. 8). This emphasis on societies (or cultures) is correct only at a given moment. An historical view shows that, despite some remarkable examples of stickiness, group loyalties underpinning cultures vary over time for many reasons. The languages associated with them alter too; they have no celestial warrant and striving to preserve them is surely a nugatory exercise.

Appeals to 'identity' are ill-considered, implying as they do that people are happy prisoners of their original languages and should be left in their cells. The history of voluntary migration shows this to be incorrect. However inconvenient it may be to political nationalists and language purists, it is possible to hold more than one allegiance, for instance to country and the (Roman) Catholic church. Educated people increasingly shift between local affinities and membership of the international 'invisible colleges' that nowadays communicate chiefly in English.

The argument of this chapter is therefore that incurring costs on behalf of particular cultures or languages risks depressing economic growth, stunting cultural exchange, and fomenting collective animosities. Economists are likely to be suspicious of the alternative, which might be described as language monopoly. A language monopoly is, however, not a problem in itself, since language is merely a mode of transmission. Languages are codes. Employing more than one is a cost to be reduced. There would undoubtedly be an initial advantage for certain cultural producers if the whole world learned to speak their language (unless that language were, implausibly, an invented one). But the gains in respect of trade, peace and cultural access would surely outweigh such a passing effect. Plenty of opportunities would remain for the suppliers of goods and services to compete, free from the burdens of life in a Tower of Babel.

VIII. The Very Long Term

In the surprisingly thin literature of the economics of language discussion of a shared world language has been dismissed as uninteresting. This is an odd charge. The limiting case helps to spotlight forces tending towards either monolingualism or infinite fragmentation, while a study of the long-term reveals pressures obscured at any one period. The approach counteracts the presentism of debates about language choice. A second charge levelled against proposals for a shared world language is lack of realism. We are thus enjoined to accept as permanent the present state of the tide of linguistic change, whereas in reality languages are transient artefacts and their present distribution can claim no finality.

The number and distribution of languages is in an extreme state of disequilibrium. The course of change may be from a fragmentation that was almost at the level of one village, one language; via the present, with its set of widely-spoken languages (English of course being much the commonest when second- and third-language speakers are taken into account) and its moribund tail of minor tongues; towards a future of increasing consolidation, a more generally shared language, and conceivably at last unilingualism.

As the geographical range of *Homo sapiens* expanded over many thousands of years, small groups nevertheless settled and lived out their lives within a dozen miles of their birthplace (Diamond 1992, p. 198-9 and 225-49).[7] Tiny populations had few distant contacts and each developed a culture and a language. In old-settled regions much of this diversity has been erased during the last five thousand years by the expansion of centralised empires. The most recently occupied areas, New Guinea and the Americas,

7 The following account owes most to Diamond's bold conceptualisation though it is fair to note that his views are not uncontested; other authors find there to be no real means of reconstructing early language distributions. See e.g. the exchange in *Nature* 391 (5.2.98), p. 547, and DIXON (1998).

came to hold about half the world's languages. New Guinea, where stone-age technology, political and demographic isolation, and xenophobia, persisted into the twentieth century, gives us, according to Diamond, "a last glimpse of what the rest of the world used to be like" (Diamond 1992, p. 199).

Almost one thousand mutually unintelligible languages, including dozens with no relation to any other, are still spoken in New Guinea, which is only the size of Texas. Elsewhere, and no doubt from now on in New Guinea itself, a far smaller number of languages has prevailed. Larger and larger areas succumbed to some conqueror's tongue. Successive empires were bigger than their predecessors and contained bigger populations (Goudsblom, Jones and Mennell 1996, pp. 63-81; Taagepera 1978). Indo-European languages are prominent among those that came in this way to dominate wide areas including, once European powers acquired maritime empires, vast zones outside their continent of origin. More than mere demographic expansion was accordingly involved. The rise of Europe involved trade expansion beyond the bounds of empire. Commerce inspired the adoption of Western European languages, especially English. Learning one language need not mean abandoning another, but that sometimes happened, as when the children of non-English immigrants to the United States let lapse the languages of their parents. As Bismarck said, the most significant element in world history is that Americans speak English.

"Whenever you find the same language or related languages spoken over a wide area," states Diamond, "you know that the clock of language evolution must have been restarted recently. That is, one language must have spread recently, eliminated other languages, and started to differentiate all over again" (Diamond 1992, pp. 231-2). This rather loose transfer of evolutionary theory to social science implies a biologist's extravagant chronology. The type specimen is Latin, the basis of the Romance languages that slowly began to separate out from it and from one another soon after the Fall of Rome - though much later they were still engaged in replacing Celtic languages, like Breton, that Latin itself had never entirely supplanted.[8]

8 In the 1860s ten per cent of Frenchmen still did not speak French, let alone Latin, while the Marxist theorist Gramsci welcomed the eventual development of modern Italian because its lack had created friction, "particularly among the popular masses." [Quoted by HONEY (1997, p. 69)]

The branching of Latin into the Romance languages is often explained as a consequence of Rome's loss of power. This neglects the role of the market. Had transport and communications reached a sufficient level to sustain a large volume of trade through the Dark Ages, Latin might have survived, even expanded, as a *lingua franca* regardless of Rome's political collapse. The point is significant in view of frequent extrapolations of the supposed relationship between language and power, specifically the modern assertion that English is the global language only because the United States is a superpower. This does not necessarily follow. Language may have become substantially independent of power. The scale on which English is being used and the soaring number of exchanges of all kinds following the revolution in information technology are historically unprecedented and may lock in English.

The rise of European nationalism exemplifed simultaneous centrifugal and centripetal forces. National languages had less scope than the Latin of Imperial Rome, yet they were unifying 'locally' in that they established one language where more than one, and many dialects, had otherwise survived the spread of Latin or emerged subsequent to its decline. Each nation-state created an educational system to help homogenise its population. But although up to a point nationalism did produce language consolidation, it also erected barriers at the next level up - between national languages. Efforts at linguistic colonisation were vigorous. Thus Austro-Hungary carried out a brutal campaign before 1914 to Germanise or Hungarianise its respective parts, while Germany put down minority languages even more savagely. After 1918 German was stamped out again in some areas, only to lead once more to revengeful Germanisation during the Second World War. It may turn out that we should view the nationalistic phase as a stunted and somewhat malign staging post on the way to the larger process of unification now made possible by international economic integration.

The converse of consolidation is language extinction, the rate of which likewise suggests that the modern situation is unprecedented. The consensus is that half the total of 6,000 or so languages will disappear before A.D. 2100. Crystal however reports estimates that project loss as high as eighty per cent within a century, and McKay one of ninety per cent, while a prediction at the other extreme says that only between 5 per cent and ten per cent will vanish (Crystal 1997, p. 17; McKay 1996, p. 4; and Honey 1997, p. 15). These estimates imply that anything between 300 and 5,400 languages will vanish, a range so wide as to undermine all confidence in the numbers.[9]

IX. Number of Polities and Number of Languages

Extrapolation of the *very* long-term trend towards fewer and larger political units suggests that complete unification is still distant (Taagepera 1978, p. 119). Recent political history points in the opposite direction: the average size of states is falling and separatism increasing. This might be supposed to favour rebuilding the Tower of Babel. How, then, should we account for the ever-greater adoption of English?

One part of the answer may be that, while trade liberalisation encourages the proliferation of states, it equally favours a sharing of languages. Work by Alberto Alesina and various collaborators asserts a relationship between greater openness and the number of polities (Alesina *et al* 1997; *The Economist* 3.1.98). World trade, measured by the volume of imports plus exports as a share of world GDP, grew by 40 per cent between 1945 and 1995 in a sample of 61 countries, while the total number of countries rose from 74 to 192. Above all, the number of small countries rose: by 1995 87 states possessed fewer than five million inhabitants. On average these are far from the poorest jurisdictions. Alesina argues that free trade benefits them because the advantage of a large market within a state's borders falls and productivity ceases to be a close function of market size.

Alesina's work shows that since 1870 (a period perhaps too short to clinch his argument), spells of economic integration have been characterised by political disintegration and *vice versa*. If trade really is the key to state formation - though it seems only part of the story when one considers, say, the dissolution of the Austro-Hungarian empire - a revival of Protection would return the advantage to large states. We should however consider not only the consequences of political events scarcely connected with trade but the permanent effects of technological change: the latter means that there is trend as well as cycle. The lower cost of communications and transport has

9 This point is reinforced by the much lower estimate of 4,000 extant languages (with several dozen falling annually into disuse) cited in DIXON (1998).

made size less important, inserting a rachet which means that small states should be able to retain some advantage whatever the trade regime. Of the ten countries with the highest ratio of Internet hosts to population, seven have populations of fewer than nine million people.

Two further papers by Alesina and Spolare claim, first, that political secession is commonest in times of peace because the benefit of remaining in large units for defence falls, and secondly that democratisation favours the formation of small states. Authoritarianism, on the contrary, "maximizes rents for the rulers by keeping together large countries formed by very different individuals who would want to separate, were they not forced together by the regime" (Alesina 1997, p. 18). These relationships are certainly plausible, though no detailed historical evidence is offered.

The fragmentation of states may facilitate experimenting with lesser languages. A richer world is after all better able to indulge itself, and Kaurna and Cornish may indeed be raised from the dead. Yet trade overall encourages sharing languages. The rise of small states and the rise of English may thus prove to have been partly co-determined by free trade. It is in the larger non-English-speaking states that we find the strongest official resistance to English. Why in such countries, like France, do cultural considerations provoke defensiveness, whereas others manage the relationship between a *lingua franca* and their own tongue in a positive way? Scandinavians and Dutch learn English without resentment; the ever-rational Singaporean government has reaffirmed not only that English is the country's working language but is vital for social harmony; and Malaysia has returned to promoting English for the sake of competitiveness. France takes the opposite view and the 'Berlin Republic' may also be flirting with inwardness - it is in Sweden, not France or Germany, that Ph.D. theses are written in English.

Divergent attitudes to a *lingua franca* in general, and English in particular, coincide with differential opportunities for capturing rents by retaining local languages. In small markets, as we have seen, the costs are high. Citizens of small countries are thus generally more polyglot than those of large ones. The threat of intellectual, even cultural, isolation prompts them to acquire a major language, which for historical and other reasons tends now to be English. As *The Economist* comments, in little Iceland, "the necessity of speaking English is unquestioned" (3.1.98).

Despite exceptions like Quebec, English is generally preferred more by the people of small polities than of large ones. This can be shown by recalculating figures of the national proportions of speakers of English as a second language provided for fourteen countries by Crystal (1997, pp. 57-60).[10] The largest seven countries in terms of population (ranging from India to Sri Lanka) contain only 7.75 per cent of such speakers, whereas the smallest seven countries (ranging from Botswana to Tuvalu) contain 25.5 per cent. Large states are more likely to suffer diseconomies of scale. Their own language community seems big enough to sustain itself and accordingly they may be tempted to adopt inward-looking language policies. Their citizens may learn English privately but their governments commit resources to hampering its maximum adoption.

X. The Utility of a Standard

The opinion has developed among linguists that there is no optimal language, though occasionally the literature, even a single text, contradicts itself about this and there are some (slightly hesitant) dissenters. To take only a recent example, Dixon stresses that the belief among linguists that 'all languages are equal' is mistaken (Dixon 1998: 75 n.7, 118). Languages *are* approximately equal, he says, in that none is six times as complex as another, there are no primitive languages, and (a point made by many authors) differences exist that amount to offsetting difficulties in ability to communicate in given spheres. Dixon goes on to say that languages are not equally hard to describe and speakers master comparable points in their grammars at quite different rates. In any case, for one language to have not six times but even twice, or one-and-a-half, or one-and-a-quarter, times the complexity of another, surely torpedoes the assertion of language equality.

Optimality to linguists however refers to technical characteristics of languages rather than practical use. A majority seems to believe that, given the need and opportunity to develop appropriate grammatical structures and

10 Comprehensive data are not available by country for speakers of English as a foreign language. From Crystal's table relating to English as a second language, we have to exclude countries where figures are interpolated from levels of educational attainment, Pidgin English is widely spoken, or there are more first- than second language speakers of English (since we would learn little about the preference for English by including countries where it is the main language).

acquire a vocabulary suitable for the modern world, no language would be found wanting. But all this is beside the point, firstly because several languages can cope already, and secondly because it overlooks the inherent utility of choosing one language as the standard. Whether the choice is arbitrary or not is neither here nor there - indeed, the linguistic consensus requires that such a choice be arbitrary. Measuring in miles or kilometres is arbitrary too yet selecting one of them as a universal measure would reduce confusion.

As we have noted, if we are to continue moving towards a standard, English does have advantages. It is said to have a vocabulary three times larger than French or German. Among 'world languages' with fully-developed modern vocabularies, it possesses the largest literature and offers network advantages because of the number of users who have already selected it. Admittedly, the demographic weight behind a particular language does not guarantee permanent dominance; costs and benefits at the margin rather than size alone determine choice of language. Politics may constrain choice. But English now attracts so much talent that it creates agglomeration effects like the network of firms in a central business district.

Where minority languages are taught instead of those more widely spoken, and particularly instead of English, it can be argued that people are being steered away from a superior resource. Rather than bolstering their supposed 'identity', their adjustment to the modern world is likely to be hampered. Who benefits from setting themselves up to hinder the spread of English or indeed of any shared tongue? Those with an investment in other languages, of course. While linguists are properly interested in vanishing languages, artificial efforts at preservation, not to mention resurrecting the dead, serve the self-interest of rent-seeking groups, often battening on the residual archaisms of ethnic particularism. Suffice it to note that the IRA's so-called 'equality agenda' involves moves to further the use of the Irish language.

Beyond such efforts at reinforcing political differences, there is an authoritarian strain in the literature of linguistics itself. Thus Hall, a Cornell professor, hoped that anyone setting up as an authority on language without scientific training, "will be prosecutable under law" like anyone practising medicine unlicensed, while the Sorbonne professor, Etiemble, wrote that, "to violate [the French language] is a crime. Persons were shot during the war for treason. They should be punished for degrading the language" (Hall 1960, p. 249; Etiemble quoted in *The Australian* 28.2.98). More often diversity is endorsed without any mention of its negative aspects; nowadays such views tend to be clothed in the dogmatic terms of language 'rights' and cultural 'rights'. We might prefer to believe that the greatest right is of access to the largest linguistic community.

A guide to an outward-looking policy might be, 'thou shalt not kill but needst not strive, officiously to keep alive.' No proscription of any language is involved. Irving Horowitz asked his Dutch friends, "why do you continue to speak Dutch?" (Symposium 1995, p. 232). They replied, "this is the language of our heart; when we make love, we speak Dutch; when we have a scientific conference with foreigners we speak English." As Horowitz observes, "the corporate language as well as the scientific idiom is English, but it has not destroyed the intimacies with which we communicate - the language of love, region, and nation."

Language is a feature of cultures but seemingly not an integral one. This is captured by the following observation: "although a person from Kenya speaking English (the usual language in schools) may be more understandable to an American than [would be] a Scot from Glasgow, many white Americans may well identify with the latter more than the former because of other considerations" (Seelye and Howell Wasilewski 1996, p. 49). After all, the dumb can share in culture; the British, Americans and Australians differ culturally while speaking the same language; and Debussy would remain French even if the speaking of French were abandoned. No-one's culture is threatened by learning to speak another language; to think otherwise is to mistake form for cultural function.[11] "The apparent dependence of thought on language may be an illusion that derives from the fact that it is hard to obtain evidence of thought without using language" (Anderson 1980, p. 384).[12]

XI. Conclusions: A Shared Future

Honey points out that there is no escaping the fact that English is foremost among the major languages helping to kill the minority ones that per-

11 See RODRIGUEZ (1981, p. 35) for an eloquent testimony.

12 I owe the reference and other points in this paragraph to Ekkehart Schlicht.

ish every year. Certainly many languages are being drastically altered by the impact of English on their grammar, vocabulary and so forth. In the *very* long term, English may supersede other languages, in the way Noah Webster anticipated that the dialects imported by early immigrants to the United States would be "gradually destroyed" by "the intercourse among *the learned* of the different states" (quoted in Honey 1997, p. 82). Honey suggests that over the next five hundred or a thousand years even the more prominent European languages may succumb: "it is not entirely fanciful to think that Gaelic or Albanian may have limited life; when you talk, in millennial terms, of languages like French sharing the same fate, there is real horror and incredulity, but the possibility, at least, is surely there" (Honey 1997, pp. 252-3). The force pulling in the opposite direction is the other main function of language, beyond communication - the alternative purpose of solidarity, of expressing one's membership of tribe, community or nation. It remains to be seen whether this can resist the spread of monolingualism, but in truth there is no contest. Most people in the world already speak more than one language and they may choose to share English with people at large and some other tongue with those dearest to their heart.

Modern communications may even promote this dual outcome. Writing in 1978, Colin Cherry thought that broadcasting would revive lesser languages (Cherry 1978, pp. 179-85). These had been under siege because the great bulk of books were published in a mere half-a-dozen languages, whereas international broadcasters operated in many more. When Frances Cairncross wrote on a similar theme in 1997, she too concluded that modern communications may benefit languages other than English (Cairncross 1997, pp. 244-9). They seem to do so - a twin process is at work, for example within the European Union: English increasingly dominates official discussions yet the proponents of regional languages clamour for representation, while television programmes are being broadcast in once-spurned dialects. But Cairncross also referred to "the coming global tongue" and pointed to the need for a standard for international communications. In practice the standard is English, which dominates the Internet and navigational languages. This magnifies its impact since the Internet is the vehicle of choice among the creative young, who have a disproportionate influence and need accept no geographical limitations on their audience.

The world has a better chance than ever to exchange knowledge. The costs of access to education are falling and with this comes the prospect of a fresh rise in productivity, besides the creation of astonishing cultural syntheses. Although Protectionism remains able to hamper Free Trade in ideas, it has less scope nowadays. The progress of English towards the status of the world's first universally-shared language continues. Efforts to hamper this are misguided, since the benefits promise to be so much greater than the costs.

References

ALESINA, A. ET AL: "Economic Integration and Political Disintegration", NBER Working Paper No. 6163, Sept. 1997.

AMIS, K.: *Memoirs,* London (Penguin) 1992.

ANDERSON, J. R.: *Cognitive Psychology and its Implications,* San Francisco (Freeman) 1980.

ARCAND, J-L.: "Development Economics and Language: The Earnest Search for a Mirage", *International Journal of the Sociology of Language,* 121 (1996).

BASU, K., JONES, E. L., SCHLICHT, E.: "The Rise and Decline of Custom: The Role of the New Institutional Economics in Economic History", *Explorations in Economic History,* 24 (1987).

CAIRNCROSS, F.: *The Death of Distance: How the Communications Revolution Will Change Our Lives,* Boston, Mass. (Harvard Business School Press) 1997.

CHERRY, C.: *World Communication: Threat or Promise? A Socio-technical Approach*, Chichester (John Wiley & Sons) revised edition, 1978.

CRYSTAL, D. (1997a): "The Future of English", Unpublished lecture at Melbourne University, 17/7/97.

CRYSTAL, D. (1997b): *English as a Global Language*, Cambridge (Cambridge University Press) 1997.

DIAMOND, J.: *The Rise and Fall of the Third Chimpanzee*, London (Vintage) 1992.

DIXON, R. M. W.: *The Rise and Fall of Languages*, Cambridge (Cambridge University Press) 1998.

DORIAN, N. C.: "Purism Versus Compromise in Language Revitalization and Language Revival", *Language in Society,* 23 (1994).

EASTERLY, W., LEVINE, R.: "Africa's Growth Tragedy: Policies and Ethnic Divisions", *Quarterly Journal of Economics,* November (1997).

GOUDSBLOM, J., JONES, E. L., MENNELL, S.: *The Course of Human History: Economic Growth, Social Process, and Civilization*, Armonk, N.Y. (M. E. Sharpe) 1996.

GRIN, F.: "Towards a Threshold Theory of Minority Language Survival", *Kyklos,* 45 (1992).

GRIN, F.: "The Economics of Language: Match or Mismatch?", *International Political Science Review*, 15 (1994).

GRIN, F. (1996a): "Economic Approaches to Language and Language Planning: An Introduction", *International Journal of the Sociology of Language*, 121 (1996).

GRIN, F. (1996b): "The Economics of Language: Survey, Assessment, and Prospects", *International Journal of the Sociology of Language,* 121 (1996).

HALL, JR., R. A.: *Linguistics and Your Language*, Garden City, New York (Anchor Books) 1960.

HONEY, J.: *Language is Power: The Story of Standard English and its Enemies*, London (Faber and Faber) 1997.

HUGHES, A.[13]: "Multilingualism in Europe", Unpublished lecture at La Trobe University, 2/6/97.

JONES, E. L. (1995a): "Culture and its Relationship to Economic Change", *Journal of Institutional and Theoretical Economics*, 151 (1995).

JONES, E. L. (1995b): "The Price of Information", *The National Interest,* 41 (1995).

KURAN, T.: *Private Truths, Public Lies: The Social Consequences of Preference Falsification*, Cambridge, Mass. (Harvard University Press) 1995.

MCKAY, G.: *The Land Still Speaks: Review of Aboriginal and Torres Strait Islander Language Maintenance and Development Needs and Activities*, Canberra (Australian Government Publishing Service) 1996.

MOISI, D.: "The Trouble with France", *Foreign Affairs*, 77 (May-June, 1998).

MUELLER, D.: *On the Decline of Nations*, Jena (Max-Planck-Institut, Lectiones Jenenses) Heft 9, 1996.

Nature, 391 (5/2/98).

RODRIGUEZ, R.: *Hunger of Memory*, Boston (David R. Godine) 1981.

SEELYE, N., J. HOWELL WASILEWSKI: *Between Cultures: Developing Self-Identity in a World of Diversity*, Lincolnwood, Illinois (NTC Publishing Group) 1996.

SINGER, M. R.: "Language Follows Power: The Linguistic Free Market in the Old Soviet Bloc", *Foreign Affairs*, 77 (1998).

SYMPOSIUM: "The New World of the Gothic Fox: Culture and Economy in English and Spanish America", *Partisan Review*, LXII, (1995).

TAAGEPERA, R.: "Size and Duration of Empires: Systematics of Size", *Social Science Research*, 7 (1978).

13 Head, Delegation of the EC to Australia and New Zealand.

Periodicals

The Age.
The Aaustralian, various issues.
The Economist.
The Economist Atlas, London (Hutchinson Business Books) 1989.
The European, various issues.
The Financial Times, various issues.
Frankfuter Allgemeinerzeitung.
The Guardian Weekly.
The Independent.
The International Herald Tribune, various issues.
The Spectator.
Der Tagespiel.
The Times, various issues.

List of Authors

FRED V. CARSTENSEN is Professor at the Department of Economics, the University of Connecticut, USA.

MARK C. CASSON is Professor of Economics at the Department of Economics, the University of Reading, Reading, United Kingdom.

KEN R. DARK is Lecturer in International Business at the Department of Economics, the University of Reading, Reading, United Kingdom.

STEPHAN R. EPSTEIN is Reader in Economic History at the Department of Economic History, LSE, London, United Kingdom.

FRANCESCO GALASSI is Lecturer in Economics at the Department of Economics, the University of Warwick, Warwick, United Kingdom.

ANDREW GODLEY is Lecturer in Economics at the Department of Economics, the University of Reading, Reading, United Kingdom.

ERIC L. JONES is Professorial Fellow at Melbourne Business School, the University of Melbourne, Australia, and Visiting Professor at the Department of Economics, the University of Reading, Reading, United Kingdom.

BART NOOTEBOOM is Professor in the Erasmus Research Institute of Management, Erasmus University, Rotterdam, Netherlands.

William D. RUBINSTEIN is Professor of History at the Department of History, the University of Wales, Aberystwyth, Wales, United Kingdom.

Index of Names

Page numbers in italics refer to quotations in footnotes or references

Studies in Economic Ethics and Philosophy

P. Koslowski (Ed.)
Ethics in Economics, Business, and Economic Policy
X, 178 pages. 1992
ISBN 3-540-55359-2 (out of print)

P. Koslowski and Y. Shionoya (Eds.)
The Good and the Economical: Ethical Choices in Economics and Management
X, 202 pages. 1993
ISBN 3-540-57339-9 (out of print)

H. De Geer (Ed.)
Business Ethics in Progress?
IX, 124 pages. 1994
ISBN 3-540-57758-0

P. Koslowski (Ed.)
The Theory of Ethical Economy in the Historical School
XI, 343 pages. 1995
ISBN 3-540-59070-6

A. Argandoña (Ed.)
The Ethical Dimension of Financial Institutions and Markets
XI, 263 pages. 1995
ISBN 3-540-59209-1 (out of print)

G.K. Becker (Ed.)
Ethics in Business and Society Chinese and Western Perspectives
VIII, 233 pages. 1996
ISBN 3-540-60773-0

P. Koslowski (Ed.)
Ethics of Capitalism and Critique of Sociobiology. Two Essays with a Comment by James M. Buchanan
IX, 142 pages. 1996
ISBN 3-540-61035-9

F. Neil Brady (Ed.)
Ethical Universals in International Business
X, 246 pages. 1996
ISBN 3-540-61588-1

P. Koslowski and A. Føllesdal (Eds.)
Restructuring the Welfare State
Theory and Reform of Social Policy
VIII, 402 pages. 1997
ISBN 3-540-62035-4 (out of print)

G. Erreygers and T. Vandevelde
Is Inheritance Legitimate?
Ethical and Economic Aspects of Wealth Transfers
X, 236 pages. 1997
ISBN 3-540-62725-1

P. Koslowski (Ed.)
Business Ethics in East Central Europe
XII, 151 pages. 1997
ISBN 3-540-63367-7

P. Koslowski (Ed.)
Methodology of the Social Sciences, Ethics, and Economics in the Newer Historical School
From Max Weber and Rickert to Sombart and Rothacker
XII, 565 pages. 1997
ISBN 3-540-63458-4

A. Føllesdal and P. Koslowski (Eds.)
Democracy and the European Union
X, 309 pages. 1998
ISBN 3-540-63457-6

P. Koslowski (Ed.)
The Social Market Economy
Theory and Ethics of the Economic Order
XII, 360 pages. 1998
ISBN 3-540-64043-6

Amitai Etzioni
Essays in Socio-Economics
XII, 182 pages. 1999
ISBN 3-540-64466-0

P. Koslowski (Ed.)
Sociobiology and Bioeconomics
The Theory of Evolution in Biological and Economic Theory
X, 341 pages. 1999
ISBN 3-540-65380-5

J. Kuçuradi (Ed.)
The Ethics of the Professions:
Medicine, Business, Media, Law
X, 172 pages. 1999
ISBN 3-540-65726-6

S.K. Chakraborty and S.R. Chatterjee (Eds.)
Applied Ethics in Management
Towards New Perspectives
X, 298 pages. 1999
ISBN 3-540-65726-6

P. Koslowski (Ed.)
The Theory of Capitalism in the German Economic Tradition
Historism, Ordo-Liberalism, Critical Theory, Solidarism
XII, 577 pages. 2000
ISBN 3-540-66674-5

P. Koslowski (Ed.)
Contemporary Economic Ethics and Business Ethics
IX, 265 pages. 2000
ISBN 3-540-66665-6

M. Casson, A. Godley (Eds.)
Cultural Factors in Economic Growth
VIII, 244 pages. 2000
ISBN 3-540-66293-6

Printing: Weihert-Druck GmbH, Darmstadt
Binding: Buchbinderei Schäffer, Grünstadt